N INFORMATION SYSTEMS

Video training courses are available on the subjects of these books in the
James Martin ADVANCED TECHNOLOGY LIBRARY of over 300 tapes and disks,
from Applied Learning, 1751 West Diehl Road, Naperville, IL 60540 (tel: 312-369-3000).

Database	Telecommunications	Networks and Data Communications	Society
AN END USER'S GUIDE TO DATABASE	TELECOMMUNICATIONS AND THE COMPUTER (third edition)	PRINCIPLES OF DATA COMMUNICATION	THE COMPUTERIZED SOCIETY
PRINCIPLES OF DATABASE MANAGEMENT (second edition)	FUTURE DEVELOPMENTS IN TELECOMMUNICATIONS (third edition)	TELEPROCESSING NETWORK ORGANIZATION	TELEMATIC SOCIETY: A CHALLENGE FOR TOMORROW
COMPUTER DATABASE ORGANIZATION (third edition)	COMMUNICATIONS SATELLITE SYSTEMS	SYSTEMS ANALYSIS FOR DATA TRANSMISSION	TECHNOLOGY'S CRUCIBLE
MANAGING THE DATABASE ENVIRONMENT (second edition)	ISDN	DATA COMMUNICATION TECHNOLOGY	VIEWDATA AND THE INFORMATION SOCIETY
DATABASE ANALYSIS AND DESIGN	**Distributed Processing**	DATA COMMUNICATION DESIGN TECHNIQUES	**SAA: Systems Application Architecture**
VSAM: ACCESS METHOD SERVICES AND PROGRAMMING TECHNIQUES	COMPUTER NETWORKS AND DISTRIBUTED PROCESSING	SNA: IBM's NETWORKING SOLUTION	SAA: COMMON USER ACESS
DB2: CONCEPTS, DESIGN, AND PROGRAMMING	DESIGN AND STRATEGY FOR DISTRIBUTED DATA PROCESSING	ISDN	SAA: COMMON COMMUNICATIONS SUPPORT
IDMS/R: CONCEPTS, DESIGN, AND PROGRAMMING	**Office Automation**	LOCAL AREA NETWORKS: ARCHITECTURES AND IMPLEMENTATIONS	SAA: COMMON PROGRAMMING INTERFACE
SQL	IBM OFFICE SYSTEMS: ARCHITECTURES AND IMPLEMENTATIONS	OFFICE AUTOMATION STANDARDS	SAA: AD/CYCLE
Security	OFFICE AUTOMATION STANDARDS	DATA COMMUNICATION STANDARDS	
SECURITY, ACCURACY, AND PRIVACY IN COMPUTER SYSTEMS		CORPORATE COMMUNICATIONS STRATEGY	
SECURITY AND PRIVACY IN COMPUTER SYSTEMS		COMPUTER NETWORKS AND DISTRIBUTED PROCESSING: SOFTWARE, TECHNIQUES, AND ARCHITECTURE	

SYSTEMS APPLICATION ARCHITECTURE:
COMMON USER ACCESS

A _____ BOOK

THE JAMES MARTIN BOOKS

currently available from Prentice Hall

- Application Development Without Programmers
- Building Expert Systems
- Communications Satellite Systems
- Computer Data-Base Organization, Second Edition
- The Computerized Society
- Computer Networks and Distributed Processing: Software, Techniques, and Architecture
- Data Communication Technology
- DB2: Concepts, Design, and Programming
- Design and Strategy of Distributed Data Processing
- Design of Real-Time Computer Systems
- An End User's Guide to Data Base
- Fourth-Generation Languages, Volume I: Principles
- Fourth-Generation Languages, Volume II: Representative 4GLs
- Fourth-Generation Languages, Volume III: 4GLs from IBM
- Future Developments in Telecommunications, Second Edition
- Hyperdocuments and How to Create Them
- IBM Office Systems: Architectures and Implementations
- IDMS/R: Concepts, Design, and Programming
- Information Engineering, Book I: Introduction and Principles
- Information Engineering, Book II: Planning and Analysis
- Information Engineering, Book III: Design and Construction
- An Information Systems Manifesto
- Local Area Networks: Architectures and Implementations
- Managing the Data-Base Environment
- Principles of Data-Base Management
- Principles of Data Communication
- Recommended Diagramming Standards for Analysts and Programmers
- SNA: IBM's Networking Solution
- Strategic Information Planning Methodologies, Second Edition
- System Design from Provably Correct Constructs
- Systems Analysis for Data Transmission
- Systems Application Architecture: Common User Access
- Technology's Crucible
- Telecommunications and the Computer, Third Edition
- Telematic Society: A Challenge for Tomorrow
- VSAM: Access Method Services and Programming Techniques

with Carma McClure

- Action Diagrams: Clearly Structured Specifications, Programs, and Procedures, Second Edition
- Diagramming Techniques for Analysts and Programmers
- Software Maintenance: The Problem and Its Solutions
- Structured Techniques: The Basis for CASE, Revised Edition

SYSTEMS APPLICATION ARCHITECTURE
Common User Access

JAMES MARTIN

with

Kathleen Kavanagh Chapman / Joe Leben

PRENTICE HALL
Englewood Cliffs, New Jersey 07632

Library of Congress Cataloging-in-Publication Data

MARTIN, JAMES (date)
    Systems application architecture : common user access / James
Martin with Kathleen Kavanagh Chapman, Joe Leben.
      p. cm.
    "The James Martin books"—P. preceding t.p.
    Includes bibliographical references and index.
    ISBN 0-13-785023-9 :
    1. IBM Systems application architecture. 2. User interfaces
(Computer systems) 3. Application software. I. Chapman, Kathleen
Kavanagh. II. Leben, Joe. III. Title.
QA76.9.A73M374 1991
004.2′2—dc20
                       90-22272
                       CIP

Editorial/production supervision: *Kathryn Gollin Marshak*
Jacket design: *Bruce Kenselaar*
Manufacturing buyers: Kelly Behr and Susan Brunke

Published by Prentice-Hall, Inc.
A Simon & Schuster Company
Englewood Cliffs, New Jersey 07632

The publisher offers discounts on this book when ordered
in bulk quantities. For more information, write:
        Special Sales; Prentice-Hall, Inc.
        College Technical and Reference Division
        Englewood Cliffs, NJ 07632

Printed in the United States of America

10 9 8 7 6 5 4 3 2 1

ISBN   0-13-785023-9

PRENTICE-HALL INTERNATIONAL (UK) LIMITED, *London*
PRENTICE-HALL OF AUSTRALIA PTY. LIMITED, *Sydney*
PRENTICE-HALL CANADA INC., *Toronto*
PRENTICE-HALL HISPANOAMERICANA, S.A., *Mexico*
PRENTICE-HALL OF INDIA PRIVATE LIMITED, *New Delhi*
PRENTICE-HALL OF JAPAN, INC., *Tokyo*
SIMON & SCHUSTER ASIA PTE. LTD., *Singapore*
EDITORA PRENTICE-HALL DO BRASIL, LTDA., *Rio de Janeiro*

TO CORINTHIA
—*JM*

TO JOHN AND MY PARENTS
—*KKC*

CONTENTS

PART **III** # THE CUA BASIC INTERFACE

17 The OfficeVision Product Family 277

18 ISPF 293

19 The OS/400 Operating System 315

PREFACE

On St. Patrick's Day in 1987, IBM announced *Systems Application Architecture (SAA)*. Systems Application Architecture provides a standard set of interfaces to computing for both application developers and end users. IBM's intent is that these interfaces should provide a framework for developing applications that are consistent and operable across all the major IBM computing environments. IBM's goal is to provide improved interoperability among its major computing environments.

One of IBM's motivations for developing SAA is to address the problems caused by the lack of commonality among the different computing environments that it supports. Although the same general functions are provided in each of the environments, different programs are used to provide the functions, and these programs often are very dissimilar in how they are used and what they produce. In a broader sense, SAA provides a strategic direction for the use of computing and has the potential to become the standard that defines a universal computing environment. In this environment, applications can be developed without regard to the underlying hardware or operating system.

This book provides a general introduction to the goals and interfaces that Systems Application Architecture defines, as well as a detailed examination of the Common User Access (CUA) interface that defines the way an application developer creates an SAA-compliant user interface. Companion volumes describe other SAA interfaces: The *Common Communications Support (CCS)* component of SAA specifies standard data streams and communication services that can be used to support the transmission of information between computing systems, and the *Common Programming Interface (CPI)* component of SAA specifies a standard set of languages and a standard set of services that can be used for application development.

ACKNOWLEDGMENTS The authors wish to thank Kim Wenzel of IBM, who provided us with information about the OS/400 implementation of SAA and access to an AS/400 system to produce the screen examples in the chapter on the OS/400 operating system. John Gridley, also of IBM, supplied much helpful information and put us in touch with the right people in IBM who were able to answer our many questions.

James Martin
Kathleen Kavanagh Chapman
Joe Leben

PART **I** INTRODUCTION

1 INTRODUCTION TO SAA

INTRODUCTION   IBM markets computing systems that are based on
many different hardware and software architectures.
By supporting a diversity of hardware architectures and system software environments, IBM has been able to offer equipment and software to support general-purpose computing systems that span a nearly thousandfold capacity range. Systems Application Architecture is an attempt to bring coherence to IBM's wide range of products. It is a comprehensive architecture that consists of a collection of published software interfaces, protocols, and conventions that address three key areas:

- **End-User Interface.** One key to the effective deployment and efficient use of computer applications is ease of use for the application user. The interface that the application end user employs must be well designed and easy to learn. Interfaces should be consistent from application to application in the same environment and from application to application across different computing environments. For example, a database query application running on a 3090 processor complex should employ the same user interface principles as a spreadsheet application running on a personal computer. The *Common User Access* component of SAA includes specifications for the design and use of the screen panels that the end user sees and defines standard techniques for interaction between the end user and the computer system.

- **Programming Interface.** It is becoming increasingly common for enterprises to employ computing systems of varying sizes to meet their computing needs. In such an environment, it is often desirable to run the same application on more than one type of computing system. The *Common Programming Interface* component of SAA provides specifications for a standard set of languages and a standard set of services that can be accessed using those languages. These languages and services can then be used in a consistent manner by application developers. In such an environment, an application developed using standard tools can be moved easily from one computing environment to another. In theory, for example, a spreadsheet application for a personal computer that is written in an SAA standard language and that uses only SAA standard services should run on an AS/400 processor simply by the programmer's making a few minor changes and recompiling it using an AS/400 compiler.

- **Communication Support.** Enterprises not only employ a variety of different computing environments, but they are also beginning to connect different types of computing systems to create extensive networks of great complexity. In such an environment, it is desirable for applications to be able to communicate with one another and to access resources that are distributed throughout the network. The *Common Communications Support* component of SAA specifies standard data streams and sets of communication services that can be used to support the transmission of information between computing systems and between the programs running on them.

WHY SAA?   The development of Systems Application Architecture required a considerable investment of resources on the part of IBM, and full implementation of the architecture, which may run over a decade or more to accomplish, will take even more. Why was IBM willing to make this investment? Not surprisingly, the answer is that IBM felt that such an architecture was needed to ensure its own growth and continued success in the information systems business.

Over the years, IBM's product line has become exceedingly complex. IBM markets and supports many different, and basically incompatible, hardware families. These include the following:

- The System/370 and System/390 lines, with processors ranging from small uniprocessors to various very large processor complexes
- The AS/400 line and its predecessor, the System/3X family
- The 8100
- The Series/1
- The System/88
- Various personal computer and personal workstation lines, including the original PC family, the PS/1 and PS/2 lines, and various UNIX workstation models

In addition to supporting multiple hardware architectures, IBM also has developed, and must continue to support, multiple operating systems. At the time of the SAA announcement, IBM offered 14 different operating systems, which provide a wide diversity of interfaces. This diversity also extends to the major system software products used in the different operating environments. Box 1.1 lists key system software products for just a few of IBM's operating systems. Some products operate in more than one environment, but there are

BOX 1.1 System software in the SAA operating environments.

System Control

MVS	VM	AS/400	OS/2
Info family	Info family	OS/400 functions:	EZ-VU
SMP/E RMF	PPF	system mgmt	Presentation
Data Facility	VSAM	storage mgmt	Manager
VSAM	PSF	dialog mgr	Dialog Mgr
PSF	ISPF	presentation mgr	Batch File
ISPF	GDDM	workstation	Utility
GDDM	CMS	support	
TSO/E	CMS Batch	work mgmt	
JES2, JES3	RACF	security	
RACF		GDDM	

Communication

MVS	VM	AS/400	OS/2
VTAM	VTAM	Token Ring	Token Ring
NCP	NCP	3270 emulation	3270,3103,VT100
Netview	Netview	APPC	emulation
DSX	DSNX	SNA upline	APPC
X.25 interface	RSCS	APPN	PC Network
		DSNX	Asynchronous
		X.25 interface	X.25 interface
		Netview alert	Netview alert
		DDM	

Application Enablers

MVS	VM	AS/400	OS/2
COBOL	COBOL	COBOL	COBOL
FORTRAN	FORTRAN	FORTRAN	FORTRAN
C	C	C	C
PL/I	PL/I	PL/I	Basic
CSP	CSP	Application Dev.	Application
ADF	REXX	Tools	Generator
QMF	QMF	RPG	Query Mgr
IMS/DB	SQL/DS	Basic	Database Mgr
IMS/DC	CICS/VM	Pascal	
IMS Fastpath		AS/400 Query	
DB2		SQL/400	
CICS/VS		Database Mgr	
		ICF	

still considerable differences, even in the same subsystem, in moving from one environment to another.

The cost of this complexity is very high, to both IBM and its customers. For IBM, there is the investment in money and resources that is required to maintain and enhance each of these separate systems and products. Resources have also been consumed in "reinventing the wheel," where multiple products provide essentially the same function, such as IMS/VS and DB2 in database access, ISPF and CMS in time sharing, and JES2 and JES3 in job entry facilities. In cases like these, IBM must continue to devote resources to providing the same range of functions in different environments rather than being able to use those resources to add new functions or develop new products. The net result of this for IBM has been a limitation on how rapidly it has been able to enhance or develop critical new system and application software. One obvious concern for IBM is that this situation is having a significant impact on software revenue, which is an increasingly important part of IBM's business.

This product and operating environment complexity has also had a direct impact on IBM's customers. In dealing with enterprisewide needs for computing, companies need to employ all manner of computing systems ranging from personal computers, through midrange systems, to the large-system host processors. Because of incompatibilities among different systems, companies often have had to create duplicate system support staffs and application development staffs for each of the different computing system environments. Many of IBM's customers have found it difficult to develop applications that operate in multiple computing system environments or that communicate from one environment to another. The drain on company resources caused by dealing with such complexity has slowed the rate at which IBM's customers have been able to develop and install applications. This, in turn, has slowed the rate at which these companies have needed to install new computing capacity. For IBM, growth in its customers' computing capacity requirements represents an opportunity to sell more hardware and software.

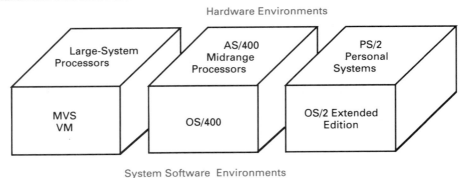

Figure 1.1   SAA interfaces address three categories of hardware and system software.

Support for SAA will be provided across a wide range of hardware and software environments, by both IBM and other vendors that produce SAA-compliant hardware and software. However, IBM has committed to broad support for SAA to provide a consistent system image across all future offerings that operate in the system software environments (see Fig. 1.1) described below:

- **Multiple Virtual Storage.** Multiple Virtual Storage (MVS) refers to a family of operating systems that runs on IBM's large-system processors. Much of the software that runs under the various MVS operating systems is already SAA compliant. All new IBM software for MVS/ESA (Multiple Virtual Storage/Enterprise Systems Architecture), the latest version of MVS, will be SAA compliant. Important MVS subsystems included in SAA are DB2 (Data Base 2) and IMS (Information Management System) for database access and CICS (Customer Information Control System) for transaction processing.

- **Virtual Machine Facility.** The Virtual Machine (VM) and Conversational Monitor System (CMS) are alternative system software for IBM large-system processors. All new IBM software for the VM environment will be SAA compliant.

- **Operating System/400.** OS/400 is the operating system for IBM's AS/400 line of midrange processors. All new IBM OS/400 software will be SAA compliant. The AS/400 and the OS/400 operating system constitute the successor computing environment to IBM's System/36 and System/38 lines of midrange computing systems.

- **Operating System/2 Extended Edition.** OS/2 EE is the operating system that runs on IBM's Personal System/2 line of small computing systems. OS/2 EE also runs on many personal computers that are compatible with the PS/2, on many of IBM's older personal computers, such as the PC/AT, and on personal computers compatible with the PC/AT.

Support for other environments is likely to be included in SAA over time. An application that is developed in conformance with SAA specifications should operate consistently across all SAA-supported environments. This means the following:

- An SAA application should be able to be compiled and run in any of the supported environments without extensive reprogramming.

- An SAA application's interface to the end user should appear the same regardless of the environment in which it is run.

- An SAA application should be able to communicate with other SAA applications running in any of the environments.

GOALS OF SAA   One of IBM's overriding goals in developing and promulgating SAA, then, is to reduce complexity, both for IBM itself and for its customers. In turn, reduced complexity should lead to greater productivity—for IBM in the development and support of software products and for its customers in the development and use of computer applications. SAA reduces complexity by defining standard interfaces for both application developers and application users and then supporting those interfaces across IBM's major operating environments. The use of SAA standard interfaces, protocols, and conventions in the areas of Common User Access, Common Programming Interface, and Common Communications Support provides three primary benefits:

- **Consistent User View.** The end-user interface standards that are part of SAA provide for the development of applications that offer a consistent view to the application user. This promotes user productivity—the learning curve for new applications is reduced, and the user is not required to learn a new interface if an application is moved from one computing environment to another.

- **Application Portability.** The programming interface standards are designed to support application portability—an application developed in one environment can be compiled and executed in any of the other environments. This promotes programming productivity, since an application need not be rewritten or extensively modified in order to run in another environment. The standard programming interfaces also promote programming productivity by making the same programming skills learned in one environment usable in the other environments.

- **Connectivity.** By defining standard methods by which systems and programs can communicate, SAA makes it easier to develop networks that connect different types of computing systems and that allow applications to communicate with one another using that network. This cross-system communication may be used to access geographically distributed resources or to develop distributed processing applications where part of the processing is performed on one system and part on another.

STRUCTURE OF SAA

SAA builds on the approach that IBM has been using for some time in structuring its system software and application software. All SAA environments employ three types of product that form the consistent software foundation shown in Fig. 1.2. *Application enablers* encompass a range of tools and services that includes programming languages, tools for computer-aided systems engineering (CASE), application generators, database management systems, teleprocessing monitors, and system services for data presentation and dialog management. *Communications subsystems* allow a computing system to communicate with its own peripheral devices and with other computing systems that are attached to a computer network. *System control programs* make up the operating system and its extensions that control a computing system in a specific hardware environment. Products that form the software foundation are different for each hardware family and operating system environment.

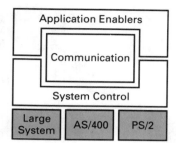

Figure 1.2   Three categories of SAA components support the three IBM computing system environments.

Standard Interfaces

With SAA, IBM has designed a way of providing compatible interfaces to the different computing environments. The three types of interface that SAA standardizes, shown in Fig. 1.3, are summarized below:

- **Common User Access.** The Common User Access (CUA) interface provides end users with a consistent view of the different applications they use.

- **Common Programming Interface.** The Common Programming Interface (CPI) defines a set of languages and services for the application developer that are consistent across the different environments in how they are used and in the results they produce.

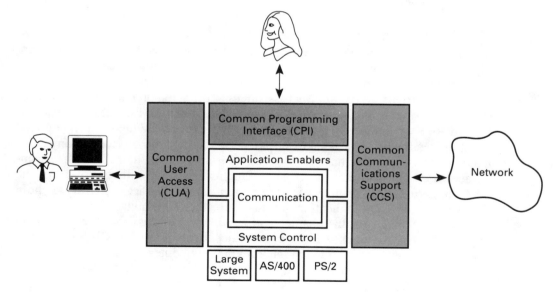

Figure 1.3   SAA defines three interfaces to the SAA components.

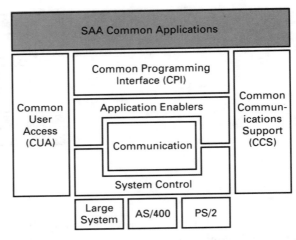

Figure 1.4   IBM and other vendors will supply SAA common applications.

- **Common Communications Support.** The Common Communications Support (CCS) interface provides consistent methods for exchanging data across a network.

Any application that is developed using these interfaces is shielded from the complexities and incompatibilities that exist in the different underlying computing environments.

Common Applications

In addition to defining the three SAA interfaces and providing system software support for those interfaces, IBM has also stated its intent to develop applications that conform to SAA standards and guidelines. Thus, these applications will be consistent and usable across all of IBM's major computing environments, as shown in Fig. 1.4. The first application that IBM developed that conformed to SAA guidelines was the *OfficeVision Product Family,* an integrated set of applications that provide extensive office automation services. Many other major software vendors have announced their support of the SAA standard interfaces and will also develop common applications that will run on all of the SAA-supported IBM computing system environments. There is likely to be a very rich set of SAA applications available for the IBM environment.

The remainder of this chapter will continue to discuss the three major interfaces that SAA defines. Although the major focus of this book is on Common User Access interface, the Common Programming Interface and the Common Communications Support interface are introduced as well. These last two interfaces are discussed in detail in other James Martin books on SAA.

COMMON USER
ACCESS
SAA *Common User Access (CUA)* is a set of rules and guidelines that help to guide the development of the interface between a computer application and an end user of that application. The two main aspects of the Common User Access interface concern presentation and user interaction. *Presentation* is concerned primarily with the way in which the computer application presents information to the user of the application. *User interaction* is concerned with the ways in which a user specifies actions and provides information to the application.

Presentation

An application normally displays information to the end user on a screen that is part of a computer workstation or terminal. The way in which that information is formatted and displayed depends on the type of device the user is employing. SAA defines the use of two different types of terminal device: nonprogrammable terminals *(NPT),* such as 3270 display terminals, and programmable workstations *(PWS),* such as an IBM personal computer.

For a *nonprogrammable terminal,* a particular arrangement of information that appears on the screen is called a *panel.* All panel types share a common format that divides the panel into five areas: the *action bar,* the *work area,* the *message area,* the *command area,* and the *function key area.* The CUA panel layout for a nonprogrammable terminal is shown in Fig. 1.5. The action bar area is used to provide the user with a set of currently available action choices. The work area is used for the general display or entering of information related to the application. The message area is used by the application to display messages to the user. The command area enables the user to enter commands directly. The function key area displays the action choices that can be selected using the keyboard's function keys.

For a *programmable workstation,* such as a personal computer, information is displayed in windows. A *window* is a bounded portion of the display screen that is used to display information. CUA defines standard elements that make up a window and provides guidelines on formatting these elements. Multiple windows can be used to display information from multiple applications simultaneously. Multiple windows can also be used for a single application. CUA defines certain standard ways of using multiple windows. For example, a Help window is used to assist the user in understanding information displayed or choices available in an application panel being displayed in some other window. Figure 1.6 shows how the screen of a programmable workstation might look with two windows displayed. The figure also points out the various elements that make up PWS windows.

In addition to defining standard panel and window layouts, CUA provides guidelines for the use of icons, color, and emphasis. Guidelines are designed to allow these facilities to be used in a way that reinforces the user's understanding

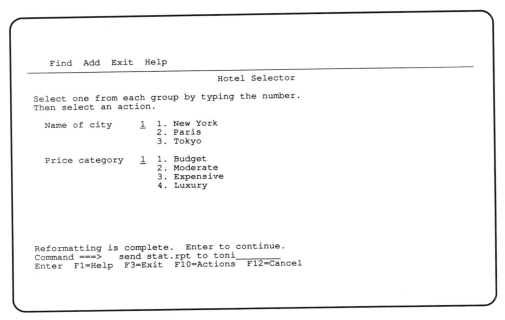

Figure 1.5   Nonprogrammable terminal panel layout.

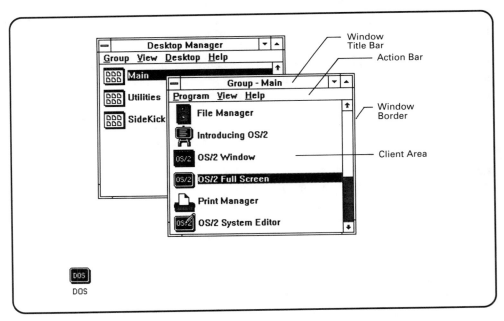

Figure 1.6   Programmable workstation screen with two windows displayed.

of how the user interface operates and that is consistent both within an application and from one application to another.

Interaction Techniques

CUA defines standard methods for user interaction where the interaction may be used to make a selection, enter information, or perform standard actions. CUA supports four techniques for making a selection:

1. A selection cursor can be moved to the desired choice, using standard techniques for moving the cursor. Once the cursor is positioned, a Select action makes the selection.
2. Mnemonics or numbers associated with given choices can be entered.
3. Function keys or pushbuttons can be used to select certain predefined actions.
4. Commands can be entered directly to specify actions.

CUA also specifies methods of defining a field into which a user will enter data and different ways in which the data can be entered. CUA scrolling techniques allow the user to control and change the information that is displayed on the screen when there is more information than can be displayed at one time.

Standard Actions

Typically, an application interface will require more than one display of information and will involve a series of interactions between the user and the application. The application displays information, the user requests an action, the application supplies additional information, the user requests another action, and so on. This series of requests and responses between the user and the application is known as a *dialog*.

As part of dialog design, CUA defines standard actions that can be made available to the user as part of the interface. These actions may be part of an action bar or may be accessible through the use of function keys or pushbuttons. Many of the standard actions are designed to help the user control the dialog that takes place with the application. Others can be used to invoke application functions directly.

The key benefit to be gained from adhering to the Common User Access rules when designing an application interface is increased productivity, for both end users and application developers. End users benefit from reduced learning time as they move from one application to another or from one computing environment to another. Productivity of application developers increases because they need not design the user interface from the ground up for each new application. SAA standard panel and window layouts and standard interaction techniques can be used as a basis for the interface. They then can be modified as necessary to meet each new application's unique requirements.

COMMON PROGRAMMING INTERFACE

The SAA *Common Programming Interface (CPI)* defines a set of languages and programming services that application developers can use in developing SAA applications. The CPI language set includes specifications for procedural languages that are widely used in the different IBM computing environments, including C, COBOL, FORTRAN, PL/I, and RPG. It also includes a specification for an application generator based on IBM's Cross System Product (CSP) and for a procedure language based on the REXX program product. These various language specifications define the features that must be included when implementing a language in one of the SAA computing environments. Figure 1.7 shows the SAA specification for the IF statement in COBOL. The specifications for all the SAA language statements are written with a consistent format using a diagramming technique that lists parameters and options in a concise, easy-to-read manner.

CPI also includes specifications for various types of programming service that can be used by an application. These services are defined in terms of the application program interfaces that are used to invoke them:

- **Communications Interface.** The *communications interface* is used to provide program-to-program communication. It is based on SNA's logical unit (LU) 6.2 architecture and includes the services needed to start and end a conversation with a remote program, send and receive data, synchronize processing between programs, and notify a partner of errors in the communication.

- **Database Interface.** The *database interface* allows applications to define, retrieve, and manipulate data from a relational database. It employs the Structured Query Language (SQL), as defined in the American National Standard Database Language—SQL standard and as used in IBM's relational database products, DB2 and SQL/DS.

- **Query Interface.** The *query interface* allows end users to access and update a relational database and request the formatting of reports using the results of queries. The functions that are part of the query interface are designed to be easy to use and accessible via menus. The query interface is based on the Query Management Facility (QMF) that is used with the DB2 database management system.

- **Dialog Interface.** The *dialog interface* provides services used to control user interaction with the application. These services support the display of information on the screen, the passing of data and function requests from the user to the application, and the flow of panels that make up the dialog. The dialog interface specifications are based on the ISPF and EZ-VU program products.

- **Presentation Interface.** The *presentation interface* provides formatting services for information presented on displays and printers. It includes specifications for both alphanumeric and graphic information. Features supported by the presentation interface include the use of windows, color, fonts, the double-byte character set for international languages, and both line and picture images. The presentation interface specification is based largely on the GDDM product.

IF Statement

TSO/E	CMS	OS/400	OS/2	IMS	CICS
X	X	X	X	X	X

The IF statement evaluates a condition and provides for alternative actions in the object program, depending on the evaluation.

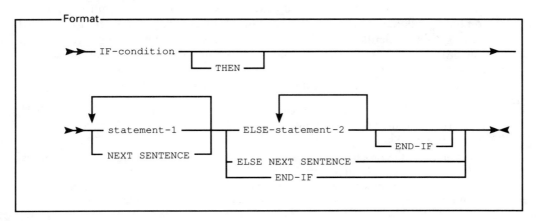

condition
    May be any simple or complex condition, as described in "Conditional expressions" on page 139.

statement-1
statement-2
    Can be any one of the following:

- An imperative statement
- A conditional statement
- An imperative statement followed by a conditional statement.

NEXT SENTENCE
    If the END-IF phrase is specified, the NEXT SENTENCE phrase must not be specified.

ELSE NEXT SENTENCE
    May be omitted if it immediately precedes a separator period that ends the IF statement.

END-IF Phrase
    This explicit scope terminator services to delimit the scope of the IF statement. END-IF permits a conditional IF statement to be nested in another conditional statement.

For more information, see "Delimited Scope Statements" on page 155.

Figure 1.7 SAA COBOL specification for the IF statement.

Both the dialog interface and the presentation interface are closely related to Common User Access. Panels and dialogs generated through these interfaces are designed to be consistent with the rules and guidelines that make up CUA.

The specifications that make up CPI are intended to provide application developers with a set of languages and services that can be used in any of the supported SAA environments. Although the specifications cover many aspects of an application developer's responsibilities, not every function of application development is included. For example, certain features that are specific to the hardware or to a particular operating system, such as job control language, installation procedures, tuning considerations, and compile-time and runtime options, are not included in the CPI specifications.

The Common Programming Interface has four objectives:

1. To provide consistency for the end user. This objective is met through the dialog interface and the presentation interface, which support Common User Access and its goal of consistent and easy-to-use end-user interfaces.

2. To enhance the productivity of application developers. This objective is met in two ways: through application portability and through skill portability. Applications developed in conformance with the CPI specifications are more easily moved from one computing environment to another, with minimal rewriting required to achieve this portability. The standardization of application development languages and services also allows a developer to move more easily between environments and to become productive in a new environment with a minimum of retraining.

3. To make it possible for applications to access programs, data, and other resources that are part of a different computing environment. The communications interface specifies a standard method for program-to-program communication. The database interface and the file statements in the procedural languages allow access to data. Underlying Common Communications Support facilities allow the CPI interfaces to be used to access remote data in a way that is transparent to the application and to the application developer.

4. To provide an enterprise-wide application development environment, where designing, modeling, developing, testing, and maintaining applications can be done in an integrated fashion. Providing such an environment requires the specifications that make up CPI, and also the full set of application development tools that are consistent with the specifications.

Users and vendors alike are realizing the value of specifying standard application-enabling architectures. Whenever a repetitive aspect of application development can be identified, a standard way of doing it can be specified, a tool to make it happen can be built, and the time it takes to build an application can be reduced.

COMMON COMMUNICATIONS SUPPORT

Common Communications Support (CCS) is a set of protocols, services, and standardized data stream formats that can be used to interconnect applications, systems, networks, and devices in a way that permits useful data interchange. The elements that make up CCS are drawn primarily from SNA, IBM's wide area network architecture, but there are also selected portions of international standards developed by organizations such as ISO, CCITT, and IEEE. CCS elements are divided into six categories: objects, data streams, application services, session services, network services, and data link controls.

Objects

Various types of data, such as text, images, and graphics, can be included in the data streams used to interchange data across the network. Each type of data is contained in the data stream as an *object*. Different object architectures define the structures of the objects used for different types of data. CCS currently includes definitions for six object content architectures and an object method architecture:

1. **Formatted Data Object Content Architecture.** This architecture is used to express the format and meaning of data elements that are stored in files and databases.

2. **Graphics Object Content Architecture.** This architecture defines the structure and content of graphic objects that contain such elements as lines, arcs, and character strings.

3. **Extended Graphics Object Content Architecture.** This architecture can be used to describe complex objects that can combine text, graphics, and bit-mapped images.

4. **Presentation Text Object Content Architecture.** This architecture defines the structure and content of objects containing text that has been formatted for display.

5. **Image Object Content Architecture.** This architecture defines the structure and content of objects containing bit-mapped images.

6. **Font Object Content Architecture.** This architecture defines the structure and content of objects containing information about type fonts that can be used control the appearance of printed or displayed text.

7. **Object Method Architecture.** This architecture defines elements called *methods* that can be carried with a revisable document. They carry information that describes how a data object should eventually be presented on an output device.

Data Streams

A *data stream* is a continuous stream of characters that conforms to a defined format. The format typically specifies the characters that are allowable within the data stream and the syntax and meaning of control codes that are embedded in the data stream. Five data stream definitions are included in CCS:

1. **3270 Data Stream.** This data stream is used for transmitting data between an application program and a 3270-type terminal. A 3270 data stream contains user data, commands, and control codes that govern the processing and formatting of data. For

data sent from a program to a terminal, the data stream controls how information is formatted and displayed on the device's display screen or printer. For data sent from a terminal to a program, it controls how the program interprets the data.

2. **Intelligent Printer Data Stream (IPDS).** This data stream is used to send data from an application program to an all-points-addressable printer. IPDS supports presentation of high-quality text, image, vector graphics, and bar code data, and control of device functions such as duplexing and media-bin selection.

3. **Mixed Object Document Content Architecture (MO:DCA) Data Stream.** This data stream is used to store and exchange composite documents, which may consist of a combination of text, graphics, and images. A MO:DCA (often pronounced to rhyme with vodka) data stream consists of data objects and control information, where the data objects can be of different types. The individual object content architectures described previously define the structure of data objects of a particular type.

4. **Character Data Representation Architecture.** This data stream is used to carry character data and information identifying the graphic character set, called a *code page*, used to display or print each character in the data stream.

5. **Revisable-Form Text Document Content Architecture (RFT-DCA) Data Stream.** This data stream is used to store and exchange text documents in an office system. An RFT-DCA data stream contains both text representing the content of the document and control information that specifies how the document is to be formatted. RFT-DCA specifies the structure used within the data stream to represent both text and control codes and how systems are to interpret the text and control codes. Revisable-form text documents are in a form that permits them to be easily modified by anyone who receives the document or has access to it. RFT-DCA is not a strategic data stream and is included in CCS only for migration purposes.

Application Services

Application services are those services that can be requested by SAA application processes. SAA application services enhance the services offered by the network itself by allowing SAA systems to distribute files, exchange documents, and exchange electronic messages. These services are defined by a number of IBM architectures, ISO standards, and CCITT Recommendations.

The CCS application services that are included in CCS for the SNA networking environment are the following:

- **Document Interchange Architecture (DIA).** This architecture specifies the means by which documents are exchanged between application processes running in SAA systems that are currently communicating with one another.

- **SNA/Distribution Services (SNA/DS).** This architecture specifies the means by which documents are exchanged between application processes on an *asynchronous* basis. Asynchronous in this context means that the recipient of the document need not be currently active in the network. Documents are stored until the recipient becomes active, at which time the document can be delivered.

- **SNA/Management Services (SNA/MS).** This portion of the SNA architecture defines services that allow users to plan, organize, and control the network in a consistent fashion.

- **Distributed Data Management (DDM).** This architecture defines the means by which files can be shared among SAA computing systems. It defines a data connectivity language that allows data to be interchanged in a consistent fashion among different types of SAA systems.

- **Distributed Relational Database Architecture (DRDA).** This architecture defines the way in which remote access to remote relational databases is handled.

The International Organization for Standardization (ISO) in Geneva, Switzerland, has documented a generalized model of system interconnection, called the *Reference Model of Open Systems Interconnection,* or *OSI model* for short. The primary purpose of the OSI model is to provide a basis for coordinating the development of standards that relate to the flexible interconnection of systems using data communication facilities. IBM has included OSI protocols in the application services component of the Common Communications Support interface as a way of supporting communication between IBM and non-IBM systems. The following OSI-related application services are included in CCS:

- **Association Control Service Element.** This is an ISO standard that specifies services and protocols that define how an application running in one open system forms an association with an application program running in another open system for the purposes of communication in the OSI environment.

- **File Transfer, Access, and Management (FTAM).** This is an ISO standard (also adopted by CCITT as a CCITT Recommendation) for the OSI application layer that specifies services and protocols that define a standardized way for accessing and transferring files between open systems.

- **X.400 Message Handling System.** This is a CCITT Recommendation (also accepted as an ISO international standard) for the OSI application layer that specifies services and protocols that define standard methods for transferring electronic mail messages between open systems.

Session Services

Session services are used to establish and terminate communication between two application programs and to transfer data between them. For SNA, CCS employs the formats and protocols that are defined by the *SNA Logical Unit Type 6.2 (LU 6.2)* architecture. LU 6.2 provides for program-to-program communication across an SNA network. LU 6.2 services are accessed via a protocol boundary that is defined in terms of a set of protocol boundary verbs. Each verb and its associated parameters provide a specific function, such as starting or ending a conversation between programs, sending or receiving data, synchronizing processing, or notifying a program of an error condition.

For OSI, CCS session services also support the following protocols:

1. **Presentation Layer—Kernel and ASN.1: ISO 8823, 8824, and 8825.** These protocols provide for connection establishment and release, for data transfer with synchronization and resynchronization capabilities, and for the use of contexts for determining data values. Data encoding is based on the use of self-delimiting values, where a value consists of an identifier, the value length, the value contents, and an optional end-of-value indicator.

2. **Session Layer—Versions 1 and 2: ISO 8327.** This protocol provides for both half-duplex and full-duplex transmission with expedited data transfer and exception reporting.

3. **Transport Layer—Classes 0, 2, and 4: ISO 8073.** This protocol provides for multiplexing of transport connections onto a network connection, the use of checksums and sequence numbers for error detection and recovery, and the use of sequence numbers for flow control.

Network Services

The *network services* category in CCS consists of the protocols used to provide routing services across a network. For SNA, it uses the protocols associated with SNA *Type 2.1 Nodes*. The facilities supported by Type 2.1 nodes are often described as SNA *Low Entry Networking (LEN)* facilities. The LEN protocols allow peer-to-peer connections between type 2.1 nodes. They provide the connectivity required to support LU 6.2 sessions, including the use of multiple and parallel sessions.

For OSI, two protocols are supported by the CCS network category:

1. **Connectionless Network Services (CLNS) Using the ISO 8473 Internet Protocol.** This protocol provides a best-efforts, or datagram, network layer service that includes no error handling or acknowledgment facilities.

2. **Connection-Oriented Network Service (CONS) Using Subnetwork Interface to X.25 (CCITT 1980 and 1984 Versions): ISO 8878.** This protocol provides a reliable, positive notification of failure network layer service that includes facilities for data transmission with acknowledgments, sequence preservation, and error detection and recovery.

Data Link Controls

Data link controls are responsible for the transmission of data between two nodes in a network over a particular physical link. This may involve sequence checking, flow control, and error detection and recovery. The data link control protocols included in CCS are *Synchronous Data Link Control (SDLC), CCITT Recommendation X.25,* and *Token Ring.* SDLC is used for managing synchronous, code-transparent, serial-by-bit transmissions between nodes that are connected by telecommunications links. CCITT Recommendation X.25 is used for packet-mode transmission between devices attached to a packet-switched data network (PSDN). Token Ring is used for transmission across a shared physical medium by stations attached to a local area network using a token passing access control method. The Token Ring protocols are based on the IEEE 802.2 and 802.5 standards (also described by ISO standards 8802-2 and 8802-5).

The Goal of CCS

The primary goal of Common Communications Support is to provide connectivity between applications across networks in order to support distributed application processing, distributed file processing, and distributed database processing. CCS includes protocols that allow non-SAA systems to participate in the connectivity and to exchange data with SAA systems. An SAA application accesses the various Common Communications Support components through the Common Programming Interface (see Fig. 1.8). For example, if an SAA application needs to communicate with another application, it does so using high-level language statements to invoke the services that are part of the CPI communication interface. These statements generate code that uses the protocols and formats defined by the LU 6.2 component of CCS to accomplish program-to-program communication during program execution. In this way, the application is shielded from the details involved in the CCS protocols. Similarly, an application uses the database interface (SQL) or file I/O statements that are part of one

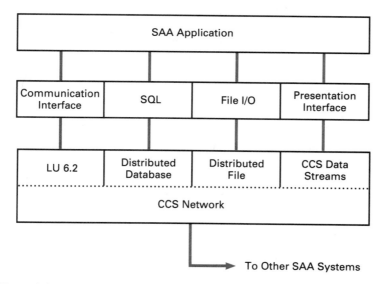

Figure 1.8 The CPI and CCS interfaces work together in handling communication functions for an SAA application.

of the CPI languages to access data. The underlying CCS protocols then provide the facilities needed to access distributed data in a manner that is transparent to the application. The CPI presentation interface allows an application to process data that are to be displayed or printed using one of the CCS data streams, again without the application being involved with the details of the CCS protocols and formats.

ARCHITECTURE VS. IMPLEMENTATIONS

SAA is an *architecture* and is not itself a product or set of products. A good architecture relates primarily to the needs of the end users rather than to enthusiasms for particular techniques. A well-architected house, for example, is one that reflects the desired life style of its owners rather than one that is designed to exploit a building technique that is currently in vogue. An architecture is independent of any particular hardware or software products that implement it. Often products do not implement all functions defined in an architecture because of constraints in the environment in which they are developed and must operate. However, product limitations are not necessarily architectural limitations. Different products may also choose to implement an architecture in different ways. As long as they conform to the rules of the architecture, they can use different techniques to implement the rules. The underlying architecture does not dictate, nor is it affected by, these implementation choices.

Although architectures provide rules for the development of new products, these rules can change. Computing requirements are extensive and are complex to define and implement. The architectures must be able to grow and adapt to new ideas and technologies. This means that the development of architectures like SAA is an evolutionary process. The term *architecture* in the computer industry often implies an overall scheme or plan that has not necessarily yet been fully implemented. It is the goal toward which its implementors strive. Thus architectures are bound to change as new hardware, software, and techniques are developed.

In describing SAA, IBM has defined the term *architecture* in the following way: "An architecture is a set of design principles that define the relationships of and interactions between various parts of a system or network of systems."

As an architecture, SAA defines a set of interfaces that, as we have seen, can be used consistently across multiple computing environments. The specification of these interfaces consists of data formats, protocols, and conventions. They define standard interfaces for end users interacting with applications and systems, for application developers creating programs and applications, and for programs and systems communicating across a network.

Many different hardware and software products have been and are being developed in the different computing environments. For these widely varying products to be used effectively and efficiently by applications in complex configurations involving multiple computing environments, they must be compatible; if compatibility is not achieved, complex interfaces would have to be built for meaningful interaction to take place. One of the primary reasons for developing architectures is to facilitate this compatibility.

By conforming to SAA, applications can be developed that are compatible with the different hardware and software products and can be used in or interlinked across multiple environments. When new products are developed that conform to the architecture, they will also be compatible, and can used with existing applications without major disruptions.

The goals and standards of architectures are important to both customers and vendors. The architectures must provide customers with a variety of choices in the development of applications, and they must allow customers to continue using the applications with relative ease as their overall computing environment evolves. Architectures should permit vendors to mass-produce hardware or software building blocks that can be used in a variety of different environments. They should also allow the development of new products that are compatible with existing products and can be integrated into existing systems without the need for costly interfaces and program modifications.

SAA: STRENGTHS AND WEAKNESSES

SAA, according to IBM Chairman John Akers, is the technology that will have the largest effect on IBM customers over the next five to ten years. In many ways, the transition to SAA represents the most significant change in IBM software environments since the introduction of the System/360 in 1964.

As its name implies, SAA is an architecture for building enterprisewide systems of applications. It is a consistent, open set of specifications for how these applications will be built. Many vendors, including IBM, have recognized the need for integrated computing environments. Today, organizations often mix many types of computers. All the machines serve different, but sometimes overlapping, functions. They are programmed differently and have different user interfaces, and there is little communication between them. It is not easy to build applications that can make the best use of differing machine capabilities.

The objective of integrated computing environments is to provide seamless connections between all the machines, so information and processes can be distributed freely among them. Additional objectives include the provision of consistent user interfaces for all applications. Such an environment provides programmers with a consistent development environment that makes it easy to build applications for a distributed environment.

SAA is the architecture that will accomplish these objectives in the IBM environment. It is the architecture that will help IBM customers to build the distributed processing applications of the 1990s. IBM's SAA is an impressive effort to unify IBM's application environments under a single architecture.

However, we must recognize also that SAA is still in a formative stage. A well-designed architecture should reflect a unified and all-encompassing structure or model within which detailed specifications can be developed. At this point, SAA is more of a collection of interfaces and protocols that have been designated as standard across the SAA-supported computing environments. The underlying model for integrating the various specifications has not yet been fully developed. In a number of instances, the individual interface specifications have been developed based on existing products rather than being designed as part of an overall logical model. Since these products are not fully integrated, the specifications that make up SAA do not yet define a totally seamless environment. As SAA continues to evolve, it will undoubtedly become more complete and comprehensive. IBM's development of an application-development model, AD/Cycle, with its underlying repository, is a step in this direction.

SAA: An Open Architecture

There is also the question of whether SAA is truly an open architecture. One of the major limitations of vendor-developed architectures is their proprietary nature. SAA is a proprietary architecture from IBM, not the result of a standards-setting organization. SAA is open in that it specifies a common set of software interfaces across multiple hardware platforms. It supports both proprietary services and protocols, such as SNA and LU 6.2, as well as international standards, including support for ISO protocols for communications.

However, we must understand that SAA plays a critical role in IBM's strategy to increase its dominance in the 1990s in both hardware and software systems. This strategy does not necessarily conflict with the needs of IBM's customers. Customers of IBM are currently expressing a growing need for greater connectivity and distributed-processing capability. SAA is designed to meet that need. However, SAA may tend to lock IBM in as a vendor. If SAA becomes the standard for an organization, then IBM or IBM-compatible hardware and software will be preferred in that environment. Competing vendors may be forced either to accept the SAA standard or to develop their own. Customers may then be forced either to accept SAA as the standard or to forgo its benefits.

IBM is responsive to the demands of the marketplace for an open architecture, as can be seen in its support for ISO protocols under the SAA umbrella. SAA had originally used IBM's proprietary SNA for communications, but many customers asked for support of the ISO protocols that were being developed in support of the OSI model. That support has been announced and partially implemented. In addition, much of the marketplace prefers UNIX as the environment for programmable workstations. IBM is responding to this demand with AIX, its version of UNIX, which is evolving to maintain compliance with the communication and programming interfaces of SAA. This will allow IBM customers to use either UNIX or OS/2 as the operating system for programmable workstations.

Still, difficulties remain, because the programmer must choose between the SNA or OSI communications interface. The same problems exist with the programming interfaces, database services, and the user interface. Sensitive to language standards, IBM will most likely continue to support international language standards. The database standards will be driven by its own products, as will the user interface standards.

SAA Implementation

Another current limitation of SAA is the lack of system software and tools that can be used to develop and execute SAA-compliant applications in all the designated computing environments. IBM has committed to provide products in all environments within two years of the publication of an SAA specification. Doing this will be a major challenge for IBM and will continue to be a challenge as SAA expands and evolves. IBM has also indicated that SAA-enabling products may be implemented in different ways. Some products will have versions available in each of the SAA environments—MVS, VM, OS/400, and OS/2. In this case, an application can be developed and run in any of the environments as a stand-alone system and can also be ported from one environment to another. Some SAA functions that are intended to be used where processing is distributed across different systems may be implemented in products that involve distributed processing. In a case like this, the SAA-enabling tool may require both OS/2 and a connected host, with the function not available on a stand-alone basis in a single environment.

THE FUTURE OF SAA

SAA has the potential of having great impact on the future of computing. For IBM, it will eventually reduce the resources required to support overlapping products and allow more resources to be invested in providing new functions and new products. SAA holds the promise of increasing application development productivity, for IBM, for other vendors, and for customers. The skills of application developers will be leveraged across multiple environments, and the multisystem use of applications will be facilitated.

SAA also facilitates the use of multisystem computing and enterprisewide networks that combine different computing environments. SAA applications will be able to employ distributed application processing, distributed file processing, and distributed database processing. The use of these types of processing effectively and efficiently is key to IBM's view of the future, where workstations are on every desk, connected to medium and large-scale processors acting as departmental and corporate systems. The workstation provides a consistent user interface—based on the Common User Access—to the network and to host systems. The workstation may also perform parts of the application processing, as appropriate to the power of the workstation and the particular application. IBM's hope is that SAA will facilitate application growth, and that application growth will, in turn, drive the demand for IBM's computing systems.

In a broader sense, SAA provides a strategic direction for the use of computing and has the potential to become the standard that defines a universal computing environment. In this environment, applications can be developed without regard to the underlying hardware or operating system. For this to happen, SAA has to be accepted as a de facto standard, by vendors and by customers. IBM has been successful in the past with establishing de facto standards. Its System/360 architecture underlies the current family of IBM processors that range from very small to very large and also underlies a number of plug-compatible processors. SNA has become the most widely used network architecture, with a large number of non-IBM vendors providing products and interfaces that support SNA. The SQL language is well on its way to becoming a standard for database processing.

For SAA to be successful in achieving widespread acceptance, several things must occur. IBM must, in a reasonable time period, implement the system software and application development tools needed to develop and execute SAA-compliant applications in all the designated computing environments. There also is a need to have a critical mass of SAA applications developed, by IBM, by other vendors, and by customers. Finally, SAA must continue to expand and evolve, so that it addresses all areas required for true cross-system consistency and connectivity. SAA has already evolved since its original announcement by adding RPG, PL/I and the communications interface to the Common Programming Interface, and by adding the Distributed Data Management architecture and the OSI protocols to Common Communications Support. The original Common User Access specifications have also been expanded to provide separate models for nonprogrammable terminals and programmable workstations. Areas expected to be addressed within SAA in the future include security, distributed database processing, knowledge-based systems, the use of a central repository, and transaction processing.

The future of SAA, either in its development as an architecture or its success in terms of implementation, will not be determined in the short term. As with SNA, an architecture of this magnitude may well take eight or ten years before its full impact is felt. In the meantime, even partial observance and implementation can be valuable, by providing greater consistency and connectivity across different computing environments.

2 SAA APPLICATION DESIGN

INTRODUCTION   As system software and application development tools are developed that support SAA, many of the features and benefits of SAA will be incorporated in applications automatically through standard options and defaults within the tools. However, even with this automatic support, applications will need to be properly designed to take full advantage of the cross-system consistency and connectivity possible with SAA. The general design principles that are important in the SAA environment are the subject of this chapter.

DESIGN GOALS   One of the goals of SAA is to increase application portability, where an application developed in one environment can be compiled and executed in any of the other environments. Portability provides for more efficient and economical operation in several ways: Applications do not have to be rewritten for each environment, thus reducing development and maintenance costs. Programmers and users can be more productive, since they are not required to learn a new set of skills when an application moves to a new environment. As an application evolves and is modified over time, programming resources do not have to be expended to maintain significantly different versions of the application in different environments.

A second goal of SAA is to support connectivity between computing systems and between applications on different computing systems. This connectivity can be the basis for *distributed processing,* where the processing of an application is spread across two or more processors.

DISTRIBUTED PROCESSING   At the strategic level, the most important benefit of SAA is support for a distributed processing environment. Distributed processing implies that different functions of an application reside on different machines and the different components of an application on each machine work together. This is different from *function distribution* where similar components of applications reside on different machines.

A distributed processing approach supports the distribution of both processing power and data throughout a computer network. In a distributed processing application each processor attached to the network is assigned the functions that it performs best. For example, the functions assigned to host processors and programmable workstations may be completely different. Host processors are best at serving multiple users and coordinating access to large corporate databases. Workstations are best suited for user interface support and local analysis functions. Some specific application functions might be assigned to one or more computing environments. Both a host environment and a workstation environment are needed for most business applications. Until now, it has been necessary to assign applications to one environment, forgoing the advantages of the other. With the advent of integrated environments such as SAA, however, applications can be built that take advantage of both environments in a distributed manner.

With any one application, there are three components that might be separated using a distributed approach:

- User interface
- Application logic
- Database access

All three components of an application might run on a single machine (host or workstation), or the three components might be run independently on different machines. Depending on where these three application components are located, we can place applications into the following four major categories:

- Local processing
- Cooperative processing
- Distributed function processing
- Distributed data access

The following sections discuss each of these four categories of application. Keep in mind that complex applications may have some of the characteristics of more than one category.

Local Processing

With *local processing,* illustrated in Fig. 2.1, all programs and data reside at the same location, and thus all three application components reside on the same ma-

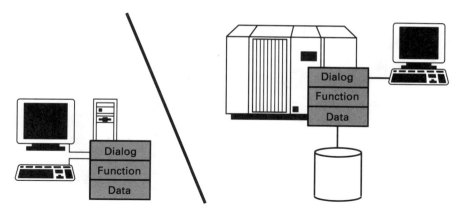

Figure 2.1   With local processing, the application's dialog processing, all of its dialog, function, and data access processing are all performed on the same computing system.

chine. The location might be the site of the user and might employ a programmable workstation to run all three application components, as illustrated on the left in the figure. Alternatively, the location might be the site of a centralized host processor, where the user communicates with the application using a terminal attached to the host via a telecommunications link, as illustrated on the right in the figure.

Cooperative Processing

One form of distributed processing, illustrated in Fig. 2.2, is *cooperative processing*. Here the processing needed to present panels, accept user input, and possibly validate that input is performed at the user's location. The application's general processing logic is performed at some other location. Information to be displayed is returned to the user's location for formatting and interaction. The data interface between the two computing systems allows data entered by the user to flow to the application and data generated by the application to be returned to the user.

Cooperative processing is typically performed using a personal computer for the user interface–related processing and either a midrange or large-system processor to handle other application functions. A personal computer offers several capabilities that can be used to make the user interface easier to use, including the following:

- Keystroke tracking
- Field highlight options

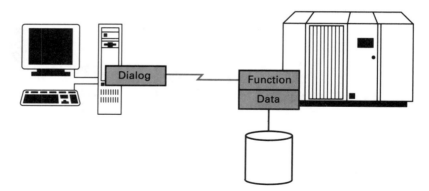

Figure 2.2 With cooperative processing, dialog processing is performed on a computing system at the user's location; function processing and data access processing are performed on a computing system at some other location.

- Color and graphics
- Automatic horizontal scrolling on data entry
- Single keystroke responses
- Multitask windowing
- Use of a mouse or other pointing device
- Predictable, fast responses to user input

Distributed Function Processing

Figure 2.3 illustrates *distributed function processing,* where application functions are divided into multiple segments. Each of the segments may be executed at a different location. Program-to-program communication facilities are used to invoke functions as they are required and to pass data between segments. Distributed function processing allows the unique processing capabilities of different processors to be used to best advantage. For example, graphics processing might be handled best by a personal computer, whereas computationally intense processing may require the use of a large-system processor. The key to this form of distributed processing is to design the data interfaces between the segments in a way that minimizes data transfer. Distributed function processing can be combined with cooperative processing.

Distributed Data Access

Another form of distributed processing, shown in Fig. 2.4, is *distributed data access,* which allows programs and data to be stored at different locations. Requests for accesses to data are sent from the processors that perform application processing logic to the processors on which the information resides. The proces-

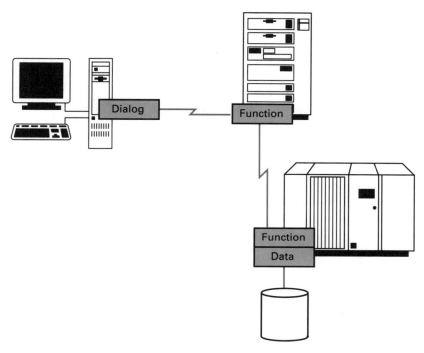

Figure 2.3 With distributed function processing, different application functions are executed on computing systems at different locations. Distributed function processing can be combined with cooperative processing.

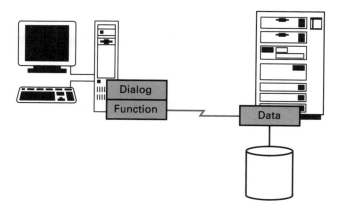

Figure 2.4 With distributed data access, dialog processing and function processing are performed at the user's location; data access processing is performed by a computing system at some other location. Distributed data access can be combined with cooperative processing and distributed function processing.

sors that maintain the files or databases process data requests and return the requested data to the application processors. This type of distribution can be implemented using distributed database systems, distributed file systems, or file server systems on a local area network. Distributed data access allows for the widespread access to data often demanded by the demographics of modern business while still maintaining security through centralized access control. This approach may also be used where local processors cannot provide the required data storage capacity. Distributed data access can be combined with distributed function processing and cooperative processing.

DESIGNING FOR DISTRIBUTED PROCESSING

Even though an application may not be implemented initially in a distributed processing environment, designing the application with these types of processing in mind will make it easier to migrate progressively to a full distributed processing environment at a later time. Isolation of modules is the key to designing applications for a distributed processing environment.

The first step is to isolate the user interface processing and the data access processing from the remainder of the application's processing. These are the two components of an application most readily adapted to a distributed processing environment. The user interface and data access components should be designed and implemented as separate modules, with the application using standard interfaces to invoke their services. Isolating these components makes it easier to move them later to a separate processor without having to make fundamental changes to the application. The next step is to separate application functions into modules whose services can be invoked by a high-level controlling function. These application function modules can then be located on the workstation or a host processor, as appropriate.

Good application design practices use isolation techniques to shield details of data access, user interface, application services, communication services, and security functions from other parts of the application. These techniques make it easier to maintain and port application modules regardless of whether SAA is used. SAA adds to the formula by providing tools and services for incorporating the isolated modules within a distributed processing environment.

DESIGNING THE USER INTERFACE

In addition to having the user interface isolated from the rest of the application, an application designed for an SAA environment should follow Common User Access specifications. As we have seen, the CUA interface of SAA defines a set of rules and guidelines that guide the design of the application's user interface. Following these guidelines will help maintain consistency in the user interface, both as the application moves from one computing environment to another and as a user moves from application to application.

Object-Action Principle

The CUA rules and guidelines are based on an underlying principle called the *object-action principle*. The object-action principle states that the user should first select the *object* to be acted upon and then select the particular *action* to take with respect to that object. To be consistent with this principle, an application should always begin by displaying a panel that allows the user to select an object and should then follow with a list of possible actions that can be applied to that object. An important benefit of the object-action approach is that the list of actions can always be tailored to the specific object chosen.

Presentation and Interaction

The design of the information that an application displays is an important part of the user interface. CUA defines general panel and window formats. These should be used as the basis for designing application displays. CUA also provides guidelines for the use of color and emphasis within panels. Because of the differences in capabilities between a nonprogrammable terminal and a programmable workstation, presentation techniques can affect application portability. Formatting decisions may, then, need to reflect the types of workstation supported by the application. CUA also defines standard methods of user interaction. The methods chosen for a particular application may also be determined in part by the hardware on which the application will run. Certain interaction techniques, such as the use of a mouse or other pointing device, may only be available if the application is run on a programmable workstation.

Message Design

Another part of the design of the user interface involves designing the *messages* to be displayed when different conditions occur. CUA provides guidelines for formatting and displaying different types of message, including system, warning, notification, and error messages. The design of the user interface should also address the use of help information. CUA includes standards for displaying different levels of help.

Dialog Flow

A fourth aspect of user interface design concerns the application's *dialog flow*. The application designer needs to ask the following questions when choosing the sequence in which to display panels and determining the options the user will have for continuing or terminating the dialog:

- **Normal Workflow.** In what sequence will functions normally occur in the application?

- **Possible Return Sequences.** How will the user terminate a particular function? How will the entire application be terminated? Can the user back up step-by-step within a function? When should the user be prompted to save data?

- **Restart Sequence.** How should a function be restarted if the user is interrupted for a period of time?

- **Help and Message Panels.** In what sequence should message and help panels be displayed? How does the user return to the normal dialog flow?

CUA provides guidelines for developing a dialog flow that will be consistent with the dialog flow of other SAA applications. Consistency in dialog flow is important so that the user can expect consistent results when taking similar actions.

DESIGNING FOR DISTRIBUTED DATA

CCS provides comprehensive support for distributed file processing, when an application is located on one SAA computing system and the data it processes resides in a file on another SAA computing system. Support is also provided for accessing remote relational databases. There are several challenges to providing distributed file and database processing in the SAA computing environments. Different file systems, different file formats, and different database management systems are used in the various SAA computing environments. Also, applications specify file and database requests using different types of I/O statements that are part of the SAA languages. The various languages have different I/O capabilities, and these differences must also be accommodated as part of distributed file and database processing.

Two architectures are included in CCS that define how distributed file and database access is performed: *Distributed Data Management* and *Distributed Relational Database Architecture*.

DISTRIBUTED DATA MANAGEMENT

The *Distributed Data Management (DDM)* architecture defines a standard file model and a set of standard file commands. A file request received from one file system is translated first into DDM standard commands. The request is then routed to the system containing the file to be processed. There, the standard DDM commands are translated into file requests appropriate for the target system. The request is processed and the results are returned to the requesting system using DDM formats.

DDM defines a standard set of commands for passing requests between file systems. These include OPEN, READ BY KEY, READ NEXT, CLOSE, etc. The portion of DDM that translates the original request into DDM format is called the *source DDM server*. The portion that translates from the DDM format to the format of the receiving system is called the *target DDM server*. Figure 2.5 illustrates the different environments that must be supported as part of distributed file processing in SAA.

Level 3 of DDM also provides facilities that operate in support of DRDA

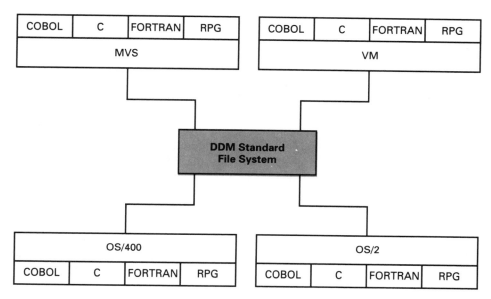

Figure 2.5   The SAA distributed file environments.

(described in the next section). DRDA allows application programs to access relational databases stored on remote systems. The DDM facilities required to implement distributed relational databases include definition of a standaradized relational database model and an application manager for the Structured Query Language (SQL). SQL is used to access relational databases. DDM packages the following into the proper data stream format for transmission over the network:

- Requests for access to a remote relational database.
- Replies from the remote system that maintains the relational database.
- Data from the relational database for transmission over the network.

DISTRIBUTED RELATIONAL DATABASE ARCHITECTURE

The *Distributed Relational Database Architecture (DRDA)* defines the way in which access to remote relational databases is handled. DRDA builds on the database interface defined by the Common Programming Interface (CPI) and on the relational database facilities of DDM. CPI defines a version of Structured Query Language (SQL) that is consistent across the various SAA computing environments. With a consistent language interface, support for distributed database facilities can be performed by an underlying database management system (DBMS). The DBMS can then process the SQL statements appropriately, regardless of the location of the application and the data. DRDA defines a CCS application service that operates in conjunction with Level 3 of DDM to provide support for a certain type of distributed database access called *remote unit of work*. The remainder of this section introduces this form of distributed database access and introduces the more powerful forms of distributed database access that will eventually be addressed in CCS.

The goal of the distributed database environment is to make the location of data being processed totally transparent to the user and to the application. The user should be able to make requests for data, and the application should be able to issue the appropriate SQL statements without regard to where the data is stored. From a practical standpoint, this complete transparency will take time to achieve. In the meantime, other levels of distributed database processing may be employed.

Application programs can employ two forms of distributed database access without requiring the use of any specific CCS application services for distributed database access:

- **User-Assisted Processing.** This is the simplest form of distributed database processing. With user-assisted processing, the user (possibly at a personal computer) makes a connection with the system on which the desired data is located (possibly on a large system processor). The user formulates a request to extract the required data from the large-system database and transfers the data back to the personal computer. Then the user processes the data on the personal computer. With this approach, the user must know where the data is located and be able to access and interact with both computing systems.

- **Remote Request Processing.** A second form of distributed database processing is *remote request processing*. Here the user interacts with an application running on one computing system to generate a data request. This application then sends the request to a second application located on the computing system that maintains the database containing the requested data. The second application submits the request to the DBMS on that computing system and returns the results of the data access to the first application. In this approach, the first application is known as the *requester* and the second application is called the *server*.

With remote request processing, CCS facilities are used only for ordinary communication between the requester and the server, and the DBMS in the database processor is unaware that distributed processing is taking place. The data request is submitted to the DBMS by the server application, which looks to the DBMS like any other local application. The DBMS holds and releases locks and performs recovery based on the server application. If there is a failure in the network or in the requester application, the DBMS is unaware of the failure.

Remote Unit of Work

The Distributed Relational Database Architecture defines a more powerful form of access to remote relational databases, called *remote unit of work*. In remote unit of work processing, the DBMS must be aware that distributed processing is taking place. In the remote unit of work form of distributed database access— the only form of distributed database access currently addressed in CCS—data requests are submitted directly from an application on one system to a DBMS on another system. Since a single SQL request can result in the DBMS making a great many database accesses, the idea of passing the SQL request itself to the remote DBMS can result in a reduction of network traffic that is required to satisfy the request. The remote application is then involved in the releasing of locks through its own COMMIT/ROLLBACK processing. The DBMS must be notified if the application fails so that it can take appropriate recovery action. With remote unit of work processing, the user does not have to know where the DBMS or the data is located, but the operating system at the application site must be prepared to communicate with the DBMS in the event of an application failure.

Other Forms of Distributed Database Access

IBM has described two other, more powerful forms of distributed database access that are not yet addressed in CCS:

- **Distributed Unit of Work.** With this form of distributed database access, data in multiple locations may be updated within the scope of a single transaction. The DBMS is responsible for knowing which systems manage the affected data and for coordinating the different accesses and updates. If a problem occurs during a unit of work, the DBMS performs recovery on all systems. With distributed unit of work processing, data can be updated in several locations within a single unit of work. However, separate SQL statements must be used for each location, and a given statement can affect data at only one location. This means that the application must be sufficiently aware of the location of data to avoid issuing an SQL statement that might reference tables residing in more than one location. IBM has announced that CCS will eventually include application services for implementing distributed unit of work processing, but the current version of DRDA does not support it.

- **Distributed Requests.** In this form of distributed database access, a single SQL statement can reference data from more than one location. The DBMS is responsible for determining where data is located, accessing it, and coordinating COMMIT/ROLLBACK and recovery processing among the different systems. With this form of distributed database access, data and application location is totally transparent to the user and to the application. The DBMS provides all the support necessary for distributed database processing. Although IBM has described this form of distributed database access, no plans for its inclusion in CCS have yet been announced.

3 INTRODUCTION TO CUA

INTRODUCTION   As we noted in Chapter 1, the Common User Access (CUA) component of SAA defines a standard set of components that are intended to be used in designing the user interface for an application. The user interface is the boundary at which a person and a computer application communicate. This communication typically takes the form of a *dialog,* where information passes back and forth between the person and the computer application in a manner similar to a conversation that might take place between two people. CUA specifies the characteristics of this dialog, both in terms of the appearance of information that is displayed on a workstation screen and in how users interact with the information using a keyboard or a pointing device, such as a mouse.

USER INTERFACE MODEL   Over the years, IBM has evolved a general model of the user interface. This model has guided the development of the SAA Common User Access interface and is based on three user interface components:

- **How the Computer Communicates with the User.** This component addresses how information that is accessed and computed by an application is translated into understandable form and presented to the user.

- **How the User Communicates with the Computer.** This component addresses how the user enters information, selects options, and indicates responses to a computer application.

- **What the User Thinks About the System.** Users develop conceptual models of the systems they work with. Such a conceptual model reflects the user's expectations of what the system is, what it does, and how it works. These expectations influence the way the user tries to use the interface to the system. A

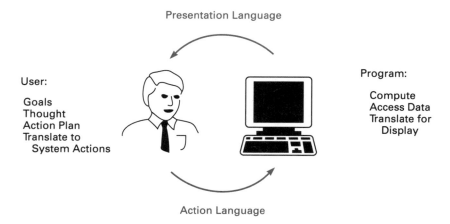

Figure 3.1   The SAA user interface model.

good user interface will help develop and reinforce correct expectations in the user's mind.

Figure 3.1 illustrates the major characteristics of IBM's view of a user interface model. The *presentation language* represents the ways in which the computer communicates with the user. The *action language* represents the ways in which the user communicates with the system.

INTERFACE DESIGN PRINCIPLES

The rules and guidelines for panel design and user interaction defined by CUA are based on a set of underlying design principles. One such design principle is the *object-action principle*. With the object-action principle, the user first selects an object to be acted upon and then selects the action that is to be applied to that object. Another principle is that an effective interface should enable users to develop an appropriate *conceptual model*. As described earlier, a user's conceptual model consists of the user's understanding of what the interface does and how it works. A good interface is one that is easy for users to understand and is consistent with the conceptual model the user develops. A third principle is that the *user,* and not the computer application, should be in control of the dialog. Users should be able to perform any actions in any sequence they choose in order to complete their work.

THE OBJECT-ACTION PRINCIPLE

In an object-action process sequence, the user first selects an object and then selects an action that operates on that object. With this approach, the user is able to perform a series of actions on a particular object without having to select it repeatedly. For example, the user could select a document, such as a spreadsheet, and then perform a series of actions on it, such as printing it, sending it to another user, and filing it away. An interface that requires the document to be selected for each operation is less convenient for the user. The object-action approach also allows the user to explore an application. The user can browse through the actions that are available for a given object without actually having to perform any of those actions.

An important part of designing the user interface for an application involves identifying the objects that the user will manipulate and defining the actions the user can apply to each of those objects. CUA guidelines define how the objects and actions should be presented to the user and how the user should interact with them. An interface designed in this way tends to focus the user's attention on the objects and actions that are available in an application rather than on the details concerning how the application performs its functions.

DEVELOPING THE USER'S CONCEPTUAL MODEL

A good user interface helps a user to develop an appropriate conceptual model and reinforces that model by providing expected outcomes for any user actions. For this to happen, the application model must match the user's conceptual model. Several techniques can be used to ensure that the application model and conceptual model correspond. A discussion of some of these techniques follows.

Reflecting the User's Work Environment

One approach is to have the user interface reflect a metaphor or analogy that is based on the user's real-world work environment. CUA, in defining standard actions and, in particular, as part of the *workplace extension* (discussed later in this chapter), takes activities that are typical of an office environment—processing files, editing documents, using the phone, processing mail, and so on—and reflects them in an electronic workplace.

Making the Interface Consistent

Another way of reinforcing the user's conceptual model is to make the user interface consistent. There are three different types of consistency that need to be addressed:

- **Physical Consistency.** This refers to physical positioning of hardware elements involved in the interface, such as a keyboard or a mouse. Having the function keys in the same position on the keyboard in all the various computing system environments is an example of physical consistency.

- **Syntactic Consistency.** This refers to the arrangement and position of elements on the screen and to the sequence of actions required to obtain a particular result. Examples of syntactic consistency are always to display the action bar at the top of a panel and always to display help information when the user presses the F1 key.

- **Semantic Consistency.** This refers to the *meanings* associated with the objects and actions that are part of the interface. For example, the cancel action normally causes the currently active panel or window to be removed and the previously active panel or window to become active. This allows the user to back up in a dialog.

There are several reasons for maintaining consistency, even though this may require making trade-offs against maximizing use of special features and facilities that are not available in all computing environments. Consistent interfaces reduce learning time for users, since the conceptual model developed initially still applies as the user gains experience with the application or moves to a new application. A consistent interface also increases a user's comfort with an application, which typically leads to increased use of it. Application development time can also be reduced by using standard basic building blocks to implement the user interface rather than designing and developing it from scratch for each new application. Reusable screen designs can also increase development productivity.

CUA supports consistency by establishing an interface with common presentation characteristics, common interaction techniques, a common processing sequence (object-action), and common actions. CUA defines standard forms of visual appearance for the components that are presented by the interface and specifies standard ways of arranging components in panels and windows. It also defines standard interaction techniques that help to ensure that the user always receives the same type of response when using a particular technique. The object-action process sequence provides a consistent method of interaction between the application and the user. The standard actions defined by CUA provide a common language between the computer and the user, making it possible for the user to predict the meaning and result of a given action wherever it occurs in a dialog.

Making the Interface Transparent

A user's conceptual model should include using an application to get specific tasks accomplished and should not focus on the mechanics of the application itself. To this end, the user interface should be simple and natural to use so that the user focuses on using objects and performing actions, and not on how the interface works. One way of doing this is to use work-related metaphors, as described previously.

Another way of keeping the interface simple is to avoid *modes* or *states* of the user interface where user interactions are constrained to a specific sequence or where the same action has different results in different situations. CUA does not employ modes for its normal interactions, although an application may need to use modes in certain situations. For example, when an error occurs, the application may enter an error mode where the user may be required to perform only error-correction actions before being allowed to continue with the task in progress. CUA guidelines specify that modes should be used only when necessary, and visual techniques should be employed to make it clear to the user when a particular mode is in effect.

PUTTING USERS IN CONTROL OF THE DIALOG

Users are in control of the dialog when they can explore options within the application without actually taking actions, can switch from one task to another, and can discontinue or suspend an activity that has not been completed without destructive results. Here are some ways of putting the user in control:

- **Automatically Reversing User Actions.** During a dialog, the user should always be able to leave the current panel or window, undo any changes that were made there, and return to the previous state. This allows a user to explore an application by selecting various options, seeing what results are produced, and backing up if the option chosen does not provide the desired result. The user should also be able to reset to their original state any values in a panel that are altered.

- **Providing Context Information.** The information displayed by an application should help a user to remain oriented within the dialog and within the application. Ways of providing context include providing panel titles, displaying scrolling location information, using windows to provide concurrent display of related information, and positioning a sequence of windows offset from one another to indicate their relationship.

- **Minimizing Reliance on User Memory.** A number of techniques can be employed to provide the user with memory aids and reminders. These include displaying currently available actions and currently active function key assignments. The general technique of allowing the user to make a selection by positioning the cursor on a choice or by entering a number or mnemonic rather than typing a command reduces demands on the user's memory. Graphics and icons can also be used to make controls more concrete and visible.

- **Providing Immediate Feedback.** Feedback should be provided following each user interaction. This can be done by using color or emphasis to highlight the cursor position after the user makes a selection. Audio beeps can also be used to alert the user to an incorrect action or a request that has not produced normally expected results.

- **Asking for Confirmation of Destructive Actions.** Before a potentially destructive action is taken, confirmation should be obtained from the user that the action is, in fact, desired.

CUA MODELS FOR MULTIPLE ENVIRONMENTS

As part of SAA, CUA must define standards and guidelines that are usable in a consistent manner in any of the SAA computing environments. This presents a significant challenge, since the different environments have significantly different capabilities, some of which have a big effect on user interface capabilities. One of the key differences is whether the user interface is implemented using a programmable workstation (PWS) or a nonprogrammable terminal (NPT).

In order to handle the great differences in capability between a nonprogrammable terminal and a programmable workstation, IBM defines two user interface models, with two versions defined for one of them.

- **Entry Model.** This model, sometimes referred to as CUA-1, is intended to be used for applications that support nonprogrammable terminals, such as a 3270 display. It is described by the SAA *Common User Access Basic Interface* and is documented in IBM's *SAA Common User Access Basic Interface Design Guide*.

- **Graphical Model.** This model, sometimes referred to as CUA-2, is intended to be used for applications that support a programmable workstation, such as a personal computer—specifically a personal computer that supports the Presentation Manager component of the OS/2 operating system. It is described by the SAA *Common User Access Advanced Interface* and is documented in IBM's *SAA Common User Access Advanced Interface Design Guide*. The CUA design guidelines that apply to user interfaces that employ programmable workstations are described in Part II of this book.

- **Text Subset of the Graphical Model.** This subset maintains a similar appearance to the panels defined by the graphical model. The text subset of the graphical model can be implemented on nonprogrammable terminals in situations where an application must support both programmable workstations and nonprogrammable terminals and needs to display similar-appearing panels on both types of equipment. The text subset of the graphical model is documented in *SAA Common User Access Basic Interface Design Guide*. The design guidelines that apply to the entry model and the text subset of the graphical model are described in Part III of this book.

IBM has identified a third user interface model, sometimes referred to as CUA-3. CUA-3 describes the user interface implemented by NeXT Corporation for its line of computing equipment, which runs a variation of the UNIX operating system. IBM has licensed the NeXT user interface for possible use on a UNIX workstation of its own. Since at the time of writing IBM has not published specifications for the CUA-3 user interface model and has not yet announced its intentions to implement this user interface on an actual product, this book does not describe CUA-3 further.

THE GRAPHICAL MODEL

The graphical model, used for programmable workstations, is based heavily on the Presentation Manager facilities of the OS/2 operating system. The graphical model presents information in windows, where a window is a bounded portion of a screen that displays related information. Multiple windows can be displayed on the screen at the same time.

Window Types

There are three major types of window that an application can display when it employs a programmable terminal to implement the user interface:

- **Primary Windows.** A *primary window* is used to carry out the primary dialog between the user and the application. It presents to the user the application objects and actions. Multiple primary windows can be displayed on the screen, each representing a different application.

- **Secondary Windows.** A *secondary window* is always associated with a particular primary window. It is used to support an independent, parallel dialog that is part of the same application. For example, help information is presented in secondary windows. The user can interact with the help information or can continue to interact with the application through the primary dialog in the primary window.

- **Pop-Up Windows.** A *pop-up window* is a window that is typically displayed for a short period of time on top of some other window. There are two types of pop-up window. A *dialog box* is a pop-up window that is used to extend a dialog and obtain additional information needed to complete an action. A *message box* is a pop-up window that is used to display messages to the user.

Window Components

The CUA graphical model defines a set of standard window components. Figure 3.2 shows the components used with primary and secondary windows. At the top of the window is a *title bar*, containing a *system menu icon*, the *window title*, and *window sizing icons*. The system menu icon provides access to different actions that can be performed on the window as a whole. The window sizing icons allow the user to increase or decrease the size of the window. The window also has a visually distinctive border.

The window may contain an *action bar*, which lists the actions available as part of the application dialog. The *client area* is used to present objects to the user. It may contain various types of displayed information, selection fields, and entry fields. *Scroll bars* are used when there is more information to be displayed than can be shown in the window at one time. The user can control the portion of the information that is displayed with the scroll bars.

Figure 3.3 shows the general window format used for a *pop-up window* that implements a dialog box or message box. Again, there is a title bar, but no

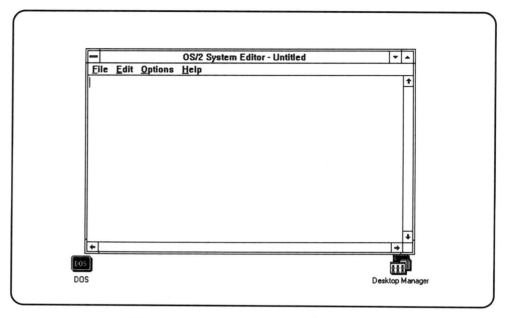

Figure 3.2   Window components used with primary and secondary windows.

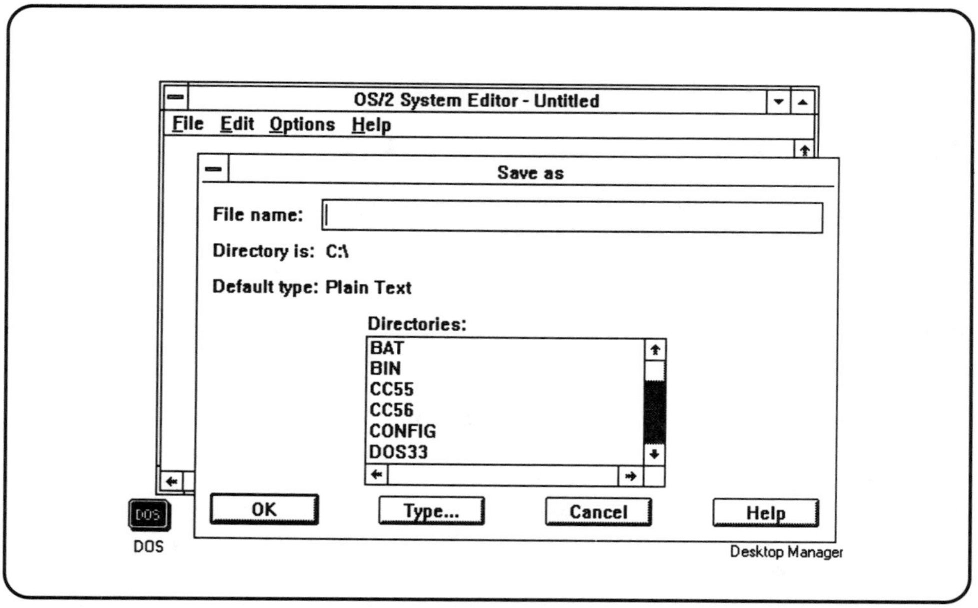

Figure 3.3   General window format for a pop-up window.

window sizing icons. The user cannot change the size of a pop-up window. The window has a border and a client area that can contain displayed information, selection fields, or entry fields. *Pushbuttons* at the bottom of the window show the actions that are available from this window.

Interaction Techniques

As we have discussed, the user interacts with an application by identifying an object and then specifying the action to be applied to the object. The two most common forms of user interaction for identifying objects and actions are *selecting options* and *entering information*. The primary method of selection used with the graphical model is the *point-and-select technique*. With this method, the user positions a pointer or selection cursor over a particular choice and then takes an action that indicates selection. This method can be used with either a keyboard or a pointing device. An alternate method of selection with the keyboard is to enter a *mnemonic* associated with a particular choice. For entering information, CUA specifies how the user moves the cursor, scrolls fields, and corrects typing errors.

Other general types of user interaction are *scrolling* and *switching areas*. When there is more information to be displayed than will fit in a window, scrolling can be used to move through the information. Scrolling can cause the information to move up and down or left and right. CUA defines the ways in which a user can cause scrolling to take place, as well as how scrolling is indicated in the window. CUA also defines the ways in which a user can switch positions from one area within a window to another or from one window to another. These interactions can be implemented with either the keyboard or a pointing device.

A user can also interact with a window as a whole. When multiple primary windows are displayed on the screen, the user can select the window that is to be the active window. The user also can change the position of any window on the screen, as well as the size of primary and secondary windows. CUA defines the techniques used for these window interactions.

Standard Actions

The graphical model defines standard actions that should be included in the action bar when certain types of processing are supported:

- **System Menu Actions.** The system menu actions are actions that can be performed on a window as a whole, such as moving, sizing, or closing it.
- **File Actions.** File actions allow the user to manipulate a file as a whole, including opening, printing, or saving it.
- **Edit Actions.** Edit actions allow the user to perform common document processing activities, such as moving or copying text.

- **View Actions.** View actions allow a user to display an object in various ways without modifying the object itself.

- **Options Actions.** Options actions allow the user to change the appearance of an object.

- **Help Actions.** Help actions provide the user with access to different types of help information.

Standard actions are also available through the use of pushbuttons. These actions generally allow the user to control interactions with the portion of the dialog that takes place in pop-up windows.

Workplace Environment

In addition to defining general guidelines and techniques for the user interface, CUA also defines an extension of the graphical model called the *workplace environment*. Together the graphical model and the workplace environment make up the CUA advanced interface. The CUA workplace environment is an electronic simulation of a real-world work environment. It uses icons to represent data objects, such as messages, text documents, spreadsheets, charts, and files, as well as functions that can be applied to data objects, such as storing, retrieving, editing, printing, and deleting. Users perform tasks in the workplace environment by directly manipulating the icons that represent data objects and functions. The CUA workplace environment also defines presentation formats, interaction techniques, and standard actions that are used in implementing a user interface to the workplace environment. By following CUA guidelines, applications can be highly integrated with the environment and can portray their functions as an extension of the real world.

NONPROGRAMMABLE TERMINAL USER INTERFACE MODELS

As introduced earlier, two models have been developed for user interfaces that are implemented using nonprogrammable terminals: the *text subset* of the graphical model and the *entry model*. These two models make up the CUA basic interface. With both of these user interface models, information is displayed in *panels*. The primary dialog with the application takes place using panels where one panel occupies the entire terminal screen. *Pop-up windows* in panels may be used to extend the dialog or to display information, such as help or messages.

Text Subset Panel Format

Figure 3.4 shows the general panel format used with the text subset of the graphical model. There is an *action bar* at the top. The *work area* contains the

```
      Find  Add  Exit  Help
_____
                       Communications Choices
    Select one.

       1. Received mail
       2. Messages pending
       3. Outgoing mail
       4. Mail log
       5. Action items
       6. Mail status




    Reformatting is complete.  Enter to continue.
    Command ===>     send stat.rpt to toni_____
    F1=Help  F3=Exit  F9=Actions  F12=Cancel
```

Figure 3.4　Text subset panel format.

panel title. Optionally, a *panel ID* can appear to the left of the panel title (not included in the figure). The rest of the work area is used to present information and to provide selection and entry fields to allow user interaction. The *message area* is used by the application to display messages to the user. The *command area* allows the user to enter commands directly. The *function key area* displays standard actions that are currently available and can be invoked by pressing a function key.

Figure 3.5 illustrates the use of an action bar *pulldown* menu. A pulldown specifies the specific actions that are available when the user selects a particular item in the action bar. Pop-up windows can also be used with the text subset. The pop-up window shown in Fig. 3.6 is an example of a *dialog box,* which displays additional information that the user needs to specify an action completely. Pop-up windows can also be used for command entry and for displaying messages, prompts, and help information.

The primary differences between the text subset and the full graphical model are that

- The text subset does not use icons or other graphical elements.
- Windows are not movable or sizable and do not have window title bars or window borders.

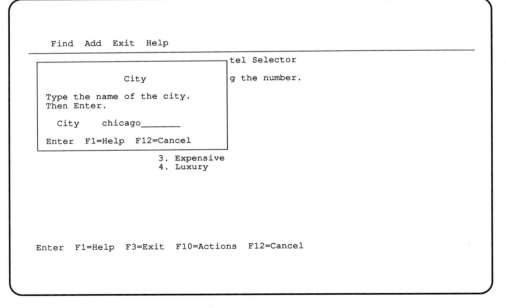

```
      Find   Add   Exit   Help
    ┌──────────────────────────────────┐ Selector
    │      1. One hotel...             │
Selec │      2. Many in same city...   │ e number.
Then  │      3. Many with same name... │
      │                                │
  Nam │  ──────────────────────────────│
      │  F12=Cancel                    │
      └──────────────────────────────────┘

      Price category    1  1. Budget
                           2. Moderate
                           3. Expensive
                           4. Luxury




      Enter  F1=Help  F3=Exit  F10=Actions  F12=Cancel
```

Figure 3.5 Action bar pulldown menu.

```
      Find   Add   Exit   Help
    ┌────────────────────────────────┐ tel Selector
    │              City              │ g the number.
    │ Type the name of the city.     │
    │ Then Enter.                    │
    │   City    chicago_____       │
    │ Enter  F1=Help  F12=Cancel     │
    └────────────────────────────────┘
                      3. Expensive
                      4. Luxury




      Enter  F1=Help  F3=Exit  F10=Actions  F12=Cancel
```

Figure 3.6 Dialog box pop-up window.

Entry Model Panel Format

Figure 3.7 shows the panel format used with the entry model. The entry model does not support the use of action bars and pulldowns. Also, the use of pop-up windows is optional. If pop-up windows are not supported, full-screen panels are used to extend the dialog and to display prompt and help information.

Interaction Techniques

Users with a nonprogrammable terminal interact with the application via a keyboard. CUA does not support the use of a mouse or other pointing device with nonprogrammable terminals. Users typically make selections by entering a number or mnemonic associated with a particular choice or a particular selection character alongside a choice. The point-and-select technique is more limited in its use. A special type of selection field, called an *action list,* allows the user both to select objects and specify actions to be applied to the objects. Scrolling is supported and is controlled using function keys.

Standard Actions

The basic interface, used with nonprogrammable terminals, also defines standard actions that should be included in the action bar when the actions are appropriate. These actions are a subset of the graphical model actions and include

```
                        Communications Choices
     Select one.

     _ 1. Received mail
       2. Messages pending
       3. Outgoing mail
       4. Mail log
       5. Action items
       6. Mail status




     Reformatting is complete.  Enter to continue.
     Command ===>    send stat.rpt to toni_____
     F1=Help  F3=Exit  F9=Instruct  F12=Cancel
```

Figure 3.7   Entry model panel format.

the File, Edit, View, Options, and Help actions. Standard actions are also defined that can be invoked using specific function keys. These actions generally allow the user to control the interaction between the application and the user, including such functions as scrolling, moving from one panel to another within a dialog, or obtaining different forms of assistance.

CUA: AN EVOLVING STANDARD As with all of SAA, CUA is in a state of evolution. It has undergone change since it was first announced and will continue to change in the future. The first version of the CUA specifications, published in 1987, was built on essentially a single model that was applied to both programmable workstations and nonprogrammable terminals. The specifications contained a large number of options and restrictions aimed at adapting the model to different device characteristics, such as supporting graphics vs. operating in character mode or being programmable or nonprogrammable. However, this approach, with its all-encompassing single model and single specification, proved to be very complex. Software developers found it difficult to work with in designing application interfaces. This version of CUA also failed to exploit the full capabilities of some environments (i.e., the programmable workstation operating under OS/2).

In 1989, a second version of the CUA specifications was released. In this version, nonprogrammable terminals and programmable workstations are addressed separately. The basic interface, covering the entry model and the text subset of the graphical model, specifies interface guidelines suitable for a character-oriented device with limited windowing capabilities. The advanced interface defines guidelines and a model that reflect the more powerful capabilities associated with a programmable workstation, such as graphics-based icons, windowing, and mouse interactions. Even within the second version of CUA, evolution continues. The appearance of certain icons used in the advanced interface has changed over time.

IBM has also indicated that new elements and interaction techniques will be added to CUA in the future, to reflect additional technologies that may be part of the user interface and as user requirements change. Areas of potential change that have been identified by IBM include touch input, full-motion video, standard actions for database applications, user ability to tailor mouse or keyboard interactions, and the use of context menus to provide actions associated with a particular object.

PART **II** THE CUA ADVANCED INTERFACE

4 ADVANCED INTERFACE
PRESENTATION TECHNIQUES

INTRODUCTION

In CUA, *presentation* is concerned with what the user sees on the screen, the way information is visually presented. For the graphical user interface model, the primary presentation component is the window. Multiple windows may appear on the screen at the same time. For primary and secondary windows, if there is sufficient space, they are positioned so they do not overlap. If necessary, one window can overlap another, as shown in Fig. 4.1. When windows overlap, a secondary window is positioned overlapping the primary window to which it relates. If primary windows overlap, the primary window for the currently active application is shown on top of the other primary windows.

A pop-up window (dialog box or message box) generally appears within or overlapping the window with which it is associated, as shown in Fig. 4.2. If a series of pop-up windows is required, they are positioned overlapping one another, each offset to the right and down.

WINDOW LAYOUTS

The graphical model defines the general layout to be used for windows and specifies the appearance of the different components that make up a window. CUA specifies the positioning of the elements within the title bar and the appearance of the system menu and window sizing icons. CUA also specifies the appearance and positioning of the scroll bars. The arrows in the scroll bar indicate the direction in which scrolling is possible. A scroll bar also contains a slider box between the arrows. The position and size of the slider box within the scroll bar represent the amount and location of the information being displayed relative to the total information available for display. For dialog boxes and message boxes, CUA specifies the positioning of pushbuttons and the appearance of the icon used to represent them.

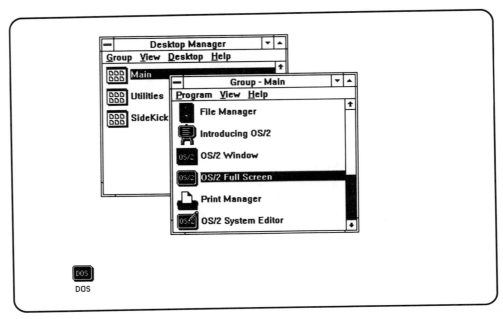

Figure 4.1 Overlapping windows.

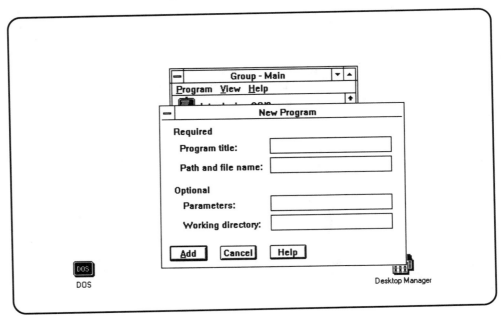

Figure 4.2 A pop-up window generally appears within or overlapping the window with which it is associated.

THE ACTION BAR AND PULLDOWNS

When a window contains an action bar, it appears directly below the window title bar. The choices in the action bar are listed horizontally. If mnemonics are used for the choices, the mnemonic for each choice is indicated by underlining. When an action bar choice is selected, a pulldown appears, as shown in Fig. 4.3. The pulldown is positioned directly under the choice that triggered it. The pulldown contains choices that represent specific actions that the user can perform in the action category indicated by the action bar choice. The choices in the pulldown are listed vertically, and if mnemonics are assigned they are indicated by underlining. Horizontal lines may be used to divide pulldown actions into logical groups.

Selecting an action from a pulldown can complete the user's interaction. However, at times there may be a need for further selections or information provided. When this is the case, a dialog box is used to continue the dialog with the user. An ellipsis (. . .) following a choice in the pulldown indicates that a dialog box will be used to gather the additional information needed for this action. Sometimes a pulldown action can be specified using a function key or control key combination. These are called the *accelerator keys*. If accelerator keys have been assigned to any pulldown actions, they are shown to the right of the action. If one of the choices in the pulldown has already been selected or is already active as a default, this is shown by a check mark, called the *current state indicator,* to the left of the choice.

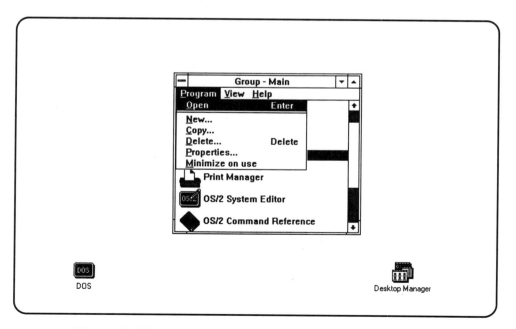

Figure 4.3   When an action bar choice is selected, a pulldown appears.

PUSHBUTTONS   Dialog boxes and message boxes use pushbuttons to specify actions, rather than an action bar and pull-downs. As shown in Fig. 4.4, pushbuttons appear at the bottom of the box. Each action is enclosed in a rectangular box. Mnemonics can also be used with pushbuttons. The default action for the box is shown with a bold border. Pushbuttons are arranged horizontally unless layout restrictions require them to be placed vertically. If a pushbutton action will cause another dialog box to appear, an ellipsis follows the action text.

THE CLIENT AREA   The application is responsible for determining what information should be displayed in the client area of a window and how it should be positioned and visually presented. However, CUA provides guidelines for methods of presentation and methods of interaction for the two most common types of field used in the client area: selection fields and entry fields.

SELECTION FIELD FORMATTING   A selection field presents the user with a list of choices. Three general layouts can be used to arrange the choices in a selection field: vertically in a single column, vertically using multiple rows and columns, or horizontally. The action

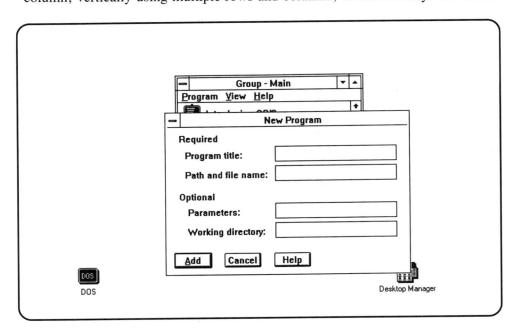

Figure 4.4 Pushbuttons appear at the bottom of a dialog or message box.

bar at the top of the window is an example of a selection field that lists choices horizontally. A pulldown menu is an example of a selection field that lists choices vertically. There are also a number of methods that can be used to identify fields, including column headings and field prompts.

The choices themselves can be represented by one or more words or by symbols that represent the choices visually. The examples here illustrate two types of selection field.

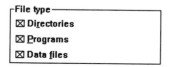

In this selection field, the choices are represented by words.

In this selection field, graphics are used to illustrate the choices that are available.

As with the action bar and pulldowns, mnemonics can be used in a selection field, with the individual mnemonics indicated by underlining. A mnemonic is a single character that identifies a particular choice. Where possible, the mnemonic should be the first letter in the choice. If that letter has already been used for another choice, then some other consonant should be chosen. If all consonants have been used, any other character in the choice can be used. If all the characters have been used, a character that is not in the choice can be used and added as a suffix character in parentheses.

USE OF EMPHASIS

A method commonly used in CUA to select a choice is the point-and-select technique. With this technique, the user moves a visual cue called the *input focus* to the desired choice (point) and then specifies an action that selects that choice (select). The input focus is an element on the screen that identifies the place at which the user's interaction will occur. The appearance of the input focus depends on whether the user is employing the keyboard or a pointing device to make the selection. With a mouse, the input focus takes the form of a *mouse pointer,* which normally appears as an arrow on the screen. With the keyboard, the input focus takes the form of a *selection cursor,* which takes the form of an area of the screen that is highlighted using a particular form of highlighting called *selection cursor highlighting.* Selection cursor highlighting normally takes the form of a dotted box that surrounds the current choice. Pointing to a choice with the selection cursor or mouse pointer allows the user to select that choice. When the user selects a choice, that choice is highlighted using another form of highlighting called *selected emphasis*. Selected emphasis usually takes the form of the colors of the choice being inverted. A selection choice can be in one of four possible states:

- **Uncursored/Unselected.** The selection cursor is not on the choice and it has not been selected.
- **Cursored/Unselected.** The selection cursor is on the choice but it has not been selected.
- **Uncursored/Selected.** The selection cursor is not on the choice and it has been selected.
- **Cursored/Selected.** The selection cursor is on the choice and it has been selected.

Use of the CUA-recommended techniques for selection cursor emphasis and selected emphasis allows these four states to be visually distinguished from one another. When selection fields are initially displayed, an application can provide default choices for the user. Default choices are indicated in the same way as selected choices, using the two highlighting techniques just described. CUA also defines ways of indicating choices that are currently unavailable. An unavailable choice is deemphasized by using reduced contrast or a color that contrasts less with the background color.

TYPES OF SELECTION FIELDS

The graphical model defines the appearance of certain types of field, called *controls*, that allow the user to select choices or enter information. Controls that allow the user to select choices include the following:

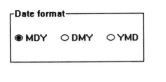

Radio Button. A *radio button* control consists of a circle icon followed by text describing a choice. Radio buttons are used in a selection field in which the user can select only one choice. The selected choice is indicated by a dot in the center of the circle.

Value Set. A *value set* is a single-choice selection field in which choices are presented without radio button icons. Choices are represented using either text or graphic elements. The currently selected choice is indicated by selected emphasis (normally inverse color).

Check Box. A *check box* control consists of a square box icon followed by text describing a choice. A check box functions like a switch, with the choice either "on" (selected) or "off" (not selected). A group of check boxes can be used for a related set of choices. With check boxes, the user can select any number of the choices in the group. Each selected choice is indicated by an X in the check box for that choice.

List Box. A *list box* consists of a rectangular box that contains a scrollable list of choices from which the user can select only one choice. Scroll bars are used to indicate and control scrolling. The currently selected choice is indicated by selected emphasis.

Dropdown List. A *dropdown list* is a list box that initially shows a single choice and a downward-pointing arrow.

When the user selects the downward-pointing arrow icon, the rest of the list box appears.

ENTRY FIELDS

An *entry field* is an area in which the user can enter information. It consists of a rectangular box containing one or more lines for entering data.

Name: ⬚

A field prompt, consisting of text that identifies the field, appears to the left of the box.

Date: ⬚ / /

Separator characters, such as the slashes shown here, can be used to help with the positioning of the data to be entered.

Number of copies: ⬚ 1-99

A description of possible values to enter may appear to the right of the box.

THE TEXT CURSOR

The *text cursor* is a symbol that indicates where typed information will be entered. The text cursor must be located in an entry field before data can be entered into that field. When the user moves the selection cursor or mouse pointer to an entry field, the selection cursor or mouse pointer turns into the text cursor. The appearance of the text cursor is determined by the application and is different depending on whether the insert mode or the replace mode is in effect. In insert mode, as new information is typed in, existing information shifts to the right. In replace mode, information typed in overlays existing data. The text cursor is normally a vertical bar (|) when in insert mode and an inverse video box when in replace mode.

COMBINED FIELDS

Certain controls combine the capabilities of selecting choices and entering data:

Combination Box. A *combination box* control consists of an entry field and a list box. The user can enter information into the entry field or select one of the choices from the list box.

Dropdown Combination Box. A *dropdown combination box* control is initially displayed with no list.

The list is displayed when the user points to the downward-pointing arrow icon.

Spin Button. A *spin button* control is an entry field in which the user can select a value by scrolling through a ring of choices. Spin buttons are commonly used for time and date values, where there is a fixed set of possible values.

FORMATTING GROUPS OF CONTROLS

Various types of control can be grouped together in a client area or dialog box to allow the user to select and enter information that is logically related. CUA provides guidelines to help format a group of controls as a field and in arranging multiple interactive fields. Various types of identifiers can be used to describe a field or a group of fields.

Field Prompts and Column Headings. A *field prompt* is text describing the purpose of a selection or entry field. It appears above or to the left of the field. A *column heading* can be used for a field that has items listed vertically in a column. It is located above the field. For an entry field, text describing possible values to enter can appear to the right of the field.

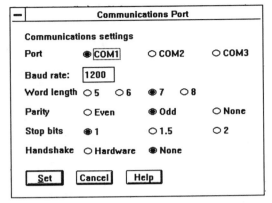

Group Heading. A group of related fields can be described with a group heading. A *group heading* is descriptive text that appears above a group of related fields. Field prompts can be used to identify individual fields.

Group Box. A *group box* can also be used with related fields. It consists of a title and a rectangular form enclosing the related fields.

CUA also provides general guidelines for arranging fields within a display area. These are summarized in Box 4.1.

USER FEEDBACK

The CUA graphical model specifies certain forms of graphical feedback that should be used to alert the user that specific conditions have occurred. The feedback keeps the user informed of the status of the application and indicates the progress that has been made in processing a request.

BOX 4.1 Guidelines for arranging controls.

- Arrange a group of controls that make up a single field as a single row or column.
- Align multiple selection and entry fields vertically and horizontally so the cursor is able to move in a straight line from one to the next.
- Arrange controls and fields in the order most users would logically process them.
- Arrange logically related fields in groups and identify them with a group heading or group box.
- Align group boxes where possible.

APPLICATION STATUS

The multitasking nature of a programmable worksta-tion means that the user may be able to continue the dialog and request a second action while the process-ing of a previous request is still in process. The application must have a way of informing the user that processing is in progress and when it is finally com-pleted.

Hourglass. For relatively simple oper-ations, processing in progress is indi-cated by changing the shape of the mouse pointer from an arrow to an *hourglass*.

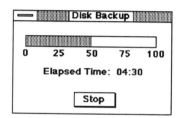

Progress Indicator. For a more com-plex operation that may take longer to complete, a *progress indicator* can be used. A progress indicator is a dialog box that provides information about an operation in progress. The bar at the top is used to indicate visually the per-centage of the processing that has been completed, if this can be calculated. The amount of time that has elapsed since the start of the operation is also shown. The Stop pushbutton can be in-cluded to allow the user to interrupt processing. Messages can be displayed to reflect any exception conditions that have been detected or other relevant information.

MESSAGES

Message boxes are used to display messages to the user when something has happened in response to a request. CUA defines three types of message, each of which has a unique icon:

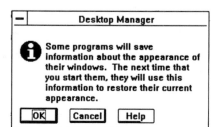

Information Message. An *informa-tion message* informs the user that an operation is in progress or has com-pleted normally.

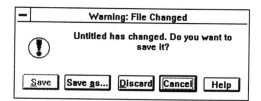

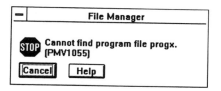

Warning Message. A *warning message* alerts a user to a condition that may require an action by the user in order for processing to continue.

Error Message. An *error message* indicates that an exception condition has occurred and that the application cannot continue until the user corrects the condition.

5 ADVANCED INTERFACE
INTERACTION TECHNIQUES

INTRODUCTION   As we have already described, consistency is important in the visual appearance of the applications a user works with. With a consistent appearance, users are better able to recognize or find the information they need to deal with. Consistency is also important in the ways in which a user *interacts* with an application. When users want a particular action to take place, they should be able to invoke it with the same interaction technique and should receive the same type of response from the application. CUA defines standard methods of interaction for selection and entry fields and for moving around within and between windows. With the graphical model, interaction can be done using either a keyboard or a pointing device, such as a mouse.

In CUA, interaction is concerned with the ways in which the user interacts with the application through the user interface. The two basic forms of interaction available to the user are *selecting choices* and *entering information*. We will look first at general techniques used for selection and entry, and then see how these techniques are applied to different window components.

KEYBOARD   Using various keys on the keyboard, the user is able
INTERACTION   to

- Move the selection cursor
- Select a choice
- Select a segment of text
- Enter data in an entry field
- Scroll information displayed on the screen

In the following sections we shall see how each of these keyboard interactions is performed.

MOVING THE SELECTION CURSOR

The cursor arrow keys (left, right, up, and down) can be used to move the selection cursor within a field or from field to field. Within a selection field, the cursor moves from choice to choice. Within an entry field, it moves from one character position to the next. Moving the cursor to a choice in a selection field causes the choice to be highlighted with cursored emphasis. Moving the selection cursor to an entry field causes the selection cursor to change into the text cursor.

The TAB/BACKTAB key can be used to move directly from one field to another. TAB moves the cursor to the next field, in a left-to-right and top-to-bottom direction, and BACKTAB (SHIFT + TAB) moves it to the previous field, in a right-to-left and bottom-to-top direction. If the cursor reaches the end of a window area, it wraps around to the field at the opposite end. If TAB or BACKTAB is used to move to a selection field, the selection cursor is positioned at the first choice within the field. If the move is to an entry field, the text cursor appears within the field.

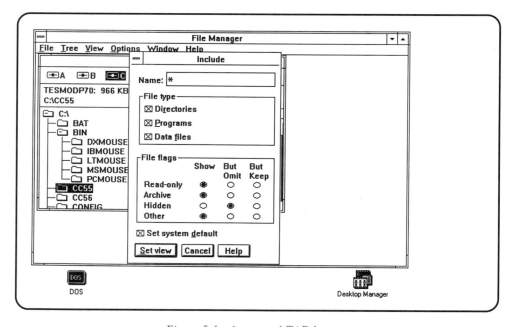

Figure 5.1   Arrow and TAB key use.

Figure 5.1 illustrates how the arrow keys and TAB key could be used. Assume the cursor is in the leftmost position of the first field, the NAME entry field. The right arrow key can be used to move the text cursor to the right within the entry field. When it reaches the last position in the field, the right arrow key moves the cursor to the next field, the FILE TYPES selection field. The down arrow could also be used to move directly to the FILE TYPES field. When the cursor is moved to the selection field, it is positioned on the first choice in the field. The down arrow or right arrow can be used to move to successive choices. After reaching the last choice, the selection cursor moves to the next field, the FILE FLAGS selection field. The TAB key could also be used to move directly to the FILE FLAGS field. The TAB key could then be used to move successively to the SET SYSTEM DEFAULT field and the pushbuttons.

A number of keys cause the cursor to move in various ways. These are described in Box 5.1.

Moving the Selection Cursor by Typing Letters

When a selection field contains a list of choices where mnemonics have not been assigned, the selection cursor can be moved within the field by entering a letter. The selection cursor then moves to the first choice that begins with that letter. The cursor always moves forward when moved in this manner. If an entry that begins with the entered letter is not found when the end of the list of choices is reached, the cursor wraps around to the top and searches from there. If no choice is found that begins with the entered letter, the cursor remains where it was before the letter was entered.

BOX 5.1   Cursor movement keys.

Key	Description
BEGINNING OF DATA (Ctrl + Home)	Moves the cursor to the top-leftmost position in the current field.
END OF DATA (Ctrl + End)	Moves the cursor to the bottom-rightmost position in the current field.
BEGINNING OF LINE (Home)	Moves the cursor to the leftmost choice.
END OF LINE (End)	Moves the cursor to the rightmost choice.

BOX 5.2 Window switching keys.

Key	Description
SWITCH TO ACTION BAR (Alt + F10)	Moves the cursor to the action bar.
SWITCH SPLIT WINDOW (F6)	Moves the cursor from one client area to the next in a split window.
SWITCH SECONDARY WINDOW (Ctrl + F6)	Changes the active secondary window in a multiple-document interface application.
SWITCH WINDOW (Alt + F6)	Changes the active window in an application.

Moving the Selection Cursor by Entering Mnemonics

When selection choices have been assigned mnemonics, the selection cursor can be moved directly to a choice by entering the mnemonic for that choice. The selection cursor does not have to be located within the selection field for a mnemonic to be entered, as long as it is located in the window area (action bar, pulldown, or client area) containing the selection field.

Moving from Area to Area

The cursor movement techniques just described can be used only within the currently active window; they cannot be used to move from one window to another. Nor can they be used to move between the client area and action bar or window title bar. Box 5.2 lists the keys that are used to switch from one window to another and from one area to another.

MAKING A SELECTION

There are three ways that the user can select a choice using the keyboard:

- **Mnemonic Selection.** If mnemonics have been assigned to choices, a selection can be made by entering a mnemonic. Entering the mnemonic also causes the selection cursor to move to the selected choice, which is shown with both selected and cursored emphases. If mnemonics are used, they must be unique within the area in which they are used—the action bar, a pulldown, or the client area.

- **Explicit Selection.** With explicit selection, the selection cursor is moved to the desired choice and the choice is then selected by pressing the SPACE BAR. When the cursor is moved to the choice, it is shown with cursored emphasis. When the choice is selected, selected emphasis is added. If the cursor is then moved off the choice, cursored emphasis is removed but selected emphasis remains.

- **Implicit Selection.** With implicit selection, a choice is selected automatically when the selection cursor is moved to it. The choice is shown with cursored and selected emphases.

Mnemonic selection can be used with radio button controls, check box controls, and value set controls where the choices appear as text. Mnemonic selection can also be used with the action bar, pulldown choices, and pushbuttons. Implicit selection is used with radio button controls and value set controls, where the user is allowed to select only one choice and all choices are visible. Other types of control use explicit selection.

Canceling a Choice

Once a choice has been selected, it can be canceled. For a selection field with radio button or value set controls, moving the selection cursor to another choice or entering a different mnemonic cancels the original choice. For a list box or combination box, explicitly selecting another choice cancels a previous choice. For a selection field with check box controls, the selection cursor must be moved to the selected choice and the SPACE BAR pressed. This acts like a switch, alternately turning the choice on and off.

Extended Selection

There may be situations where the user can select several choices, typically several objects all to be processed with the same action. The graphical model of CUA defines extended selection capabilities that allow the user to select

- A single choice
- A range or contiguous set of choices
- Multiple ranges of choices
- Multiple individual choices

To select a single choice, implicit selection is used. To select a range of choices, the cursor is moved to one end of the range, the SHIFT key is pressed and held down, and the cursor is moved to the other end of the range. Releasing the SHIFT key ends the range selection.

To select multiple ranges or multiple individual choices, the user must put the selection field in Add mode, by pressing SHIFT + F8. Once in Add mode, individual choices can be made with explicit selection by pressing the SPACE BAR when the cursor is positioned on the desired choices. Multiple ranges can be selected using the same technique as for a single range—holding the SHIFT key down while moving the cursor.

ENTRY FIELD INTERACTIONS When working with an entry field, the text cursor indicates where information will be entered when it is typed in. When the selection cursor is positioned on an entry field, the text cursor appears. As described in Chapter 3, the appearance of the text cursor varies, depending on whether the user is in Insert mode or Replace mode. Pressing the INSERT key causes the mode to be switched between Insert and Replace. As information is typed in, the text cursor moves along, indicating where the next character will be entered.

Replace Mode

When in Replace mode, the text cursor is initially positioned at the first character position in the field. When a character is typed in, it replaces any existing character in that position and the cursor moves one position to the right. The cursor automatically skips over any separator characters in the field. When the last character position in the field has been reached, the cursor stops, unless the field is an AUTOTAB field (described later). If the user overtypes the last character position, a beep sounds and an error message may optionally be displayed. The DELETE and BACKSPACE keys can be used to correct typing errors. DELETE removes the character at the current text cursor location. BACKSPACE removes the character to the left of the current text cursor location and moves the cursor one position to the left.

Insert Mode

With Insert mode, existing characters are not replaced as new information is typed in. The new character appears where the cursor was located, and the cursor and all characters following it move one position to the right. When the text cursor initially appears in the field, it is located to the right of any existing information in the field. As the cursor moves, it automatically skips over any separator characters in the field. If an attempt is made to type information into a field that is already full, a beep sounds and optionally an error message is displayed. The DELETE and BACKSPACE keys can be used to correct typing errors or to remove previously entered information from a field.

Replacing Text

An application can allow a user to mark a portion of existing information in an entry field and then replace the marked text by new information that is typed in, even though the user may be in Insert mode.

Document Name: bud**tg**137

Here, the user has marked the letters "tg" in the entry field by positioning the pointer, pressing the select button, and using the mouse to move the pointer across those two letters.

Document Name: budget137

The user has now typed the letters "get", which replaces the marked text.

Moving the Text Cursor

The text cursor can be moved within an entry field by using the cursor positioning keys. The left and right arrow keys move the cursor one character position left and right, respectively. Separator characters are skipped over. The WORD LEFT (Ctrl + ←) and WORD RIGHT (Ctrl + →) keys can be used to move the cursor to the first character in the word in the entry field that precedes or follows the current cursor location. The BEGINNING OF DATA (Ctrl + Home) and END OF DATA (Ctrl + End) keys can be used to move the cursor to the first or last position in the field.

AUTOTAB Option

A single-line entry field can be defined as an AUTOTAB field. When the user types a character into the last position of an AUTOTAB field, the selection cursor automatically moves to the next interactive field. If the next field is an entry field, the text cursor appears there. AUTOTAB fields are most useful in high-volume data entry applications, where they are used for fields that the user always fills in.

The ENTER Key

Normally, the ENTER key is used to submit a request for processing using the default action. However, when the cursor is in a multiple-line entry field, pressing the ENTER key moves the text cursor to the beginning of the next line. If there are text characters to the right of the cursor, they are also moved to the next line.

Marking a Text Segment

When doing text or document processing, the entire client area may act as an entry field, allowing the user to enter new data and modify existing data. For some text processing operations, the user may need to define a block of text. This may be done to move the text, copy it, change the font used for it, or perform other such actions. Marking the text is done by holding down the SHIFT key while moving the text cursor from one end of the block to the other.

Scrolling

Scrolling is used to change the information being displayed when there is more information available than will fit on the screen at one time. Entry fields and certain types of selection fields, such as the list box, can be scrollable. The entire client area can also be scrollable. Scrolling is indicated by scroll bars.

Scrolling can be either cursor-driven or cursor-independent. With cursor-driven scrolling, when the cursor reaches one edge of the scrollable field or area, the arrow keys can be used to scroll the information one line or position at a time. For a scrollable entry field, entering additional characters once the field boundary is reached will also cause it to scroll. Cursor-independent scrolling uses special keys to cause scrolling. For vertical scrolling, information can be scrolled a page at a time using the PAGE UP (PgUp) and PAGE DOWN (PgDn) keys. A page is equal to the number of lines in the visible area minus one. For horizontal scrolling, information can be scrolled left or right using the PAGE LEFT (Ctrl + PgUp) and PAGE RIGHT (Ctrl + PgDn) keys. Information is scrolled the width of the scrollable field or area minus one unit of information. Keys that move the cursor to a fixed place in the information, such as the BEGINNING OF DATA/END OF DATA or BEGINNING OF FIELD/END OF FIELD, will also cause scrolling to occur if necessary to position the cursor visibly.

MOUSE INTERACTIONS

All the interactions just described for the keyboard can also be accomplished using a mouse pointing device, except for entry of data. There are three basic operations that can be done with a mouse:

- **Click.** A click consists of pressing and releasing a mouse button without moving the mouse pointer. Clicking is used for selection. It moves the selection cursor to the location of the mouse pointer and causes that choice to be selected. Clicking is normally performed using mouse button 1 (the left-hand button on a two-button mouse).

- **Double click.** A double click consists of two clicks performed quickly in succession within a defined time limit without moving the mouse pointer. Double clicking is used to select an object and to cause a default action to be applied to it. Double clicking is also normally done with mouse button 1.

- **Drag.** Dragging consists of pressing a mouse button and holding it down while moving the mouse pointer. Dragging ends when the button is released. It is used for marking blocks of text and for direct manipulation. Dragging is done using mouse button 2 (the right-hand button) unless the mouse has only one button.

Selecting a Choice

Making a selection is done by moving the mouse pointer to the desired choice and clicking. The mouse pointer can be moved to any part of the window and from one window to another. Extended selection can also be accomplished with the mouse. An individual choice is selected by clicking. A range of choices is selected by clicking on a choice at one end of the range, pressing and holding the SHIFT key, and moving the mouse pointer to the other end of the range. Releasing the SHIFT key ends the range selection. To select multiple individual choices, the CTRL key is held down while a choice is selected by clicking. To select multiple ranges, the CTRL key is held down while the first choice is selected, and held down along with the SHIFT key while the pointer is moved. The other end of the range is established when the CTRL and SHIFT keys are released.

Entry Fields

A mouse can be used to move the cursor to an entry field by moving the mouse pointer to the field and clicking. The text cursor then appears in the field and data can be entered or modified using the keyboard. A block of text in an entry field can be marked with the mouse using a drag operation to define the beginning and end of the block.

Scrolling

Scrolling with the mouse is done using the scroll bar. Clicking on an arrow in the scroll bar causes incremental scrolling (one line or one position) in the direction of the arrow. Clicking above or below the slider box causes scrolling by one page in the appropriate direction. Scrolling can also be done by dragging the slider box. The information is positioned to correspond to the new position of the slider box.

Direct Manipulation

With direct manipulation, an implied action is performed directly on an object. For example, the window border on a primary or secondary window can be used to resize the window. A drag operation can be used to select a spot on the window border and then move it, causing the size of the window to change.

ACTION BAR AND PULLDOWN INTERACTIONS The action bar is a selection field. The mouse can be used to select one of the choices by clicking on it. The keyboard can also be used for action bar selection. The SWITCH TO ACTION BAR (F10) key is used to move the selection cursor to the action bar. A choice can then be selected with implicit selection or by entering a mnemonic. When a choice in the action bar is selected, its pulldown appears. By moving the cursor from one action bar choice to another, the user can successively see their associated pulldowns and thus explore the actions available as part of the application.

A pulldown choice can be selected using a mnemonic, by explicit selection, or by clicking it with the mouse. When the pulldown action is selected, this may complete the user's interaction with the window. In this case, the user's request (object and action) is submitted to the application for processing. However, for some actions additional information is needed. This is indicated by an ellipsis following the action in the pulldown. Selecting this action causes a dialog box to appear for the additional selection or entry needed to complete the request. For pulldown choices that have accelerator keys assigned to them, the accelerator keys can be used to select the action. An accelerator key can be used to select the action even when the pulldown is not visible.

Dialog Box Interactions

A dialog box can be either modal or modeless:

- A *modal dialog box* requires the user to complete the dialog box before continuing work in the application window that generated the dialog box. An application modal dialog box allows the user to work with other applications without completing what the dialog box requests. A system modal dialog box does not allow the user to continue working with any application until the dialog box request is handled.

- A *modeless dialog box* allows the user to continue processing in other windows before doing what the dialog box requests.

Since a modeless dialog box provides the user with more control over the processing, modal dialog boxes should be used only when necessary. For example, in opening a file, the user must provide the file name before the request can be processed. In this case, a modal dialog box might be used to ask the user to enter a file name.

Dialog Box Pushbuttons

Pushbuttons are used to specify actions that are related to dialog box processing. When a pushbutton is selected, the specified action takes place immediately. Certain actions will complete the user's interaction with the dialog box:

- **OK.** The OK action indicates that the user has finished making selections and entries and wants the request associated with the dialog box to be processed.
- **Cancel.** The Cancel action closes the dialog box without applying any changes that the user may already have made in the dialog box and without submitting a request to the application.
- **Action.** An application can define actions to be taken when the user has finished interacting with the dialog box. For example, a dialog box associated with record processing might have actions of Add, Replace, and Delete. Selecting an application action completes the object-action selection process and causes the request to be submitted to the application for processing.

The ways in which a dialog box interaction can be completed depend on the purpose of the dialog box. A modal dialog box can be completed by

- Selecting OK or an application action
- Selecting Cancel
- Closing the dialog box window

A modeless dialog box can be completed by

- Selecting Cancel
- Closing the dialog box window
- Closing the window from which the dialog box was displayed

Message Box Interactions

A user's interaction with a message box is also based on selecting an action displayed in a pushbutton. For an information message, the only action provided is OK, which indicates that the user has seen the message. When the user selects OK, the message box is removed. For a warning message, the user can select either OK to remove the message box and continue processing or Cancel to remove the message box without continuing processing. A warning message may also give the user a choice of whether or not to perform a corrective action. The Yes and No pushbuttons are used for the user's response to this choice. For an error message, the user can remove the message box by selecting Cancel. Where retrying an operation is a reasonable possibility, such as with a device error, a Retry pushbutton can be provided.

Audible Feedback

In certain situations, audible feedback, such as a beep, is used to alert the user that a problem has occurred. Beeps are used when

- A warning or error message is displayed
- An invalid mnemonic has been entered for a selection field
- An unavailable choice has been selected

Users have the option of turning the computer's beep off. If the user has specified that the beep be turned off, then an application should not generate a beep.

WINDOW INTERACTIONS

There are various operations that can be performed on a window as a whole. These include the following:

- **Move.** The user can move a window to a different location on the screen.
- **Size.** For primary and secondary windows, the user can change the size of the window. The *minimize* action can be used to remove all windows associated with an application from the screen and replace them with an icon that represents the application. The *maximize* action can be used to expand a window to its maximum size, occupying the entire screen. The *restore* action can be used to restore a window to its previous size and position after it has been maximized or minimized. When the size of a window is changed, the application determines whether the information in the window is rearranged or rescaled, or if it is clipped.
- **Close.** Close removes a window and all windows dependent on it from the screen.
- **Switch To.** The Switch To action allows the user to switch to a window for another application.

System Menu

Selecting the system menu icon in the window title bar causes a pulldown listing available window actions to appear. The user can select one of these actions, as with an action bar pulldown. Figure 5.2 shows an example of a system menu pulldown.

Window Sizing Icons

The window title bar may also contain window sizing icons for the minimize, maximize, or restore actions.

Selecting one of the window sizing icons causes the associated window action to take place.

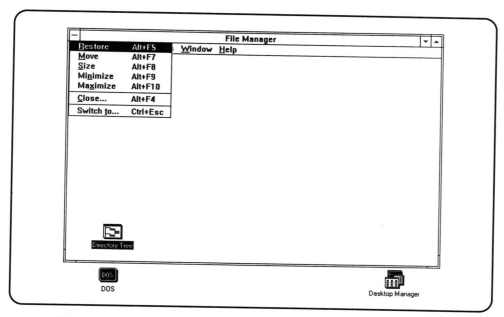

Figure 5.2 Pulldown listing the keys that are used to switch from one window to another and to move, resize, or close a window.

DIRECT MANIPULATION

The window border can be used to move or resize a window directly. The mouse pointer is moved to a point on the border, and the border is then dragged in the appropriate direction. For a primary or secondary window, dragging the border will expand or compress the window. For a dialog box or message box, it moves the window to a new location. By selecting a corner of the border, a window can be moved or sized in two directions at once.

6 ADVANCED INTERFACE DIALOG TECHNIQUES

INTRODUCTION   In addition to defining general presentation and interaction techniques, the CUA graphical model includes
specific guidelines for structuring the dialog that takes place between the user
and the application. These guidelines take the form of *standard actions* that can
be included in the action bar and its pulldowns, in the system menu pulldown,
and in pushbuttons. The graphical model also defines designs for standard interfaces that can be used to implement certain types of processing. These interfaces
include the multiple-document interface, split-window processing, and the
workplace extension. We will look first at the standard actions that the graphical
model defines.

SYSTEM MENU   The system menu icon in the window title bar of all
ACTIONS   windows provides access to a pulldown menu with a
standard set of window actions. The recommended
system menu for a primary window is shown in Fig. 6.1. These actions can be
used as follows:

- **Restore.** Returns a window to its previous size and position after it has been
  minimized or maximized.

- **Move.** Allows the user to change a window's position on the screen.

- **Size.** Allows the user to change the size of a window.

- **Minimize.** Removes from the screen all the windows associated with the currently active application and replaces them with an icon representing the application. The icon is normally placed in the lower part of the screen.

- **Maximize.** Enlarges a window so that it occupies the entire screen.

- **Close.** Removes the window and any windows dependent on it.

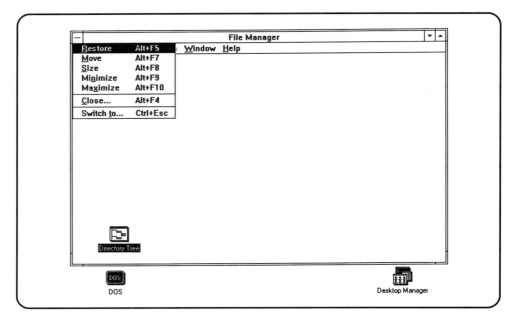

Figure 6.1   Recommended system menu for a primary window.

- **Switch To.** Allows the user to switch to another application. It causes a dialog box to be displayed that lists all active applications. The user can select an application from the list in order to switch control to that application.

For a secondary window, the Minimize and Switch To actions are not provided. For dialog and message boxes, only the actions Move and Close are included. The accelerator key assignments shown are also part of the CUA standard, and should be reserved for these window actions.

ACTION BAR CHOICES

CUA recommends that certain standard choices be included in the action bar when they are appropriate to the application:

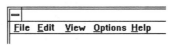

When these standard choices are included, they should be listed in the sequence shown. The functions provided by these choices are

- **File.** Enables users to manipulate an OS/2 file as a single object.

- **Edit.** Allows users to manipulate documents using typical document processing operations.

- **View.** Allows users to choose different ways of looking at an object without actually changing the object. For example, a calendar object could be viewed by day, week, or month.

- **Options.** Allows users to customize the appearance of an object. For example, in a drawing application, the user may be allowed to choose which drawing tools and color palettes are to be made available.

- **Help.** Provides users with access to various kinds of help information.

These choices are defined in CUA through associated pulldowns that provide the standard actions associated with each choice.

File Pulldown

The File pulldown provides actions that can be used to manipulate a file as a whole.

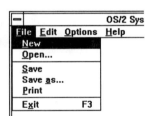

The recommended format for the pulldown is shown here. Horizontal lines are used to arrange the actions in the pulldown in logical groups of *selection* actions and *save* actions. There is also the general action Exit, which can be used to end the application. Application-specific actions for file manipulation can be added to the pulldown as needed.

The standard File pulldown actions provide the following services:

- **Open.** Finds an existing file and makes it available to the user for manipulation. A dialog box is used to allow the user to specify the name of the file to be opened.

- **New.** Allows the user to create a new file.

- **Save.** Causes a file to be written to a storage device. If the file currently being processed is unnamed, a dialog box is used to allow the user to specify the name to be used for the file.

- **Save As.** Used to make a copy of the current file. Save As causes the current file to be written to a storage device in the form of a new file that has a new name. A dialog box is used to allow the user to assign the new file name. The file also remains available, unchanged, under its original name.

- **Print.** Prepares a file for printing and submits it for printing on a user-specified printer. If the application supports the use of print options, a dialog box can be used to specify the options to be used.

- **Exit.** Ends the application and removes all of its windows from the screen. If information could be lost by exiting at this point, a message box is used that allows an opportunity to save the changed information.

Open Dialog Box

CUA defines the format of the dialog boxes to be used with the Open and Save actions. The Open dialog box, shown in Fig. 6.2, is used to identify the particular file being opened. The user can either enter or select a directory name and a file name. Application-specific options can be added to the dialog box. The user can complete the Open dialog, cancel it, or obtain help information by selecting the appropriate pushbutton.

Save As Dialog Box

The Save As dialog box is shown in Fig. 6.3. The user can select or enter a directory, and must enter the new file name under which the file is to be saved. The rest of the box is similar to the Open dialog box.

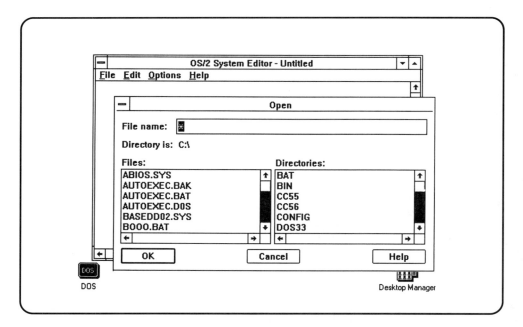

Figure 6.2   The Open dialog box.

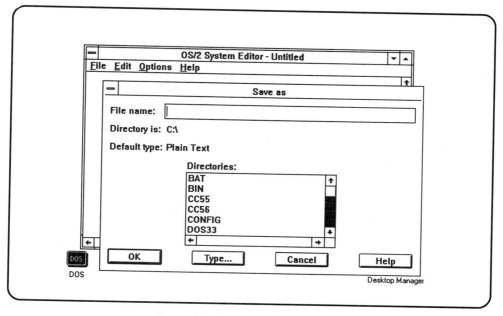

Figure 6.3   The Save As dialog box.

Edit Pulldown

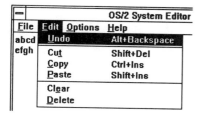

The Edit pulldown provides editing actions common to many types of objects that are based on operations typically performed in document processing.

Some of these actions support a clipboard. The *clipboard* is an area that an application makes available for the temporary storage of application data. Data placed in the clipboard can be transferred somewhere else while in the same application or can be transferred from one application to another. The actions in the Edit pulldown are logically grouped into *undo* actions, *clipboard* actions, and *nonclipboard* actions. The functions these actions provide are the following:

- **Undo.** Reverses the user action that was most recently executed.
- **Cut.** Copies a selected segment of the object to the clipboard and removes it from the object being edited.

- **Copy.** Makes a duplicate of a selected segment of the object and writes it to the clipboard.
- **Paste.** Copies the contents of the clipboard into the object being edited.
- **Clear.** Removes a selected segment of an object but leaves the space that the segment occupied.
- **Delete.** Removes a selected segment of an object and also removes the space it occupied.

View Pulldown

The View pulldown provides users with different ways of viewing an object. This can include specifying the amount of information presented, the presentation sequence, the format, and scale. The actual contents of the View pulldown will vary, depending on the type of object being viewed, so no specific View pulldown actions are defined by CUA.

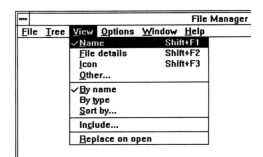

This View pulldown is used for viewing files and directories. The first set of choices determines what is displayed for each entry. The second set determines the sequence in which entries are displayed. The last two choices determine which entries are displayed.

Options Pulldown

The Options pulldown lets the user customize an object's appearance. As with View, the specific pulldown actions vary, depending on the type of object being processed.

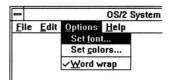

This Options pulldown is one for a text editing application.

Help Pulldown

Help information assists the user in working with the application. The information is generally intended to be used by someone who is familiar with the application but may need a reminder about syntax or about procedures associated with a particular panel. One way of obtaining help information is through selecting Help in the action bar.

This is the recommended Help pulldown used when Help is selected from the action bar in an application window. If a tutorial is provided for the application, Tutorial Help is included as a choice following Help Index.

The Help pulldown provides access to several different types of help information:

- **Help for Help.** Provides information about how to use the help facility.

- **Extended Help.** Provides information about an entire application window and the tasks that can be performed in that window.

- **Keys Help.** Provides a listing of the names and functions of all keys used by the application.

- **Help Index.** Provides an alphabetical index of help information for the application.

- **Tutorial Help.** Provides access to a tutorial on the application.

- **About.** Allows the user to view the logo window for the application.

Ways of Accessing Help

There are several ways in which the user can request help information. One is by selecting Help in the action bar of an application window and then selecting one of the pulldown choices. Alternatively, the user might place the selection cursor on a selection or entry field in the application window and press F1. A Help window explaining the indicated field then appears. This is called *contextual help*. Contextual help for a field in a dialog box or message box can be obtained by placing the selection cursor on the field and then selecting the Help pushbutton. If a window or box does not contain an interactive field, pressing F1 or selecting the Help pushbutton displays help information for the window or box as a whole.

A Help window provides access to the other forms of help by providing a Help choice in its own action bar.

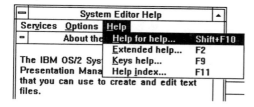

Once a Help window is displayed, accelerator keys are active for the other help options and can be used to request these additional forms of help.

Information in a Help window may contain certain words or phrases, called *reference phrases,* about which additional help information is available. These phrases are highlighted in the help text. Selecting a highlighted word or phrase causes the help information for the selected reference phrase to be displayed in another Help window.

Interacting With Help Windows

Help windows are secondary windows. When a Help window is displayed, the selection cursor is switched to that window. However, the user is able to switch back and forth between the Help window and the underlying window using the normal methods for switching between windows. This allows the user to complete interacting with the application while the help information is still available as an aid. The user's interaction with a Help window ends when

- The user selects Close from the system menu in the Help window.
- The user removes the application window from which the Help window was generated.

STANDARD PUSHBUTTON ACTIONS

In dialog boxes and message boxes, actions are provided for user selection in the form of pushbuttons rather than an action bar. When the user selects a pushbutton, the associated action is executed immediately. The graphical model of CUA defines certain standard actions to be provided in the form of pushbuttons:

- **OK.** Causes the application to accept any changes specified by the user in interacting with the box and to end the dialog with the box.
- **Apply.** Causes the application to accept any changes specified by the user in interacting with the box but does not end the dialog with the box.
- **Reset.** Cancels any changes specified by the user in interacting with the box and displays fields in the box with their original values.
- **Cancel.** Ends the dialog with the box without making any changes specified by the user in interacting with the box.
- **Help.** Causes help information to be displayed.
- **Yes.** Indicates a positive response to a question in the box and ends the dialog with the box.
- **No.** Indicates a negative response to a question in the box and ends the dialog with the box.
- **Retry.** Causes an operation to be retried after an error has occurred.
- **Stop.** Causes an in-progress operation to be stopped at the next nondestructive breakpoint.

Dialog boxes use the OK, Apply, Reset, Cancel, and Help actions. Message boxes use the OK, Cancel, Help, Yes, No, and Retry actions. A progress indicator uses the Stop action.

STANDARD INTERFACES

The graphical model provides guidelines for implementing certain standard types of interface, including the multiple-document interface, split-window processing, and the workplace extension. We now examine each of these interfaces.

MULTIPLE-DOCUMENT INTERFACE

The multiple document interface uses a series of secondary windows to let the user view different objects in the same application. The objects can be of the same type or of different types. The interface can also be used to let the user view the same object multiple times.

Window Positioning

One secondary window is used for each object or for each view of the same object. The windows can either be *tiled*, as shown in Fig. 6.4, or *cascaded*, as

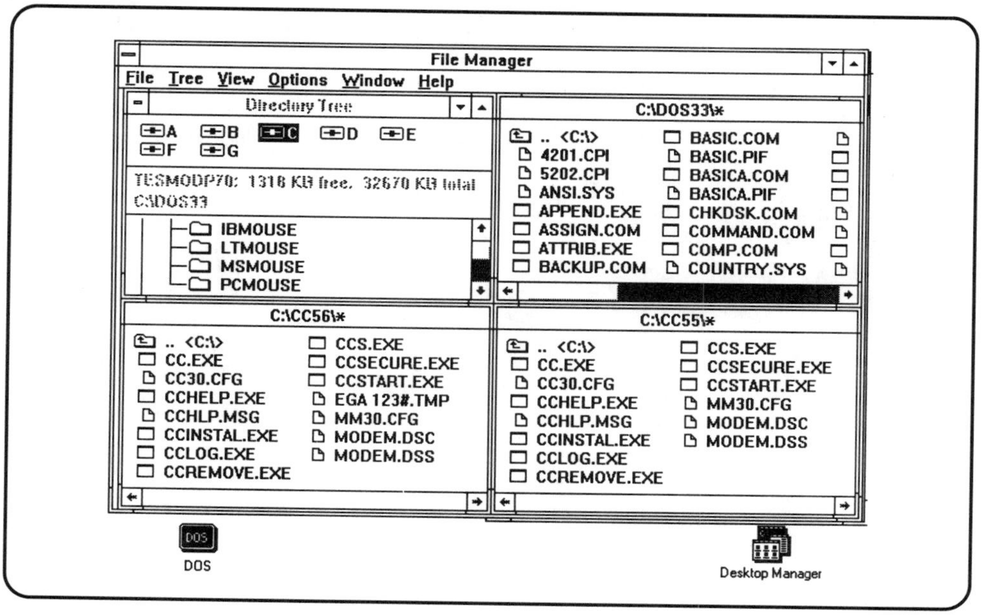

Figure 6.4 Tiled windows.

shown in Fig. 6.5. The secondary windows are movable and sizable, but only within the boundaries of the primary window. Any information that extends beyond the border of the primary window is clipped. Secondary windows can be minimized and shown as icons at the bottom of the primary window.

Window Switching

The user can interact with secondary windows only one at a time. There are several ways the user can switch from one secondary window to another:

- Move the mouse pointer to another window and click on it.
- Press Ctrl + F6 and cycle through the windows in sequence.
- Use the Window pulldown in the action bar.

Action Bar Differences

With the multiple-document interface, the secondary windows do not contain action bars. The actions associated with the object in the secondary window are shown as part of the action bar in the primary window. Since there may be different types of objects in different secondary windows, there may also be different sets of actions for the various secondary windows. Rather than try to include

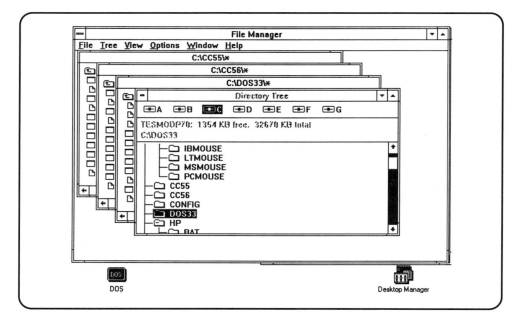

Figure 6.5 Cascaded windows.

all possible actions in the primary window action bar, a different action bar format can be defined and displayed for each secondary window when it becomes active. In this way, only the actions associated with the active secondary window need to be shown.

Because the application may be processing different types of objects, there is also a change to the File pulldown. The New action, used to create a new object, uses a dialog box that allows the user to specify the type of object being created.

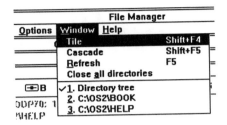

The action bar also includes a window choice. The top of the pulldown lets the user specify how the secondary windows should be arranged: tiled or cascaded. The bottom part of the pulldown presents a numbered list of the object names corresponding to the different secondary windows. The user can use this list to select the secondary window that is to be active. A check mark indicates the currently active window. The numbers in the list act as mnemonics.

If there are more than nine secondary windows, <u>M</u>ore windows . . . is added as a tenth choice in the list. Selecting this causes a list box to be displayed containing all the object names. The user can then choose an object name from the list box.

SPLIT-WINDOW PROCESSING

Split-window processing provides the capability to divide a window into sections, called *panes,* and to have different views of the same object displayed in the various panes. This capability is made available to the user by including a Split action in the system menu pulldown. Selecting Split causes a visual cue called the *split pointer* to appear. The user can move the split pointer to the desired location and then press ENTER or click the mouse. This causes the client area to be split into two or four panes, with *split bars* separating the panes. See Fig. 6.6. The user can drag a split bar with the mouse or again select Split and move the split pointer to change the size of the panes.

The different scroll bars allow the panes to be scrolled two at a time. For example, scrolling with the top vertical scroll bar scrolls the top two panes. Scrolling with the righthand horizontal scroll bar scrolls the right two panes. Using the scroll bars allows the user to view different portions of the object in the various panes.

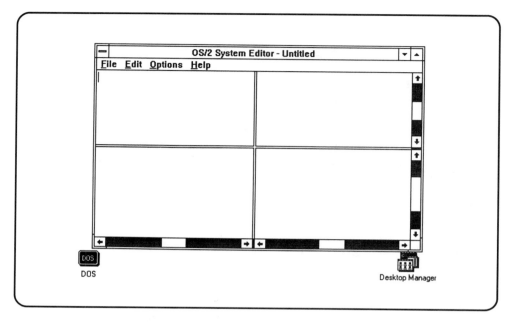

Figure 6.6 Client area split into four panes, with split bars separating the panes.

THE WORKPLACE ENVIRONMENT

The workplace environment is an extension of the graphical model describing a user interface that is intended to be an electronic representation of a real-world work environment. Objects found in the real environment are presented to the user for manipulation with operations similar to those used in the real world. The electronic environment defined by the workplace environment is referred to as the *workplace*.

Workplace Icons

The workplace uses a strongly object-oriented approach, with both objects and actions represented by icons. Icons are used for

- **Data Objects.** Objects like documents, spreadsheets and reports
- **Container Objects.** Objects like folders, file cabinets, and in-baskets that can be used to store data objects
- **Device Objects.** Objects like printers, shredders, and telephones that represent processing functions that can be performed using data objects

Figure 6.7 illustrates the types of icon that can be used in the CUA workplace. The variety of icons used allows direct manipulation to be the primary

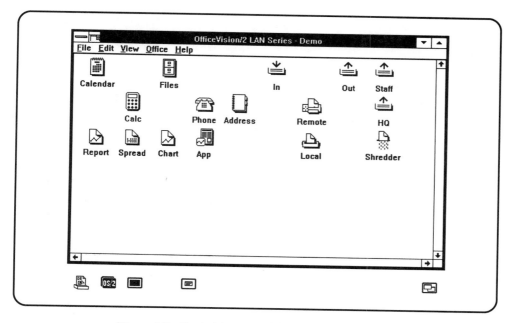

Figure 6.7   Typical icons used in the CUA workplace.

method of user interaction. For example, printing an object can be accomplished by dragging the icon representing the object to a printer icon. Similarly, an object can be stored by dragging its icon to a file cabinet icon.

Object Processing

An object is of a particular type, or *class*. For example, a spreadsheet object belongs to the *spreadsheet* class, a folder object to the *folder* class, and so on. Every object has properties associated with it. *Common properties* are properties that apply to each object, such as creation date and security class. *Class properties* apply to all objects of a given class. For example, the spreadsheet class would have rows and columns as attributes. A given object has specific values assigned to the properties. Thus, a given spreadsheet might have 20 rows and 10 columns. Users are able to change the property values for a specific object to make it suitable for their needs.

An *object handler* is a program created to process a particular class of objects. In the CUA workplace, when the user opens an object of a particular type, the object handler for that class of objects is invoked. Thus, opening a text document starts a text document processing program. An object handler lets the user change and edit both the contents of an object and the object's properties. The workplace also includes a *list handler,* which is a program designed to display the contents of container objects in icon or text form. The list handler allows the user to perform operations on the objects that manipulate an object as a whole.

Window Types

The workplace environment uses three types of primary windows:

- **Workplace Window.** The Workplace window is the initial window that is displayed. It contains icons for the container and device objects available in the workplace and may also contain data objects. Figure 6.7 is an example of a Workplace window.

- **List Handler Window.** A List Handler window displays the contents of a container object in text or icon form. The List Handler window can be used to open, move, copy, or delete entire objects. Figure 6.8 is an example of a List Handler window. Opening an object in a List Handler window invokes an Object Handler window for that object.

- **Object Handler Window.** An Object Handler window allows an object to be processed. It displays the object in the client area and provides actions that can be applied to that object. Figure 6.9 shows an Object Handler window.

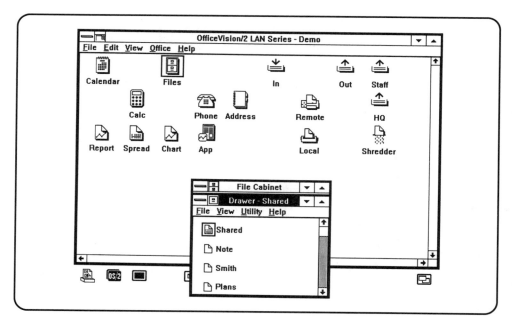

Figure 6.8   List Handler window.

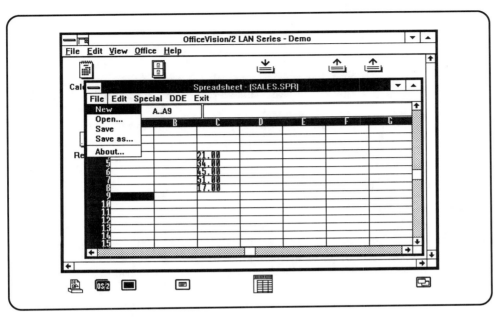

Figure 6.9 Object Handler window.

User Interactions

Users interact with the workplace either through action bars or through direct manipulation. The standard pulldown actions are supported in the CUA workplace, although there are action bar/pulldown differences based on window type. The Workplace window action bar provides the standard actions File, View, Options, and Help, but does not include Edit. The action bar in an Object Handler window supports all the standard actions. It also adds the Properties action to the File pulldown. Properties allows users to access the common properties of an object. Application-specific actions may also be added to the File pulldown. The action bar in a List Handler window does not use the Edit or Options choice. In the File pulldown, the Save and Save As actions are not provided, but the Move, Copy, Rename, and Discard actions are added.

Direct Manipulation

As discussed earlier, the CUA workplace interface is designed to use direct manipulation as its primary interaction technique. An object can be opened by double-clicking it with the mouse. Most operations can then be performed by using the mouse to move or copy the object. This is done by placing the mouse pointer on the object and dragging the object to its intended destination.

Generally, the target of the dragging operation determines whether the object is moved or copied. If the destination is a container object, such as a file cabinet or folder, the object is moved. If the destination is a device or an entry field, the object is copied. The one exception to this is the shredder. Although the shredder is a device, dragging an object to it moves the object rather than copying it. Pressing the CTRL key during the drag operation will change a move operation to a copy. Pressing the ALT key will change a copy operation to a move. Multiple objects can be processed in a single direct manipulation operation. This is done by selecting (clicking) a set of objects before performing the direct manipulation operation.

Title Bar Mini-Icons

Once an object is opened and displayed in a window, a miniature icon representing that object is added to the window title bar, just to the right of the system menu icon. This mini-icon can be used in a direct manipulation operation if the original icon used to open the object is not accessible. For example, the window containing the object may have covered the original icon.

PART **III** THE CUA BASIC INTERFACE

7 BASIC INTERFACE PRESENTATION TECHNIQUES

INTRODUCTION
Because of its more limited capabilities, the basic interface, used with nonprogrammable terminals (NPTs), does not support all the elements of the graphical model. Generally, a nonprogrammable terminal does not provide a windowing capability that allows multiple independent windows to be displayed on the screen. A nonprogrammable terminal is also more limited in its ability to support the point-and-select technique and to display graphics. With a nonprogrammable terminal, the user interface is based on presenting *panels* that the user interacts with. Basic panel formats and interactions vary to some extent, depending on whether the application is employing the entry model or the text subset of the graphical model. The primary difference between the entry model and the text subset is that the entry model does not support the use of an action bar and pulldowns.

PANEL COMPONENTS
The panel components defined by the basic interface model are shown in Fig. 7.1. An *action bar,* if used, appears at the top of the panel. Action bars are used only with the text subset, and not with the entry model. The *work area* is used to display application-specific information. Each panel contains a *message area,* which the application uses to display messages to the user. A panel may also contain a *command area,* used by the user to enter commands. The *function key area* displays function key actions that are available to the user.

WORK AREA
The *panel title* appears at the top of the work area. It is a brief descriptive phrase that indicates the function or meaning of the information contained in the panel. If a panel title is used, it is located centered in the first line of the panel. A *panel ID,* which is

```
        Find  Add  Exit  Help
                               Hotel Selector
      Select one from each group by typing the number.
      Then select an action.

          Name of city      1   1. New York
                                 2. Paris
                                 3. Tokyo

          Price category    1   1. Budget
                                 2. Moderate
                                 3. Expensive
                                 4. Luxury




      Reformatting is complete.  Enter to continue.
      Command ===>    send stat.rpt to toni____
      Enter  F1=Help  F3=Exit  F10=Actions  F12=Cancel
```

Figure 7.1 Panel components.

optional, is an alphanumeric field, ten or fewer characters long, that uniquely identifies the panel and helps the user identify the current position within a dialog. If a panel ID is displayed, it is left-justified on the first line of the panel along with the panel title.

PANEL FIELDS

The work area of a panel contains one or more *fields*. Three general types of fields can be used in the work area of a panel in whatever combination is needed for the application: *protected information, selection fields,* and *entry fields.* We describe each of these in turn.

PROTECTED INFORMATION

Protected information includes titles, headings, instructions, prompts, messages, and help information—any type of static information the user is not allowed to modify. Instructions at the top or bottom of the work area tell the user how to interact with the panel. Column headings are used to identify entry fields or selection fields that appear in a column. Group headings are used to identify a group of related fields. Field prompts identify a particular field within a group. Figure 7.2 illustrates the use of instructions and column headings. Fig-

```
                    Personal Address Book for A.C. Brown


      Select one or more by pressing /.
      Then press Enter.

          Name                     Telephone

          _  Anderson, Richard     555-8181
          _  Collins, Al G         555-7158
          _  Hanson, Charles       555-9161
          _  Lopez, Cristi A       555-7151
          _  Warner, Roxanne       555-8157







      Enter  F1=Help  F3=Exit  F12=Cancel
```

Figure 7.2   Instructions and column headings.

ure 7.3 shows a group heading and field prompts. CUA specifies guidelines for positioning, punctuating, and capitalizing these, and other types of protected information.

Displaying Copyright Information

If an application is copyrighted, copyright information should be displayed in the initial panel shown by the application. The information can be included as protected information in the work area or displayed in the message area. Figure 7.4 shows a logo panel used to display the copyright, along with information identifying the application.

SELECTION FIELDS   The basic interface uses the same general formatting guidelines for selection fields as the graphical model does. Choices can be arranged horizontally or vertically, and field prompts and column headings identify the field. However, with nonprogrammable terminals, icons, such as radio buttons and check boxes, are not used.

A selection field can be a single-choice or multiple-choice field. With a single-choice field, the user must select one and only one choice. A multiple-choice field allows the user to select any number of choices, or choose none of the entries.

```
                        Document Types

Select a document type by typing the number.
Then type new or existing document and folder names.
Enter when ready.

    Document type   1  1. Document
                       2. Memo
                       3. Note
                       4. Letterhead
                       5. Blank
                       6. Defaults

    Document identifiers
       Document name    _____
       Folder name      _____




Enter  F1=Help  F3=Exit  F9=Instruct  F12=Cancel
```

Figure 7.3 Group headings and field prompts.

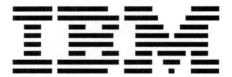

```
        ┌─────────────────────────────────┐
        │  Common User Access Samples     │
        │         Version 1.0             │
        └─────────────────────────────────┘

     (C) Copyright IBM Corp. 1987. All rights reserved.


          Enter to continue or F12 to Cancel
```

Figure 7.4 Logo panel displaying copyright information.

Single-Choice Fields

For a single-choice field, numbering and mnemonics are used as ways to identify choices. The user selects a choice by entering the number or mnemonic in a
choice entry field associated with the selection field. The choice entry field is
located to the left of the first choice. Choices are numbered sequentially, and
there are guidelines for numbering and identifying choices when the choices
themselves are numbers. Figure 7.5 illustrates the use of numbering for a single-
choice field.

      Mnemonics can also be used with a single-choice field, examples of which
are also shown in Fig. 7.5. To select a particular option, the user can enter either the number associated with it or its mnemonic, which is always under-
scored. Mnemonics are not used when the terminal used is not capable of displaying underlined characters. Guidelines for choosing mnemonic values are the
same as those for the graphical model.

Multiple-Choice Fields

With multiple-choice fields, there is an entry field alongside each choice. The
user selects a choice by entering a slash or other non-blank character in its entry
field. Figure 7.6 illustrates a multiple-choice field.

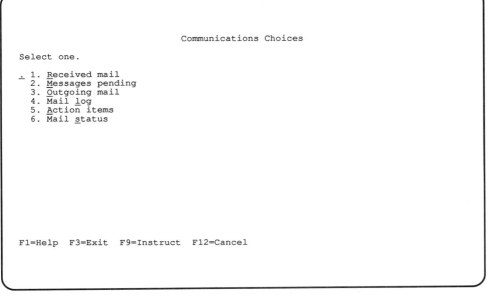

Figure 7.5   Use of mnemonics and numbering in a single-choice field.

```
                              Heading Options

     Select one or more.  Then Enter.

     /̲ Bold
     ̲ Underline
     ̲ Uppercase
     /̲ Section numbers








     Enter  F1=Help  F3=Exit  F9=Instruct  F12=Cancel
```

Figure 7.6   Multiple-choice field.

Variable Selection Fields

In some situations, the list of choices in a selection field may vary from one execution of the application to another. For example, the choices may be a list of the files currently existing in a given directory or a list of records in a given file. When a single-choice field has a variable list of choices, numbering and mnemonics are not used to identify the choices, as is illustrated in Fig. 7.7. In this case, a choice is made by placing the cursor on the choice and pressing Enter. For a multiple-choice variable field, choices still have choice entry fields and are selected by entering a character in the field.

Action Lists

An action list is a special type of selection field that consists of a list of objects, each having an entry field (see Fig. 7.8). The user can select one or more of the objects and can specify an action to be applied to each object. There are instructions and a list of action codes at the top of the field, followed by a list of choices. Each choice has an action entry field associated with it, as in a multiple-choice field. The list of choices can be scrollable. The user selects choices by entering one of the action codes in the action entry field. The action associated with that action code is then applied to that choice. Where action bars are not supported, action list fields can be used as an alternative for an interface based on the entry model.

```
      Details  Entry  Message  Exit  Help
                    Personal Address Book for A.C. Brown

   Select one.  Then select an action.


       Name                   Telephone        More:    ↓

       Anderson, Richard      555-8181
       Bettman, Marie         555-3025
       Collins, Al G          555-7158
       Dunhill, Peter         555-4734
       Hanson, Charles        555-9161
       Kavanagh, Tom          555-6426
     _ Lopez, Cristi A        555-7151
       Martin, Bob            555-2288
       Peternik, Karen        555-9007
       Thompson, Jean         555-1587
       Warner, Roxanne        555-8157


   Enter  F1=Help  F3=Exit  F10=Actions  F12=Cancel
```

Figure 7.7   Variable single-choice field.

```
                           Document List
   Type one or more action numbers next to your document
   choices and Enter.
   1=Copy    2=Delete   3=Display   4=Update   5=Print

    Action     Document

      _        Sales87
      _        Finance1
      _        Budget13
      _        Budget9
      _        Letter13
      _        Report20
      _        Letter17




   Enter  F1=Help  F3=Exit  F5=Refresh  F12=Cancel
```

Figure 7.8   Action list.

Selection Emphasis and Indicators

For a nonprogrammable terminal, there is only a single type of cursor—the *character cursor*. It always appears as a single character, whether it is positioned on a selection field choice or on an entry field. Also, there is no special visual cue to identify a cursored choice. Rather, it is indicated by the location of the character cursor.

A selected choice is indicated by the character entered in the choice entry field. For a single-choice field, the number or mnemonic is the selection indicator. For a multiple-choice field, slashes or other non-blank characters are the indicators. For action lists, action codes are the indicators. For a variable single-choice field, the position of the cursor acts as the selection indicator. A default choice is indicated in the same way.

Unavailable choices are indicated either by their display with reduced contrast or by the first character in the choice replaced with an asterisk. Reduced contrast is provided by a color change or a change in intensity. If the terminal does not support either method of reducing contrast, the asterisk technique is used. If the choice is numbered, the number is replaced; otherwise, the first character of the choice text is replaced.

Scrollable Selection Fields

When there are more choices in a selection field than will fit on the screen at one time, the field can be made scrollable. This allows the user to move up and down the list of choices, displaying different parts of the list on the screen. Scrolling is indicated with standard scrolling indicators, which are described later in this chapter. Figure 7.9 shows a scrollable selection field.

ENTRY FIELDS

An entry field is indicated by underscoring:

          Name . . . . _____

An entry field should be large enough to contain the largest value the user will enter, and may consist of multiple lines.

Separator characters can be used to help with the positioning of the data entered, and text describing possible values can appear to the right:

          start date . . . ____ /____ /____ mm/dd/yy

The position of the character cursor indicates where typed information will be entered. The user controls the appearance of the cursor when it is in an entry field. It can be either an underscore or a solid block, and it does not reflect the entry mode of insert or replace.

```
                    Outpatient Payments
    Select payment type and patient name.   Then Enter.

        Payment type     3 1. Cash
                           2. Private insurance
                           3. Government insurance

        Patient name    ┌─────────────────────────────┐
                        │                     More:    │
                        ├─────────────────────────────┤
                        │  _ Baker, R. M.      Rm 101  │
                        │  _ Chatworth, A. T   Rm 101  │
                        │  _ Edward, M. E.     Rm 101  │
                        │  _ Frank, D. L.      Rm 101  │
                        │  _ Henning, F. T.    Rm 101  │
                        └─────────────────────────────┘




        Enter   F1=Help   F3=Exit   F12=Cancel
```

Figure 7.9 Scrollable selection field.

WORK AREA FORMATTING

A typical panel consists of groups of entry and selection fields used to allow users to interact with the application. Figure 7.10 shows a sample panel. The information entered can be for different purposes. It may provide parameters associated with an action request, or it may provide information to be processed by the application or stored in a file or database. CUA defines three common formats that can be used in designing panel work areas:

- **Parameter Format.** Generally used to provide parameters, or options, associated with an action request. (See Fig. 7.10.)
- **Form Fill-in Format.** Generally used to provide information for a single item or entity to be stored in a file or database. This type of panel resembles a paper form. (See Fig. 7.11.)
- **Tabular Format.** Generally used to provide information for a series of items and entities, using a row and column format. (See Fig. 7.12.)

All three panels follow the general CUA formatting guidelines for entry and selection fields and for features like scrolling. Where appropriate, default values can be displayed in an entry field or selection field. Descriptive text can be included to the right of an entry field. The descriptive text may provide a range of values, a general description of the information to be entered, or instructions on requesting prompting information for the field.

```
                          Document Types

Select a document type by typing the number.
Then type new or existing document and folder names.
Enter when ready.

     Document type    1  1. Document
                         2. Memo
                         3. Note
                         4. Letterhead
                         5. Blank
                         6. Defaults

     Document name       _____
     Folder name         _____




Enter  F1=Help  F3=Exit  F9=Instruct  F12=Cancel
```

Figure 7.10 Work area formatting—parameter format.

```
                    Create an Entry

    Type information. Tab between entries.
    Enter when ready.


      Name  . . .      _____
      Full Name        _____
      Title  . .       _____
      Bus Phone        _____
      Home Phone       _____
      Company  .       _____
      Department       _____
      Street . .       _____
      City . . .       _____


    Enter  F1=Help  F12=Cancel
```

Figure 7.11 Work area formatting—form fill-in format.

```
                    Personal Address Book for A.C. Brown

      Type information for address book entries below.   Then Enter.

      Name                 Address              Home Phone      Work Phone
      ─────────────────    ─────────────────    ─────────────   ───────────────
      ─────────────────    ─────────────────    ─────────────   ───────────────
      ─────────────────    ─────────────────    ─────────────   ───────────────
      ─────────────────    ─────────────────    ─────────────   ───────────────
      ─────────────────    ─────────────────    ─────────────   ───────────────
      ─────────────────    ─────────────────    ─────────────   ───────────────
      ─────────────────    ─────────────────    ─────────────   ───────────────
      ─────────────────    ─────────────────    ─────────────   ───────────────
      ─────────────────    ─────────────────    ─────────────   ───────────────
      ─────────────────    ─────────────────    ─────────────   ───────────────
      ─────────────────    ─────────────────    ─────────────   ───────────────
      ─────────────────    ─────────────────    ─────────────   ───────────────

      Enter  F1=Help  F3=Exit  F12=Cancel
```

Figure 7.12 Work area formatting—tabular format.

CUA provides guidelines for spacing and sequencing entry and selection fields. Each panel format has guidelines for arranging and identifying fields. In the parameter and form fill-in panels, field prompts are recommended, and fields are arranged in a single column, with field prompts, entry and selection fields, and descriptive text aligned vertically. For the tabular panel, column headings are recommended and entry fields are aligned vertically in columns.

SCROLLING INFORMATION

The information in the work area can be made scrollable if there is more to be displayed than will fit on the screen at one time. Scrolling can be both left and right and up and down.

For a nonprogrammable terminal, scrolling is indicated by the word "More" followed by arrows indicating the possible scrolling directions:

$$\text{More: } \leftarrow \uparrow \downarrow \rightarrow$$

If the terminal's character set does not include the four arrows, other characters can be used to indicate the possible scrolling directions:

$$\text{More: } < - + >$$

The indicators correspond to scrolling to the left, up, down, and right, respectively. Figure 7.7 contains an example of scrolling indicators.

Textual information can also be used to indicate relative position of the information currently being displayed. This information takes the form:

Itemname nn to mm of xx

Itemname identifies the type of item being displayed, for example, Lines, Columns, Employees, Files, Documents. *nn* and *mm* give the boundaries of the range of items currently being displayed, while *xx* indicates the total number of items available. *nn* can also be an entry field, allowing the user to specify where the information displayed should begin. Textual scrolling information can be displayed for both vertical and horizontal scrolling. If used, it appears right-justified on the line above the scrolling indicators. Figure 7.13 shows an example of textual scrolling.

If scrolling arrows are not available and only vertical scrolling is required, an alternate form of textual scrolling information can be used. When the scrollable area is at the beginning of the information, the indicator "Top" is displayed above the area and the indicator "More. . ." below the area:

```
AAAAAAAAAAAAAAAAAAAAAAAAAAA     Top
BBBBBBBBBBBBBBBBBBBBBBBBBBB
CCCCCCCCCCCCCCCCCCCCCCCCCCC     More . . .
```

```
                         Document List
   Type one or more action numbers next to your document
   choices and Enter.
   1=Copy   2=Delete   3=Display   4=Update   5=Print

    Action    Document                           Items  8 to 14 of 22

      _       Sales87
      _       Finance1
      _       Budget13
      _       Budget9
      _       Letter13
      _       Report20
      _       Letter17




   Enter  F1=Help  F3=Exit  F5=Refresh  F7=Bkwd  F8=Fwd  F12=Cancel
```

Figure 7.13 Textual scrolling information.

If the user can scroll in either direction, "More. . ." is displayed both above and below the area:

```
                                              More. . .
    LLLLLLLLLLLLLLLLLLLLLLLLLLLLLLLLLLLL
    MMMMMMMMMMMMMMMMMMMMMMMMMMM
    NNNNNNNNNNNNNNNNNNNNNNNNNNNN
                                              More. . .
```

When the end of the information is reached, "Bottom" is displayed below the area:

```
                                              More. . .
    XXXXXXXXXXXXXXXXXXXXXXXXX
    YYYYYYYYYYYYYYYYYYYYYYYYYY
    ZZZZZZZZZZZZZZZZZZZZZZZZZZZ
                                              Bottom
```

Figure 7.14 illustrates the use of the alternate type of textual scrolling information.

```
┌──────────────────────────────────────────────────────────────┐
│                                                                │
│                         Edit Document                          │
│                                                                │
│  ────────────────────────────────────────────────────────     │
│                                                   More ...      │
│   Patricia,                                                    │
│                                                                │
│   I have just received the latest prototype of the printer adapter │
│   and its new specifications.  This is a big improvement over the  │
│   previous version.  I think it will allow us to deliver a more    │
│   attractive product - one that fits in well with the rest of the  │
│   new product line.                                            │
│                                                                │
│   Please review the attached copy of the specifications.  I hope   │
│   you will be able to save design time by following this new plan. │
│                                                                │
│   The prototype will be in my office.  When you or your department │
│   members would like to inspect it, please check with my assistant,│
│   Roy Benson.                                                  │
│                                                   More ...      │
│  ────────────────────────────────────────────────────────     │
│   Enter  F1=Help  F3=Exit  F7=Bkwd  F8=Fwd  F9=Instruct  F12=Cancel │
│                                                                │
└──────────────────────────────────────────────────────────────┘
```

Figure 7.14   Alternate form of textual scrolling information.

MESSAGE AREA   A message area located just below the work area is used when an application needs to display a message to the user. The message area can consist of one or more lines. A message can contain information, selection fields, and entry fields. The panel in Fig. 7.1 contains a message area.

COMMAND AREA   A command area is used when a user is allowed to request actions by directly entering commands. This can be done to give the experienced user a "fast path" through the application. A command area can be included as part of a panel's work area, located just below the message area. It contains a field prompt and an entry field. The field prompt consists of the word "Command" followed by a right-pointing arrow, made up of three equal signs followed by a greater-than symbol. The panel in Fig. 7.1 contains a command area.

FUNCTION KEY AREA   The function key area appears below the command area. It is used to list actions that can be invoked by pressing function keys and their corresponding key assignments. Some actions are standard dialog actions, such as Exit, Cancel, and Help; others may be actions specific to the application. Only actions that are currently available should be displayed. Choices in the function key area are displayed horizontally across the panel. The function key area is normally displayed in the last line of the screen, but multiple lines can be used if necessary. Choices are listed in function key sequence. Figure 7.1 shows a function key area. When an action in the function key area is temporarily unavailable, it is shown with asterisks replacing the function key assignment. The user can control whether or not the function key area is displayed.

ACTION BAR FORMATTING   The text subset provides formatting guidelines for the use of action bars and pulldowns. CUA recommends using an action bar when two or more application actions are available from the panel. If only one application action can be taken, an action bar is not necessary, and the panel title and instructions should be sufficient to identify the action available. The CUA formatting rules and guidelines for the action bar specify its location and layout. The bar appears at the top of the panel and extends the full width of the panel. Choices are listed horizontally. If mnemonics are used, a choice entry field is located to the left of the choices. Figure 7.15 shows an action bar with mnemonics. The action bar is separated from the work area by a solid line. When an action bar choice is selected, it is shown with selected emphasis, which is either a color change or a change in intensity.

```
      Find  Add  Exit  Help
                              Hotel Selector
      Select one from each group by typing the number.
      Then select an action.

         Name of city    1  1. New York
                            2. Paris
                            3. Tokyo

         Price category  1  1. Budget
                            2. Moderate
                            3. Expensive
                            4. Luxury




      Enter  F1=Help  F3=Exit  F10=Actions  F12=Cancel
```

Figure 7.15   Action bar with mnemonics.

CUA also provides guidelines for action bar content. Choices should be a single word, if possible. The first letter is capitalized; other letters are capitalized only if normal use of the word calls for it. Choices should be ordered with the most commonly chosen options to the left. Where standard action bar actions such as File, Edit, and Help are appropriate, they should be included.

PULLDOWN
FORMATTING

CUA specifies both the location and the layout for an action bar pulldown. Figure 7.16 shows an example of an action bar and pulldown. The pulldown should be displayed, if possible, contiguous to the bottom of the action bar immediately below the choice that triggered it. It should be aligned so that choices within the pulldown are directly below the action bar choice. However, the entire pulldown must be visible, and its location should be shifted to the side or above the bar if this is necessary to give it the required room.

A pulldown contains one or more selection fields, which can be either single-choice or multiple-choice fields. Pulldown selection fields cannot be scrollable. The general formatting rules for selection fields apply in a pulldown. Separate selection fields are separated by a blank line. Ellipses are used to indicate that further information is required to complete the dialog. If accelerator keys have been assigned to a choice, the key or key combination is shown to the right of the choice.

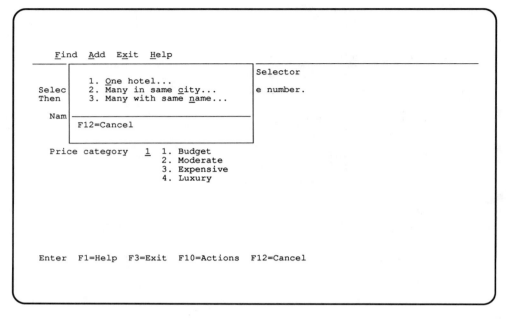

Figure 7.16 Action bar with pulldown.

WINDOWS

The basic interface uses primary and pop-up windows to display panels. Unlike the graphical model, windows do not have a window title bar or window borders, and they are not movable or sizable. A primary window is used to display the panels that implement the primary dialog between the user and the application. A primary window panel normally occupies the entire screen.

A pop-up window is an enclosed area of the screen that overlays the primary window panel. Pop-up windows are used to extend the primary dialog and provide various types of information. There are five types of pop-up window:

- **Dialog Pop-up.** Used to gather additional information needed to complete a user request.
- **Prompt List Pop-up.** Used to provide a list of possible values for an entry field when the Prompt action is selected.
- **Message Pop-up.** Used to display messages to the user.
- **Help Pop-up.** Used to display help information.
- **Command Pop-up.** Used to provide an area where the user can enter commands.

Dialog Pop-Ups

A dialog pop-up can be generated by selecting a pulldown choice. This type of pop-up functions in the same way as a dialog box. It is located in the same basic area as the pulldown but is not contiguous to the action bar. This is shown in Fig. 7.17. If a second pop-up window is necessary, it is located overlapping the first window, offset both vertically and horizontally. This is illustrated in Fig. 7.18. A dialog pop-up may contain any panel element necessary: protected information, selection fields, entry fields, message area, command area, or function key area. However, a dialog pop-up does not contain an action bar.

Message Pop-ups

All panels, including pop-ups, should contain a message area. Messages should be displayed in a pop-up rather than in the message area if the user needs to interact with the message or if it is important that the user see the message. A message pop-up may contain information, selection, or entry fields and a function key area. Figure 7.19 illustrates a message pop-up.

Command Pop-ups

A command area can be provided in a pop-up window rather than as an area in the underlying panel. This is done when the user is expected to enter commands

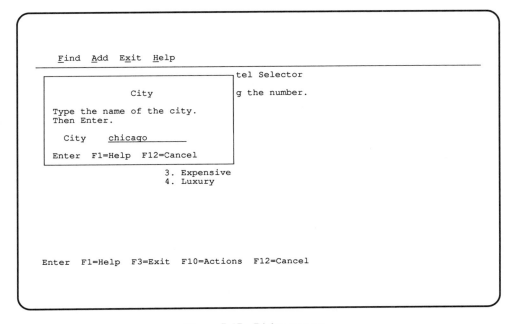

Figure 7.17 Dialog pop-up.

```
 Find  Add  Exit  Help
────────────────────────────────────────────────────────────
                                        tel Selector
┌──────────────────────────────────────┐g the number.
│                City                   │
│  Type the name of the city.          │
│  Then Enter.                          │
│                                       │
│    City    chicago_____             │
│    ┌──────────────────────────────────────┐
│    │           Hotel Information           │
│    │                                       │
│    │  Type hotel information.              │
│    │  Then Enter.                          │
│    │                                       │
│    │    Hotel name . .   _____   │
│    │    Hotel address    _____   │
│    │    Hotel phone      _____   │
│    │    Price category   _____     │
│    │                                       │
│    │  Enter  F1=Help  F12=Cancel           │
     └──────────────────────────────────────┘
  Enter  F1=Help  F3=Exit  F10=Actions  F12=Cancel
```

Figure 7.18 Multiple pop-up windows.

```
   Block   Format   Search   Exit   Help
────────────────────────────────────────────────────────────
                        Edit Document
  Make text changes. Then select an action.
                                                More:     +
────────────────────────────────────────────────────────────
  January 24, 1987

  ┌──────────────────────────────────────┐
  │  The disk is 90% full.               │
  │  Consider erasing some files or      │
  │  starting a new disk.                │
  │                                      │
  │  Enter when ready.                   │totype of the printer adapter
  │                                      │s a big improvement over the
  │  Enter  F1=Help                      │allow us to deliver a more
  └──────────────────────────────────────┘
  attractive product - one that fits in well with the rest of the
  new product line.
────────────────────────────────────────────────────────────
  Enter  F1=Help  F3=Exit  F7=Bkwd  F8=Fwd  F9=Instruct  F10=Actions  F12=Cancel
```

Figure 7.19 Pop-up window for message.

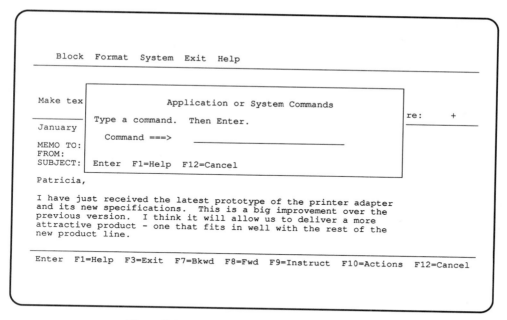

```
       Block   Format   System   Exit   Help
      ─────────────────────────────────────────────────────────────────
                  ┌──────────────────────────────────────────────┐
      Make tex    │           Application or System Commands      │  re:     +
      ─────────   │  Type a command.   Then Enter.               │
      January     │                                              │
                  │     Command ===>    ──────────────────────   │
      MEMO TO:    │                                              │
      FROM:       │                                              │
      SUBJECT:    │  Enter  F1=Help  F12=Cancel                  │
                  └──────────────────────────────────────────────┘
      Patricia,

      I have just received the latest prototype of the printer adapter
      and its new specifications.  This is a big improvement over the
      previous version.  I think it will allow us to deliver a more
      attractive product - one that fits in well with the rest of the
      new product line.
      ─────────────────────────────────────────────────────────────────
      Enter  F1=Help  F3=Exit  F7=Bkwd  F8=Fwd  F9=Instruct  F10=Actions  F12=Cancel
```

Figure 7.20   Pop-up window for command entry.

infrequently and the application needs to maximize the space available in the primary window panel. A command pop-up contains the field prompt and entry field for entering commands and should contain a function key area. Figure 7.20 is an example of a command pop-up.

Pop-up Windows and the Entry Model

With the entry model, the use of pop-up windows is optional. If pop-up windows are not supported, the command area and message area in the primary

BOX 7.1   Color and emphasis guidelines.

Action Bar Element	Large-System Color Palette	Large-System Monochrome Palette	Midrange Color Palette	Midrange Monochrome Palette
Available choice	White	High	White	High
Selected choice	Yellow	Low	Blue	Low
Separator line	Blue	Low	Blue	Low

window panel are used for entering commands and displaying messages. Help panels, prompt list panels, and dialog extension panels are displayed as full-screen panels, temporarily replacing the underlying primary window panel.

COLOR AND EMPHASIS
The basic interface provides guidelines on the use of color and emphasis for different panel elements. Separate guidelines are provided for color and monochrome terminals in a large-system environment and color and monochrome terminals in the midrange environment. Box 7.1 shows some of these guidelines.

8 BASIC INTERFACE INTERACTION TECHNIQUES

INTRODUCTION Interaction techniques for a nonprogrammable terminal involve the same basic functions as for the graphical model: moving the cursor, making selections, entering text, and submitting requests for processing. But, because of fundamental differences in the capabilities of nonprogrammable terminals and programmable workstations, there are differences in the way functions are implemented. With a nonprogrammable terminal, no mouse interactions are supported, and the point-and-select technique is more limited.

MOVING THE CURSOR For a nonprogrammable terminal, the arrow keys move the cursor one character (or line) at a time to any position on the screen. The user can move the cursor to and from the action bar, work area, or function key area, and can position it within a selection field, an entry field, or protected information. The TAB/BACKTAB key moves the cursor to the next or previous input position, which can be an entry field, or a choice entry field within a selection field. The FIRST FIELD ON SCREEN (Home) key moves the cursor to the first input position on the screen. The NEW LINE key moves the cursor to the first position on the next line where data can be entered.

SELECTION TECHNIQUES Selection can be either explicit or implicit. To perform explicit selection, the user enters a character in a choice entry field. To perform implicit selection, the user moves the cursor to a choice and presses ENTER. Similar to the graphical model point-and-select technique, this is called the *cursor-and-select* technique.

Explicit selection is used with single-choice fields that have been assigned numbers or mnemonics, with multiple-choice fields, and with action lists. For a single-choice field, the user makes a selection by entering in the choice entry field the number or mnemonic associated with the desired choice. For a multiple-choice field, there is a choice entry field for each choice. To select a choice, the user positions the cursor on a choice entry field and enters a slash or other nonblank character there. For an action list, there is a choice entry field for each choice. The user selects choices by entering an action code in each appropriate choice entry field.

Implicit selection is used with variable single-choice fields and with the action bar. Implicit selection can also be used for a single-choice field that is the only interactive field in a panel or pulldown. With implicit selection, the user positions the cursor alongside the desired choice and presses ENTER. The user employs the arrow keys to move the cursor from one choice to another within a selection field. The cursor can be moved to any position within the field. With action lists and multiple-choice fields, the cursor can be moved from choice to choice with the TAB/BACKTAB key or the NEW LINE key.

CANCELING A SELECTION

To cancel a choice in a single-choice field, a different number or mnemonic is entered in the field's choice entry field. To cancel a choice in a multiple-choice field or action list, the user positions the cursor on the choice entry field for the selected choice and either presses the DELETE key or enters a blank.

ACTION LIST INTERACTIONS

An action list, because of the range of choices it offers for both objects and actions, provides several ways for the user to interact with the field.

- **Action List as a Multiple-Choice Field.** One way of interacting with an action list is to treat it as a multiple-choice field. The user enters slashes in the action column to identify the objects being chosen, and then switches to the action bar to select an action to be performed on all the objects. An example of this is shown in Fig. 8.1.

- **Action Codes and Equal Signs.** A second form of interaction is for the user to enter the action code or mnemonic for a desired action in the action entry field for each desired choice. If the same action is desired for a series of choices, the user can enter an equal sign in the action entry field to indicate that the previous action should be repeated for that choice. This is shown in Fig. 8.2.

- **Command and Parameter Entry.** Figure 8.3 illustrates a third form of interaction. Here the user has typed a complete command and its parameters in the action entry field.

```
 Document actions  Exit  Help
_____
                        Document List
Select one or more documents.  Then select Document actions.
Or type one or more action numbers next to your document
choices and Enter.
1=Copy   2=Delete   3=Display   4=Update   5=Print

  Action    Document

             Sales87
   7         Finance1
             Budget13
   _
             Budget9
   7         Letter13
             Report20
   _         Letter17



Enter  F1=Help  F3=Exit  F5=Refresh  F9=Instruct  F10=Actions  F12=Cancel
```

Figure 8.1   Using an action list as a multiple-choice field.

```
 Document actions  Exit  Help
_____
                        Document List
Select one or more documents.  Then select Document actions.
Or type one or more action numbers next to your document
choices and Enter.
1=Copy   2=Delete   3=Display   4=Update   5=Print

  Action    Document

             Sales87
   1         Finance1
             Budget13
   2         Budget9
   =         Letter13
   =         Report20
   _         Letter17



Enter  F1=Help  F3=Exit  F5=Refresh  F9=Instruct  F10=Actions  F12=Cancel
```

Figure 8.2   Using action codes and equal signs with an action list.

```
  Document actions  Exit  Help
  _____

                              Document List
  Select one or more documents.  Then select Document actions.
  Or type one or more action numbers next to your document
  choices and Enter.
  1=Copy   2=Delete   3=Display   4=Update   5=Print

    Document    Action

    Sales87     _____
    Finance1    _____
    Budget13    _____
    Budget9     copy budget9a,c3,rfm_____
    Letter13    _____
    Report20    _____
    Letter17    _____


  Enter  F1=Help  F3=Exit  F5=Refresh  F9=Instruct  F10=Actions  F12=Cancel
```

Figure 8.3   Using command and parameter entry with an action list.

```
  Document actions  Exit  Help
  _____

                              Document List
  Select one or more documents.  Then select Document actions.
  Or type one or more action numbers next to your document
  choices and Enter.
  1=Copy   2=Delete   3=Display   4=Update   5=Print

    Action    Document
                 _____
     _           Finance1
     _           Budget13
     _           Budget9
     _           Letter13
     _           Report20
     _           Letter17


  Enter  F1=Help  F3=Exit  F5=Refresh  F9=Instruct  F10=Actions  F12=Cancel
```

Figure 8.4   Action list with an area for a new object.

- **Action List with a New Object.** Figure 8.4 shows one other possibility. The first line of the selection field is blank, allowing the user to enter information that identifies a new object. Here it is used when the user is creating a new document.

Whatever technique is used to select objects and actions, after the user has made the appropriate selections and has pressed the ENTER key, the application performs the selected actions. The actions are performed in the order in which they are displayed in the action list. The application may optionally allow the user to interrupt processing. Some actions, such as Delete, may require confirmation from the user before being performed. If so, a message is displayed telling the user to take the appropriate confirmation action. A message is also displayed if the application detects an error condition. When all processing is completed, the action list is redisplayed with an asterisk in the action entry fields of all choices that were processed.

SCROLLING A SELECTION FIELD

To scroll information in a scrollable selection field, the FORWARD (F8) and BACKWARD (F7) keys are used. Cursor-driven scrolling is not supported by the basic interface, so moving the cursor with the arrow keys will not cause information to scroll.

ENTRY FIELD TECHNIQUES

With nonprogrammable terminals, there is only one cursor. Separate cursors for selection and for text entry are not supported. The appearance of the cursor does not indicate whether the user is in Insert or Replace mode; this is indicated by an indicator on the screen. Pressing the INSERT key causes the user to be put in Insert mode; pressing the RESET key causes a switch from Insert mode to Replace mode.

Within an entry field, the cursor moves right as characters are typed in, and can also be moved in any direction with the arrow keys. The Word Left (Alt + left arrow) and Word Right (Alt + right arrow) functions may be available depending on the terminal type. The BACKSPACE key moves the cursor one character position to the left but does not erase the character to the left as it does with a programmable workstation.

Input Inhibited

If the user attempts to enter data beyond the end of a field while in Insert mode, or attempts to overtype data past the end of the field while in Replace mode, input is inhibited, an input-inhibited indicator appears on the screen, and a beep may sound. The user must press the RESET key before continuing.

AUTOTAB OPTION   An entry field can be defined as an AUTOTAB field. After the user has entered a character into the last position of an AUTOTAB field, the cursor automatically moves to the next interactive field. AUTOTAB is most useful for high-volume data entry where the user typically fills in the entire field.

INVALID VALUES   CUA does not define the types of validation that must be performed on data entered into an entry field. However, it does define the response an application should make to invalid data. According to CUA, invalid data should be displayed with error emphasis and a message should be displayed that indicates the value is in error. Help information should also be available describing valid values for the field.

SCROLLING THE   In addition to selection fields that are individually
WORK AREA   scrollable, an entire work area can be scrollable. As the area scrolls, all the fields within the area move. The FORWARD (F8) and BACKWARD (F9) keys can be used to scroll up and down. For a horizontally scrollable area, the LEFT (F19) and RIGHT (F20) keys can be used to scroll left and right.

Scrolling Classes

The extent of the scrolling that takes place depends on the scrolling class that is in effect. With *cursor-dependent scrolling,* the position of the cursor determines the extent of the scrolling. With *cursor-independent scrolling,* the amount scrolled is not affected by the position of the cursor.

Cursor-Dependent Scrolling

With cursor-dependent scrolling, information is scrolled so that the cursor and the item associated with it are repositioned to a particular place. The final position of the cursor depends on the scrolling direction:

- **Backward.** Cursor is repositioned to the bottom of the scrollable area.
- **Forward.** Cursor is repositioned to the top of the scrollable area.
- **Left.** Cursor is repositioned to the rightmost column in the scrollable area.
- **Right.** Cursor is repositioned to the leftmost column in the scrollable area.

Cursor-Independent Scrolling

With cursor-independent scrolling, information is scrolled in fixed increments. There are different types of scrolling increments that can be provided. The amount of information scrolled can be equal to:

- The size of the visible scrollable area
- The size of the visible scrollable area minus one item or one column
- A fixed portion of the visible area, such as half the area

The size of an item or a column is defined by the application. The user should be allowed to specify which scrolling increment to use. The recommended default is the size of the visible scrollable area minus one item or one column.

ACTION BAR INTERACTIONS

The cursor can be moved to the action bar with the normal cursor-movement keys or with the SWITCH-TO-ACTION-BAR (F10) key. The cursor can be moved from choice to choice in the action bar using arrow keys or the TAB/BACKTAB key. The cursor can be moved out of the action bar with the SWITCH-TO-ACTION BAR key, normal cursor movement keys, or the CANCEL (F12) key.

SELECTING AN ACTION BAR CHOICE

The action bar functions use implicit selection, so that moving the cursor to a choice selects that choice. If mnemonics are defined for action bar choices, a choice can also be selected by entering its mnemonic in the action bar choice entry field. Once a choice is selected, pressing ENTER causes its pulldown to appear.

PULLDOWN INTERACTIONS

When a pulldown is displayed, the user can use any standard selection technique for selecting choices in the pulldown. When all the necessary choices have been made, pressing ENTER submits the pulldown for processing.

Mnemonic Fast Path

When mnemonics are used for both action bar and pulldown choices, the user can select a pulldown action more quickly by entering the pulldown mnemonic along with the action bar choice mnemonic before pressing ENTER. This technique can be extended to include mnemonics used in pop-up windows associated with the pulldown. In this way, the user may be able to specify a request and submit it for processing all in one interaction.

Canceling a Pulldown

The user can cancel a pulldown and return to the action bar by requesting the Cancel action. The user can also move the cursor to the action bar, select another choice, and press ENTER. This causes the original pulldown to be removed and the one corresponding to the new choice to be displayed. The user can cancel a pulldown and return to the work area by pressing the SWITCH-TO-ACTION-BAR key (F10) or moving the cursor to the work area and pressing ENTER.

Application Response to Pulldown Selection

When the user finishes making selections in a pulldown and presses ENTER, the pulldown disappears. If this completes the information required to define the user's request, the request is submitted to the application for processing. When the processing is completed, a switch to the work area takes place. If additional information is needed, a dialog pop-up appears, and the user interacts with that. If the user selects an unavailable choice, the application displays a message. A help panel describing the choice should also be available. If the user selects an action without first selecting an object to perform it on, the application displays a message telling the user to select an object.

DIALOG POP-UP INTERACTIONS   Users interact with a dialog pop-up using the normal selection and entry techniques. When the user has completed interacting with the pop-up, pressing ENTER causes it to be processed. If no further information is needed, the user's request is submitted for processing by the application. If additional information is needed, the application displays another dialog pop-up. When all dialog pop-ups have been processed and processing of the user's request has been completed, the pop-up windows are removed. A dialog pop-up can be removed without causing processing to start by requesting the Cancel action. A dialog pop-up is modal. The user must complete the interaction with the pop-up and either submit or cancel it before being allowed to interact with an underlying panel.

ENTRY MODEL PANEL INTERACTIONS   With the entry model, action bars and pulldowns are not used. When the user completes selection and entry interactions with a panel, pressing ENTER submits it to the application for processing. If a complete request has been defined, the application processes it. If additional information is required, the application displays the appropriate panel to gather that information.

ACTION-OBJECT APPROACH

With the entry model and its lack of action bars, applications may not always be object-action oriented. The object-action approach can still be used, either by presenting users with an appropriate sequence of panels or by using action lists, allowing the user first to select an object and then to specify the action. However, in some cases an action-object approach may be used, where the user first selects an action and then the object to which that action should be applied.

The action-object approach may be used when an application has only one action. For example, a data entry application has only the action Enter Data. An application that is designed for untrained users and must lead them through choices step by step may also use the action-object approach. With automated banking terminals, the user first selects an action (withdrawal, deposit, inquiry) and then is led through successive choices for that particular transaction.

The action-object approach can be implemented in various ways. One is by presenting the user with a structured hierarchy of panels, as with an automated banking terminal application. Another way is through the use of a command interface, where the user enters a command and a set of parameters identifying both the action and the object.

Although the action-object approach may be appropriate in certain situations, CUA recommends always using the object-action approach where possible in order to maintain consistency in the user's conceptual model of how to interact with applications.

USER OPTIONS

With the basic interface, CUA recommends that users be given certain options that allow them to control the presentation and interaction techniques that the user interface supports. These options allow the user to specify

- Color and emphasis used for different panel elements
- Whether panel IDs are displayed
- Whether action codes are displayed as part of an action list
- Whether the function key area is displayed
- Whether the command area is displayed
- Which scrolling class is in effect
- The scrolling increment for cursor-independent scrolling

9 BASIC INTERFACE STANDARD ACTIONS

INTRODUCTION As with the graphical model, the CUA basic interface includes definitions of standard actions to be provided in action bars and pulldowns and in the function key area. Action bar/pulldown choices apply only to the text subset, since the entry model does not support the use of an action bar. The function key actions apply to both models.

ACTION BAR CHOICES The standard action bar choices for the text subset are the same as for the full graphical model. They include the following:

- **File.** Enables users to manipulate a file as a single object.
- **Edit.** Allows users to manipulate documents using typical document processing operations.
- **View.** Allows users to choose different ways of looking at an object without actually changing the object. For example, a calendar object could be viewed by day, week, or month.
- **Options.** Allows users to customize the appearance of an object. For example, the user may be allowed to display a document in paginated or unpaginated form.
- **Help.** Provides users with access to various kinds of help information.

These choices are defined through associated pulldowns that provide the standard actions associated with each choice.

FILE PULLDOWN The File pulldown provides actions that can be used to manipulate a file as a whole. The standard actions are the same as in the graphical model. Application-specific actions for file manipulation can be added to the pulldown. The standard File pulldown actions provide the following services:

- **Open.** Locates an existing file and makes it available to the user for manipulation. A dialog pop-up is used to prompt the user for the name of the file to open.

- **New.** Allows users to create a new file.

- **Save.** Causes a file to be written to a storage device. If the file currently being processed is unnamed, a dialog pop-up is displayed that allows the user to assign a name to the file.

- **Save As.** Makes a new copy of the current file. Save As causes the current file to be written to a storage device under a new name. A dialog pop-up is displayed that allows the user to assign a new name for the file. The file also remains available, unchanged, under its original name.

- **Print.** Prepares a file for printing and submits it for printing on a user-specified printer. If the application supports the use of print options, a dialog pop-up can be used to specify the options to be used.

- **Exit.** Terminates the current function and returns the user to a higher-level function. Exit must always be the last action in the pulldown for the leftmost action bar choice.

CUA also defines the dialog pop-ups to be used with the actions Open and Save As.

Open Dialog Pop-up

An example of an Open dialog pop-up is shown in Fig. 9.1. It is used to identify the particular file that is to be opened. The user can either enter a file name in the entry field or select a name from the selection field. Pressing ENTER then causes the open request to be processed. The user can cancel the dialog pop-up or obtain help information by pressing the appropriate function key.

Save As Dialog Pop-Up

The Save As dialog pop-up is shown in Fig. 9.2. The user enters the file name under which the file is to be saved. The selection field is an application option, allowing the user to specify where the file is to be saved. Additional application options could also be included. The user can submit the dialog pop-up for processing by pressing ENTER, or the user could request Cancel or Help by pressing the appropriate function key.

EDIT PULLDOWN   The Edit pulldown provides editing actions common to many types of objects that are based on operations

```
                    Open
File name   _____

    Sales87.txt
    Finance1.txt
    Budget13.doc
    Budget9.doc
    Letter13.txt
    Report20.rpt
    Report14.rpt
    Letter27.txt
    Budget12.doc
    Sales6.txt
    Report10.rpt


F1=Help  F12=Cancel
```

Figure 9.1   Open dialog prompt.

```
                Save as
File name   _____

Save in folder

   Budget
   Sales
   Letters
   Reports
   Charts
   Notes


F1=Help  F12=Cancel
```

Figure 9.2   Save As dialog pop-up.

typically performed in document processing. As with the Advanced Interface, some of these actions support a clipboard. The *clipboard* is an area that an application makes available for the temporary storage of application data. Data placed in the clipboard can be transferred somewhere else while in the same application or from one application to another. The functions in the Edit pulldown are

- **Undo.** Reverses the user action that was most recently executed.
- **Mark.** Indicates the beginning or end of a block of text to be processed by a subsequent Cut, Copy, Paste, Clear, or Delete operation. To mark a block of text, the user positions the cursor at one end of the block, selects the Mark action, moves the cursor to the other end of the block, and then selects the Mark action a second time.
- **Cut.** Copies a selected block of the text to the clipboard and deletes it from the object being edited.
- **Copy.** Copies a selected block of the text to the clipboard without deleting it from the object.
- **Paste.** Copies the contents of the clipboard into the object being edited at the current cursor position.
- **Clear.** Removes a selected block of text but leaves the space that the block occupied.
- **Unmark.** Deselects a block of text that was previously selected with Mark.
- **Delete.** Removes a selected block of the text and also removes the space it occupied.

VIEW PULLDOWN   The View pulldown provides users with different ways of viewing an object. This can include specifying the amount of information presented, the presentation sequence, the format, and the scale. The actual contents of the View pulldown vary, depending on the type of object being viewed, so no specific View pulldown actions are defined by CUA.

OPTIONS PULLDOWN   The Options pulldown lets the user customize an object's appearance. As with View, the specific pulldown actions vary, depending on the type of object being processed.

HELP PULLDOWN   Help information assists the user in using the application. The information is intended to be used by someone who is already familiar with the application but may need a reminder about syntax or procedures. One way of obtaining help information is through selecting the Help choice in the action bar. The pulldown used when Help is selected from the action bar provides access to several different types of help information:

- **Help for Help.** Provides information about how to use the help facility.
- **Extended Help.** Provides information about an entire application panel and the tasks that can be performed in that panel.
- **Keys Help.** Provides a listing of the functions and key assignments of all function keys used by the application.
- **Help Index.** Provides an alphabetical index of help information for the application.
- **Tutorial Help.** Provides access to a tutorial on the application.
- **About.** Allows the user to view the copyright and ownership information for the application.

METHODS OF ACCESSING HELP

The user can request help information in several ways. One is by selecting Help in the action bar. Contextual help can be obtained for a specific item by placing the cursor on the item and pressing F1. Contextual help can be obtained for

- A selection or entry field
- A choice in an action bar
- A message
- The command area
- The function key area

For the command area, pressing F1 when nothing has been entered provides help information on the commands available in the application. If a command has been entered before pressing F1, help information on that command is displayed. If the cursor is not located on one of the items listed above when F1 is pressed, extended help for the panel as a whole is displayed. A help panel may contain information only, or it may also contain selection or entry fields. Actions included in its function key area provide access to the various help options available in the Help pulldown. Figure 9.3 shows a help panel. Function keys are active for the other help options and can be used to request these additional forms of help. Information in a help panel may contain certain words or phrases, called *reference phrases,* where additional help information is available. These phrases are highlighted in the help text. Selecting a highlighted

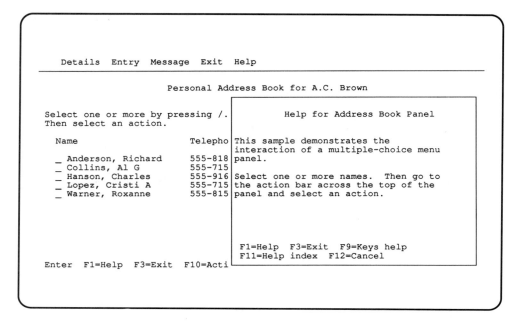

Figure 9.3   Help panel.

word or phrase causes the additional reference phrase help information to be displayed in another help panel.

INTERACTING WITH HELP PANELS

Help panels are displayed in pop-up windows if pop-ups are supported. If pop-ups are not supported, help is displayed in fullscreen panels. When a help pop-up is displayed, the cursor is switched to that window. However, the user is able to switch back and forth between the help pop-up and the underlying panel using the SWITCH CURSOR (F6) key. This allows the user to complete interacting with the application while the help information is still available as an aid. Help pop-ups are the only pop-ups that support this modeless form of interaction. The user's interaction with a help panel ends when the user requests Exit or Cancel.

FUNCTION KEY ACTIONS

With the basic interface, several standard actions can be invoked using function keys. Box 9.1 lists the actions and key assignments that can be used in primary window application panels. As shown, some of the actions must be provided and included in the function key area if it is displayed. For panels in pop-up windows other than help pop-ups, only Help and Cancel are required. Box

BOX 9.1   Function key assignments for application panels

Action	Function Key
*Help	F1
Undo	F2
*Exit	F3
Prompt	F4
Refresh	F5
Mark	F6
Backward	F7
Forward	F8
Retrieve	F9
*Switch to Action Bar	F10
Unmark	F11
*Cancel	F12
*Display Keys	F13
Left	F19
Right	F20
Command	F21

*Required actions

9.2 lists the actions and key assignments that can be included in a help panel. Exit and Cancel must always be included in a help panel.

Function key actions serve a number of purposes. The FORWARD, BACKWARD, LEFT, and RIGHT keys, as described in Chapter 7, are used for scrolling. The SWITCH-TO-ACTION-BAR key moves the cursor between the action bar and the panel work area. Function keys also enable a user to navigate, or move from one panel to another within a dialog, control what is displayed in a panel, obtain different forms of assistance, interact with the command area, and perform document editing functions.

DIALOG NAVIGATION ACTIONS

There are three dialog actions that enable a user to navigate, or move from one panel to another, within a dialog:

BOX 9.2   Function key assignments for help panels.

Action	Function Key
Help	F1
Extended Help	F2
Exit	F3
Switch Cursor	F6
Keys Help	F9
Help Index	F11
Cancel	F12
Tutorial	F14
Help for Help	F22

- **Enter.** This action causes the dialog to proceed one step. It submits a panel with interactive fields for processing, passing the information selected or entered by the user to the application. After processing the panel submitted, the dialog continues with the next panel in the path.

- **Cancel.** This action allows the user to back up in the dialog. If Cancel is requested from a pulldown, the user is returned to the action bar. If Cancel is requested from a popup window, the dialog returns to the underlying window. If Cancel is requested in a primary window, the previous primary panel is redisplayed.

- **Exit.** An application may provide a hierarchy of functions. If it does, the Exit action terminates the current function and returns the user to the next higher-level function.

Figure 9.4 illustrates how the Enter, Cancel, and Exit actions can be used to provide different paths through a dialog. Enter moves the dialog forward one step, Cancel moves it back one step, and Exit moves back to a previous function.

The Enter Action

Users request the Enter action by pressing the ENTER key. The Enter action signals that interaction with the panel has been completed and that the panel should be processed by the application. If the cursor is in a pulldown when En-

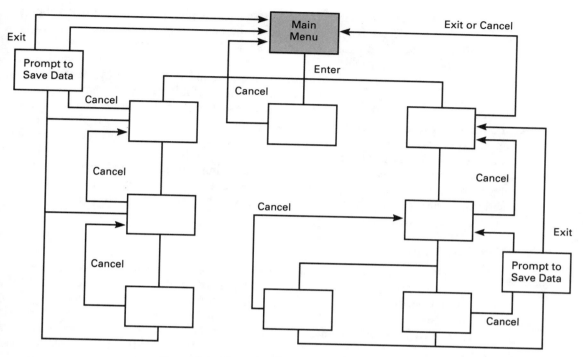

Figure 9.4   Example of a CUA dialog flow.

ter is requested, the action selected in the pulldown determines the processing performed and also the next step in the dialog. If the cursor is in the work area, the entire panel and any information selected or entered are submitted to the application. If both an object and action have been selected, the user request is processed. If the user has not selected an action, and there is an implied action for the panel, that action is performed. Otherwise, the application displays a message asking the user to specify an action. If the user has selected an action but has not specified an object for the action, a message is used to ask the user to select one or more choices from the work area.

The Cancel Action

The Cancel action allows the user to back up from one panel to the previous one. Cancel must be included in all pulldowns, and should be included in pop-up windows, except for information windows where the user can use Enter to continue processing. CUA guidelines recommend including Cancel on all panels that are part of a sequence of panels that make up a unit of work.

If the cursor is in a pop-up window when Cancel is requested, the pop-up disappears and the window immediately under it, whether another pop-up or a regular panel, becomes active. If the cursor is in a pulldown, it returns to the action bar. If the cursor is anywhere else in the panel, that panel disappears and the previously displayed panel returns. If a user has made changes to a panel by making selections or entering information, those changes can either be discarded or retained, at the application's option. If they are discarded, then the next time the panel is displayed it will contain the original default values. If they are retained, the next time the panel is displayed it will reflect the values entered by the user. If the Cancel action will cause significant information to be lost, the application should display a confirmation message that allows the user to save the information or discard it. Saving information implies that the information is put into some form of permanent storage. Retaining information means only that the information will be displayed again the next time the user sees the panel within the current application, but not that it will be kept across different executions of the application.

The Exit Action

The Exit action is used to move the user through a hierarchy of functions, where a function can consist of one or a series of panels. Exit terminates the current function and returns the user to the next higher function. Using Exit repeatedly will return the user to the highest level panel in the system.

Exit must be provided in the pulldown for the leftmost action bar choice and must also be included in the function key area if it is displayed. Typically, Exit is not included in a pop-up window. In a pop-up, Cancel is used to return to the action bar or underlying window, and Exit is requested from there. If the Exit action will cause significant information to be lost, a pop-up should be displayed, giving the user the following options:

- Save and exit
- Exit without saving
- Continue

USER GUIDANCE ACTIONS

At times during a dialog, a user may need additional information in order to continue processing. Two dialog actions are designed to provide the user with guidance in using the application:

- **Prompt.** The Prompt action helps users with entry fields by providing a list of possible entry values. This lets the user recognize and select a value rather than having to remember and type it.
- **Help.** The Help action causes help information to be displayed. Help information assists users by providing reminders about the syntax or procedures used for a panel or by explaining a message.

The Prompt Action

The Prompt action helps the user to complete an entry field. The user places the cursor on the entry field and requests Prompt. The application responds with a selection field listing valid values for the entry field. The prompt selection field is displayed in a pop-up window if pop-ups are supported; otherwise, it appears as a full-screen panel. The user can then select one or more choices from the selection field. These choices are placed in the entry field. The interaction with the prompt panel must be completed by requesting Enter or Cancel before interaction can be resumed with the underlying entry field. If Prompt is available for an entry field, a plus sign (+) is shown at the end of the field:

Document name . . . _____ +

If Prompt is requested for an entry field where it is not supported, a beep sounds and a message appears. Optionally, the application may allow the user to supply a search string in the entry field when requesting Prompt. The list of prompt values then contains only values that match the search string. A question mark (?) can be used in the search string to indicate that any character can occur in this position. An asterisk (*) indicates that any character string can occur in this position. Figure 9.5 shows an example of a search string. With this string, the prompt values will include only names that begin with the characters "Mar".

```
                          Document Types
        Select a document type by typing the number.
        Then type new or existing document and folder names.
        Enter when ready.

          Document type    1   1. Document
                               2. Memo
                               3. Note
                               4. Letterhead
                               5. Blank
                               6. Defaults

          Document name    mar*_____
          Folder name           _____




        Enter   F1=Help   F3=Exit   F9=Instruct   F12=Cancel
```

Figure 9.5   Search string for prompt.

The Help Action

The Help action provides information that assists the user in using the application. Function key actions provide access to the same help options that are found in the pulldown for the Help action bar choice:

- **Help (F1).** Provides information about a specific field in an application panel. When this basic form of help is requested, a help panel is displayed that provides access to the other forms of help.
- **Extended Help (F2).** Provides information about an entire application panel and the task it represents.
- **Keys Help (F9).** Provides a listing of the names and functions of all keys supported by the application.
- **Help Index (F11).** Provides an alphabetical index of help information.
- **Tutorial Help (F14).** Provides a tutorial on the application.

In addition, SWITCH CURSOR (F6) can be used to move the cursor back and forth between a help panel and the underlying panel from which help was requested.

**COMMAND AREA
ACTIONS**   Two dialog actions are used in connection with the command area:

- **Command.** The Command action causes the command area to appear. If the command area is already visible, the Command action can be used to switch to that area.
- **Retrieve.** The Retrieve action causes the last command that was issued to be retrieved and redisplayed in the command area. The user can then modify it, if desired, and reissue it. Retrieve may be requested repeatedly, to back through a series of previously issued commands.

The Command Action

The command area may be displayed either as part of the primary application panel or as a pop-up. If it is part of the application panel, the user should have an option of specifying whether or not the command area is always visible. If it is always visible, the Command action moves the cursor back and forth between the command area and the rest of the panel. The cursor can also be moved in and out of the command area with the normal cursor movement keys. When the cursor is in the command area, a command can be typed in and submitted for processing by pressing ENTER.

If the command area is not visible, the Command action makes it visible and moves the cursor to it. Requesting Command with the cursor in the command area then removes the command area and returns the cursor to its original location.

When a command pop-up is used for the command area, the pop-up appears and the cursor is moved to it when the user requests the Command action. A command can then be typed in and submitted for processing by pressing EN-TER. Requesting Cancel causes the pop-up to be removed and the cursor returned to the underlying panel.

The Retrieve Action

When the command area is visible, the Retrieve action can be used to redisplay the previously issued command. The command can then be modified and reissued. Retrieve can be requested repeatedly to move back through a series of previously issued commands. It is an application option as to how many commands are saved for redisplay; CUA guidelines recommend a minimum of ten.

Using Prompt with the Command Area

The Prompt action can be used with the command area. If Prompt is requested while the cursor is in the command area entry field and the entry field is blank, a list of valid commands is displayed. If the user selects one of the commands from the list, it is entered in the command area. If the command entry field contains a command or part of a command when Prompt is requested, a panel with entry fields for the command parameters is displayed. Any parameter values already entered by the user are shown in the appropriate parameter entry fields. The user can then complete the command by filling in the parameter entry fields.

PANEL PRESENTATION ACTIONS

There are three dialog actions that allow the user to control what is presented in a panel:

- **Display Panel IDs.** This action causes the display of panel IDs to be turned on and off. CUA does not specify a key assignment for this action. The application determines how to make it available to the user.

- **Display Keys.** This action controls whether or not the function key area is displayed. When the user requests this action, it toggles between displaying and not displaying the area.

- **Refresh.** This action causes the current panel to change what it is displaying. If the user has changed default values in a panel, Refresh causes the original default selections and entry values to be restored. If the panel displays information that changes continuously, Refresh causes the current status of the information to be displayed.

EDIT ACTIONS

Certain actions included in the standard Edit pull-down are also available through function keys:

- **Undo.** Reverses the user action that was most recently executed.
- **Mark.** Selects a portion of text to be processed by a subsequent Cut, Copy, Paste, Clear, or Delete operation. To mark a block of text, the user positions the cursor at one end of the block to be marked, presses the Mark function key, moves the cursor to the other end of the block, and presses the Mark function key a second time.
- **Unmark.** Deselects a block of text that was previously selected with Mark.

MESSAGES

In addition to standard actions, CUA defines standard ways of displaying messages to the user. Messages are used by the application to provide the user with unsolicited information, typically when a condition has occurred that the user should know about. CUA defines three types of messages:

- Information messages
- Warning messages
- Action messages

Information Messages

Information messages provide feedback about the state of the system or status information about user requests for action. An information message may be used to let the user know that processing is in progress and will continue for a while. The message may be general:

> Please wait

or it might be more specific:

> Document 80% reformatted.

An information message may also alert the user to the fact that processing has been completed:

> Search complete. No match found.
> Press enter to continue.

For a temporary condition, such as processing in progress, the message may be removed automatically when the condition ends. If it is important that the user see the message, the user may be required to press ENTER for the message to be removed and processing continued.

Warning Messages

Warning messages are used to identify a condition that may require the user to take an action to correct a condition, but where the application can continue whether or not the user takes the action. An example of a warning message is shown in Fig. 9.6.

Action Messages

Action messages are used when an exception condition has occurred and the user must take an action in order for application processing to continue.

- The action may be external to the application, as shown in Fig. 9.7.
- The action may alternatively involve an interaction with the application, as shown in Fig. 9.8.

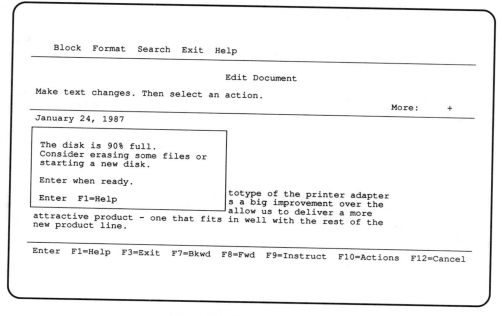

Figure 9.6 Warning message.

```
 Block  Format  Search  Exit  Help
─────────────────────────────────────────────────────────────────
                          Edit Document
Make text changes. Then select an action.
                                                    More:      +...

January 24, 1987
 ┌──────────────────────────────┐
 │ Printer is not ready.        │
 │                              │
 │ Ready printer.  Then press   │
 │ Enter to continue.           │
 │                              │
 │ F1=Help  F12=Cancel          │
 └──────────────────────────────┘t prototype of the printer adapter
and its new specifications.  This is a big improvement over the
previous version.  I think it will allow us to deliver a more
attractive product - one that fits in well with the rest of the
new product line.
─────────────────────────────────────────────────────────────────
 Enter  F1=Help  F3=Exit  F7=Bkwd  F8=Fwd  F9=Instruct  F10=Actions  F12=Cancel
```

Figure 9.7 Action message—external action.

```
 Block  Format  Search  Exit  Help
─────────────────────────────────────────────────────────────────
                          Edit Document
Make text changes. Then select an action.
                                                    More:      +

January 24, 1987
 ┌──────────────────────────────┐
 │ Directory hj22b not          │
 │ found.   Type correct     te │
 │ name and press Enter.        │
 │                              │
 │   Directory _____      │atest prototype of the printer adapter
 │                           .  │ This is a big improvement over the
 │ F1=Help  F12=Cancel          │ it will allow us to deliver a more
 └──────────────────────────────┘
attractive product - one that fits in well with the rest of the
new product line.
─────────────────────────────────────────────────────────────────
 Enter  F1=Help  F3=Exit  F7=Bkwd  F8=Fwd  F9=Instruct  F10=Actions  F12=Cancel
```

Figure 9.8 Action message—interaction with the application.

144

Message Interaction

A beep is sounded when a warning or critical message is displayed, unless the user has turned the beep option off. There are several ways in which a message panel can be removed. As shown in the information message example, a message may be removed automatically when a condition ends or changes. A message is also removed when the user performs standard actions like Enter or Cancel. When a message contains a selection or entry field, the Cancel action should always be made available.

PART IV   USER INTERFACE DESIGN

10 PRINCIPLES OF DIALOG DESIGN

INTRODUCTION   The rules and guidelines that make up the Common User Access specifications can be applied in "cookbook" fashion when designing information displays and interaction techniques as part of an application design. However, understanding the basic principles involved in an effective human/computer interface will better prepare the application developer to apply the rules and guidelines in the context of a given application. A thorough knowledge of dialog design principles will also help in the design of application-specific panels and interactions that involve requirements and techniques not addressed by CUA rules and guidelines.

INFORMATION PROCESSING CHARACTERISTICS   In designing the interface between a person and a computer, the application developer must take into account the differences in the information processing capabilities of people and computers. A computer is a machine with vast logic power, capable of storing enormous quantities of information. It operates using sequential logic, performing thousands or even millions of instructions per second. It can store both instructions and data indefinitely and performs the instructions in exactly the same way each time it executes them. A person, on the other hand, performs logical operations (thinks) much more slowly. A person is also liable to forget things and to make errors when performing the same operation repeatedly. A person, however, has capabilities that the computer does not. The human mind is remarkably adaptable and is skilled at recognizing a wide variety of visual and audible stimuli, at observing patterns in events, and detecting relevance. Humans are adept at handling unforeseen occurrences and dealing with events that have a very low probability of occurrence. They can select goals and criteria, select approaches to problems, and formulate new questions and hypotheses. They can invent.

In designing the human side of the interface, then, there needs to be provision for both human strengths and human weaknesses. The interface should be flexible enough to allow the human operator to deal with unanticipated or changing situations and requirements. The interface should also include the type of support and guidance functions needed to help the user when memory fails or errors are made. Interface design should also allow for the fact that much of the user's interaction will be based on the use of short-term memory.

SHORT-TERM MEMORY

Short-term memory can be thought of as a small buffer or working storage in which the brain stores items of information that it is currently processing. The short-term memory retains the information it receives for only a brief time—often for only a few seconds—although it can retain information for longer periods through deliberate reinforcement. The short-term memory is constantly in danger of having its contents replaced by new items that are received from the senses and by new thoughts that intervene. One factor that can affect short-term memory during a computer dialog is response time. If the computer's response is too slow, the user's mind may wander from the task at hand. However, the length of time during which short-term memory retains information is not the only consideration. There are limits to both the amount of information a person can perceive at one time and to the amount of information that can be retained in short-term memory.

Attention Channel Capacity

When a person perceives the external world through his or her senses, there is a limit to the number of different stimuli that can be transmitted to the brain. We might say that the channel from the sense organs to the short-term memory has limited bandwidth. The capacity of this attention channel has been investigated by exposing subjects to brief stimuli and then asking them what they perceived. As might be expected, when the information content of the input is steadily increased, the amount of information accurately perceived increases to a point and then reaches a limit. For most people, the attention channel limit corresponds to about seven different values for unidimensional data. For example, most people can accurately distinguish between seven different tone frequencies or tone volumes, seven colors, or the positions of seven points on a line.

There are several ways in which this limit can be increased. The first is to let the person make relative rather than absolute judgments. In a bar chart, for example, the user is usually comparing the relative lengths of the bars and not looking at their absolute lengths. The second is to organize tasks so that the subject makes several judgments in succession. The number of judgments that can be made without recording each judgment depends on the capacity of short-term memory. The third way to extend the channel capacity for perception is to use multidimensional rather than unidimensional data. For example, in addition to distinguishing points by their position on a line, we can distinguish them by varying their level of brightness and by varying their size or shape. Each dimension added increases the number of information categories that can be quickly perceived.

Short-Term Memory Capacity

A question very closely related to channel capacity is that of how many different perceived stimuli can the brain *store* for immediate use. In other words, what is the capacity of short-term memory? The items perceived by means of the attention channel are stored in short-term memory along with items retrieved from long-term memory. Just as the attention channel is limited, the short-term memory also cannot hold many items. Psychologists have measured its capacity through experiments similar to those used for measuring the capacity of the attention channel. In this case the subject is asked to withhold a response until the experimenter has given several stimuli. The results of these experiments have shown that, like the attention channel, the short-term memory can hold about seven separate items.

There is one important factor that can be used to increase the short-term memory's capacity. Up to a point, the number of items that can be stored in short-term memory is independent of the information content of the items. For example, a face can be remembered as a single item, even though it consists of a vast number of individual pieces of information, such as the color of hair, skin, and eyes and the shape of various facial features. A person is capable of recognizing and storing a pattern of sight or sound as a whole. A major design question, then, becomes that of how a problem can be encoded, and the data represented, to facilitate pattern recognition in the user. In human-computer interactions, the design of the data representation becomes important in maximizing the amount of information the user can work with in short-term memory.

Common User Access and Short-Term Memory

The Common User Access interface uses a menu-driven approach, which allows the user to make choices among items displayed rather than requiring users to remember the items. The consistent formats and interaction techniques used in CUA also help reduce memory requirements. The distributed processing techniques that underlie SAA in general can be used to place as much processing as possible close to the user, thereby reducing response time. This also lightens the burden on short-term memory.

TYPES OF USER

The design of the user interface should take into account not only general human characteristics but also traits that specific types of user can be expected to have. Some important questions that can be asked about an application's user are the following:

- **Is the user a dedicated or a casual user?** On some systems, the user spends the entire working day interacting with an application. For example, an airline clerk will work continuously with an airline reservation system. This type of user has time to practice the interactions with the system, to learn its language, and to become accustomed to its idiosyncrasies. For this type of user, efficiency in using the system may be a more important characteristic than ease of learning. On other systems the user's interaction may be more casual and not a primary part of the day's work activities. For example, a manager may need to do an occasional financial analysis using a general financial modeling package. For this type of user the interface must be easy to learn and easy to use, since problems in using the system may lead to confusion, annoyance, criticism of the system, or even refusal to use it.

- **Is the user highly trained?** Not all users can be given, or will take, lengthy and detailed training. Of course, good training is desirable as part of any system, but one cannot always be sure that the training will be taken. An engineer who is to use a sophisticated CAD/CAM system as an integral part of his or her job will probably be willing to invest several days in training. A sales manager or state legislator who will occasionally use an information retrieval system may not be able to afford more than an hour or so.

- **Is the user an active or a passive user?** While in most cases, the computer system is present as an aid to the user, in some cases a user, or operator, is present as an aid to the system. An active user is one who initiates processing. A passive user is one who takes action initiated by the computer. Process control systems, where processes are being monitored in real time, often have passive users, who may be required to react when a particular condition or problem is detected.

- **Will the user be interacting with multiple applications?** Sometimes the user may employ a variety of different applications in the course of a working day. Where this is the case, interface design must consider the similarity of dialog structures across the applications. If there were only one application, the dialog could be differently structured than if there were several. With multiple applications, it is often undesirable to employ specially labeled keyboards or to use mnemonics that could be remembered for one application but may not apply to the others. Multiple-application dialogs are often structured in a general-purpose rather than a special-purpose manner.

CUA does not attempt to address every type of user interface; it was developed to address a specific set of IBM computing environments. In general, its menu-driven approach and emphasis on ease of use are aimed more at a casual user, although its support for a command area does allow for an alternate interface for the experienced user. It also assumes an active rather than a passive user, who will exercise primary control over dialog flow and interactions. And it assumes a multiple application environment with a goal of consistency across applications.

INTERFACE DESIGN PRINCIPLES

Certain general principles can be stated for the design of the human-computer interface. The first principle is that the designer should make design trade-offs that maximize the productivity of the people who will use the system. In many cases in the past, the opposite approach had been taken, and design decisions had been made to enhance the efficiency of the computing equipment at the expense of the users. With the costs of computing equipment coming down so rapidly, there is now little justification for this type of thinking in most situations. Computer systems are intended to support people and to help them do their jobs. Wherever possible, the system should adapt to the person rather than requiring the person to adapt to the system. Computer technology certainly needs to be taken into account, and the available technology may impose restrictions on what types of interaction the system can support. The ideal interface for a particular application might be one based on the use of high-resolution graphics, but it may not be cost-effective to employ the equipment that would be required to support this type of graphic display. For example, most applications can certainly benefit from the features provided by the Advanced Interface of CUA implemented on a powerful personal computer. But for cost reasons, applications will be implemented for many years to come using less expensive, nonprogrammable terminals.

The short-term memory of users should also be taken into account. The amount of information being displayed as part of a dialog should not overload the user's short-term memory capacity. The dialog should be structured so that the user is able to complete a series of related actions without interruption. Previously entered information should be visible or easily recallable so that the user can reestablish a train of thought if it is interrupted, either by the system or externally.

Where possible, the user should be allowed to control his or her interactions with the system. This control can take the form of controlling the pacing of the interactions, deciding what information is displayed and how it is positioned and formatted, and choosing how a particular action is invoked.

INTERFACE DESIGN OBJECTIVES

Interface design principles can be embodied in a set of design objectives for the user interface. These objectives are as follows:

- **Consistency.** Consistency is an important consideration in designing all the different elements that make up a dialog. We have already touched on this important objective in Part I, as it is an important objective of CUA as a whole. An individual application can make data display be more consistent by using a standard format from one panel to another, with common information such as the title or page number always appearing in the same place. Consistency can be provided for data entry by using standard methods of identifying and formatting fields used for entry and by using a consistent method of labeling entry fields. A basic principle of consistency for interaction techniques is that the same action should always lead to the same type of result. Similarly, standard dialog actions, such as Help or Exit, provide consistency in dialog control.

- **User Efficiency.** The design objective of efficiency relates to the efficiency of the people using the system, and not necessarily to efficiency in the use of the computing equipment. This objective says that the user should not be required to take unnecessary actions. Ways of implementing this objective include providing reminders to ensure that entered information is saved and does not need to be reentered, making the most frequently used options easiest to invoke, and designing the system so it is easy to learn.

- **Minimal Reliance on User Memory.** Because of the limitations of human short-term memory, a well-designed user interface should not overload that capacity. Various techniques can be used to minimize reliance on the user's memory. A menu-driven interface allows the user to recognize choices rather than having to remember command functions and syntax. Displaying information the user has previously entered or may need to reference reduces the user's memory requirements. Maintaining consistency throughout a dialog also helps, since the user can apply the same conceptual model throughout and will not need to remember different sets of actions and syntaxes for different situations.

- **Flexibility.** A well-designed user interface is one that the user can adapt to meet a changing set of needs. Flexibility is certainly a goal to strive for, but not always one that is easy to reach. There are various ways in which flexibility can be provided. As discussed earlier, the user can be allowed to specify what data are displayed and how they are to be positioned and formatted. The user can also control displayed information through facilities like scrolling and paging. For data entry, the user can be allowed to control the pace at which data are entered, the order of the inputs, and the default values to be used. The user should also be allowed to go back and make corrections to previously entered data. Dialog actions should allow the user to interrupt one dialog function and move to another one.

Design Objective Trade-Offs

Meeting design objectives is not always easy, and trade-offs may need to be made among the various objectives. For example, a heavily menu-driven system may reduce the memory load on the user, but it might be inefficient for an experienced user who is required to progress through a series of menus, one at a time, in order to invoke a familiar action. Also, increasing the flexibility of an interface may result in more options that the user needs to understand and remember, thus increasing memory load.

In making trade-offs, the nature of the application and of the typical user must be taken into account. For example, an application that provides a specific set of predefined functions, such as that used to support bank tellers' processing standard customer transactions, may trade off some forms of flexibility in order to increase efficiency. For this type of system, the user may have little control over formatting and sequencing of data display and data entry. Direct entry of commands may be used rather than menu selection, since the user can be assumed to be both trained and dedicated. On the other hand, a general query application may expect the user to specify the data to be displayed and will let the user combine actions in any desired way. Here ease of learning and ease of use may be optimized in order to allow for users with little training and intermittent need to use the system. For an application that may have both casual and experienced users, alternative interfaces may be provided. Menus and prompting may be available to inexperienced users, to walk them through the process with the support they need, whereas experienced users can choose to enter commands and parameters directly and to use abbreviations to make their interactions more efficient.

Common User Access and Interface Design Objectives

As we have already seen, CUA embodies directly in its rules and guidelines many of the basic interface design objectives. Consistency is an important objective in CUA. Data display consistency is provided through the formatting guidelines for the different window and panel types, as well as through the formatting rules and guidelines for selection and entry fields. CUA also defines standard methods of interaction for the user, both for selection and entry techniques and for dialog actions.

CUA addresses efficiency in several ways. Its selection techniques, including point-and-select, mnemonics, and numbers, are designed to minimize data entry for the user. Users are given reminders to save data, so that data do not have to be entered twice. The emphasis on making the interface consistent within itself and consistent with the user's conceptual model makes an application easier to learn and use. This consistency also minimizes memory requirements for the user, as does the basic menu-driven approach.

Flexibility is provided by the standard dialog actions that allow the user to control dialog flow.

ALPHANUMERIC DIALOGS

Selecting a particular type or types of dialog to use as part of the user interface is a fundamental design decision. This decision will be guided in part by the nature of the information to be processed across the interface and in part by the technological capabilities that are available. Information may be basically alphanumeric in nature, consisting of data and text. Information can also be represented in graphical form, as sound, or in the form of moving images (video). Alphanumeric dialogs are still the most common, although at least limited use of graphics in the user interface is becoming more widespread. Several different types of alphanumeric dialogs can be used in applications that do not require the use of graphics, sound, or video. The next sections discuss each of them.

MENU SELECTION DIALOGS

Menu selection can be used when the valid answers or choices for the user can be predefined. The set of choices is displayed for the user, who then makes selections. This technique is particularly useful for the inexperienced user, since it provides explicit prompting and limits the scope of actions that the user can take to those provided in the menu. Figure 10.1 illustrates a menu dialog being used in an automated teller machine application that is designed to be used by a casual, untrained user.

Question-and-Answer Dialogs

A question-and-answer dialog is appropriate when the user must enter data, where the data must be entered in a predetermined sequence but where it cannot be presented in the form of selections from a set of choices. Again, question-and-answer dialogs can be useful for interacting with an inexperienced user, since it provides prompting for each required input. Figure 10.2 shows part of a

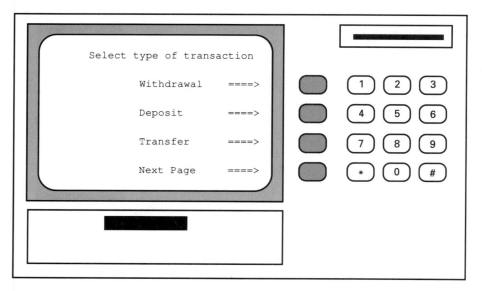

Figure 10.1   Example of a menu dialog being used in an automated teller terminal.

User:	rental
Computer:	SKIP MOST OF INPUT?
User:	n
Computer:	TAX BRACKET AS A DECIMAL
User:	.33
Computer:	MANAGEMENT RATE AS A DECIMAL
User:	.1
Computer:	UTILITIES (PER YEAR)
User:	500 + 140 + 160
Computer:	UPKEEP (PER YEAR)
User:	600
Computer:	INSURANCE (PER YEAR)
User:	350
Computer:	BASIS OF PROPERTY
User:	80000
Computer:	INTEREST ON LOAN AS A DECIMAL
User:	.10
Computer:	LENGTH OF LOAN (IN YEARS)
User:	35
Computer:	PERSONAL USE AS A DECIMAL
User:	.5
Computer:	LENGTH OF DEPRECIATION (IN YEARS)
User:	25
Computer:	MAXIMUM RENT (PER YEAR)
User:	6X400
Computer:	AMOUNT OF LOAN
User:	65000
Computer:	SKIP MONTHLY CALCULATION?
User:	n

Figure 10.2 Example of a question-and-answer dialog.

question-and-answer dialog. Here the user is prompted to enter the information necessary to do an economic analysis of a real estate property.

Form-Filling Dialogs

A common technique for data entry is to present the user with a "form" to fill in. This technique is particularly effective when the same information must be repetitively entered. Figure 10.3 presents an example of a form fill-in type panel, used for entering customer information.

Action-Based Dialogs

A common type of user interaction with an application is where the user invokes actions. These might be application-specific actions as well as standard dialog actions. When actions are a key element in the dialog, there are ways of making them easier to invoke. One way is to assign actions to different control keys, allowing the user to invoke an action by pressing a single key or a fixed combination of keys. Figure 10.4 shows a keyboard layout with the keys labeled with the functions that are provided by an airline reservation system.

Actions can also be assigned action codes, typically mnemonics, and the action codes can be entered along with other information. Figure 10.5 shows a portion of a dialog with an airline reservation system. In this example, the operator has entered the action code "L" immediately followed by "KI". The L

```
                              CUSTOMER DATA

        ENTER THE FOLLOWING INFORMATION ABOUT THE CUSTOMER:

        LAST NAME  _____    FIRST NAME  _____

        STREET     _____    CITY        _____

        STATE  __  ZIP _____ ____        PHONE  (___) ____ ____
```

Figure 10.3   Example of a form-filling dialog.

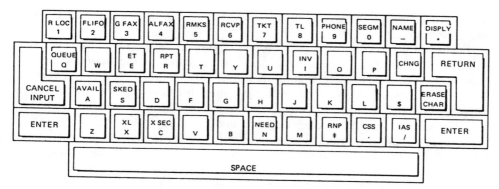

Figure 10.4   Control key assignments.

action code requests a list of passenger names; the "KI" indicates that the names should begin with those two letters. The use of control keys and action codes allows for a very terse dialog, which can provide a more efficient interface. However, such an approach often requires an experienced or well-trained operator to use it effectively.

LANGUAGE-BASED DIALOGS

The dialog types described thus far are most effective in an environment where the data to be entered can be defined by the application and thus included in a question-and-answer dialog or as part of a form fill in screen, and where user actions can be identified and included in menus or assigned to control keys. There are other types of application where the information to be entered by the user or the actions to be invoked cannot be predicted and must be left to the user. In cases like this, the interface may need to be more flexible and take the

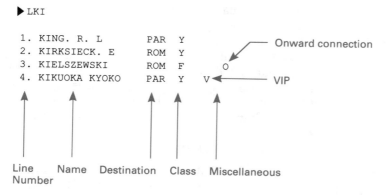

Figure 10.5   Example of an action code dialog.

form of a language, where a conversation can be carried on between the user and the computer.

The ability to communicate with a computer in the same way as one communicates with another person has long been a staple of the fictional view of computers. For example, in Stanley Kubrick's movie *2001: A Space Odyssey,* the computer controlling a space vehicle communicates with the astronauts by human voice dialog [1].

Computers do use voice answerback systems today, some capable of a rich vocabulary. There are also voice recognition systems in use, although they are still limited in their ability to recognize normal fluent speech. Flexible voice recognition systems have not yet reached the market because of the difficulties in identifying discrete words and in interpreting different accents and even variations that may occur in a single person's voice over time.

An alternative to voice recognition is to use a keyboard to type input in the form of natural language words and phrases. But there are many difficulties with even this. The computer still has to interpret human syntax. Humans use words in an enormous number of different combinations. The language we speak is very disorderly. Its words are ambiguous; its syntax confused. Many sentences are imperfect expressions of thought because the language is only partially rational. Mechanized parsing is difficult because many words can be verbs at one time and nouns at another. For example, in the sentence *Time flies like an arrow,* it is possible that either *time, flies,* or *like* could be the verb *(Fruit flies like a banana).* The language is full of irregularities and exceptions, and recognizing the meaning of sentences sometimes requires a wealth of prior knowledge, which may be difficult to program into a computer system. The magnitude of the problem is reduced greatly if the machine is required to recognize only a limited set of words and phrase structures. If it becomes too limited, however, users will require more training to know what phrases are permissible.

Command Language Dialogs

The most limited form of a language dialog takes the form of a command language. With a command language, keywords are used to identify the command, or action, being requested, and parameters are used to provide additional information needed to execute the command. A command language usually employs a specific syntax for commands and parameters and typically is used by an experienced or at least trained user. Figure 10.6 demonstrates an application-specific command language being used. With this interface, the user is able to define terms such as T1 and R2 and later reference them in a command.

Restricted Natural-Language Dialogs

Another form of natural-language dialog is one that uses a restricted form of natural language. Limitations are placed on the vocabulary that can be used and

User: aeroind = aerojet, bendix, boing, douglas, grumman
             lockheed, mcdonnell, north american, northrop,
             republic, thiokol, utd aircraft

Computer: BOING NOT IN FILE, PLEASE MAKE CHANGE

User: boeing

Computer: CHANGE ACCEPTED, PROCEED

User: get ri (mcdonnell) / average (ri (aeroind))

Computer: FOR WHAT DATES?

User: 1968 to 1972

Computer: 1968   1969   1970   1971   1972

             1.41   1.32   1.63   1.84   2.01

User: r2 = sales / equity

Computer: PROCEED

User: t1 = 1968 to 1972

Computer: PROCEED

User: get r2 (mcdonnell) and r2 (average (aeroind)) for t1

Figure 10.6   Example of a command language dialog.

on the syntax structures that are allowed. Many query languages use this approach. Query languages typically are used in conjunction with database systems and allow the user to formulate requests for the retrieval and display of all manner of data and to perform various manipulations and formatting operations. Statements in a query language still must conform to a syntax, but in general a query language is closer to natural language than a command language. Figure 10.7 shows three requests in Structured Query Language (SQL) and a typical response to one of them [2,3].

Natural-Language Dialogs

Progress has been made in the development of user interfaces that have many of the properties of a natural language. INTELLECT is such an interface [4,5]. INTELLECT is basically a query language that does not have the syntax restrictions of other query languages. Figure 10.8 shows how INTELLECT requests can be phrased in a number of different ways. All of these requests can be understood and processed by an application that supports the INTELLECT language interface.

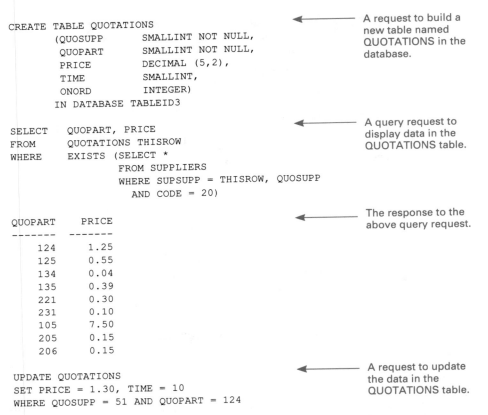

```
CREATE TABLE QUOTATIONS
        (QUOSUPP      SMALLINT NOT NULL,
         QUOPART      SMALLINT NOT NULL,
         PRICE        DECIMAL (5,2),
         TIME         SMALLINT,
         ONORD        INTEGER)
        IN DATABASE TABLEID3
```
A request to build a new table named QUOTATIONS in the database.

```
SELECT    QUOPART, PRICE
FROM      QUOTATIONS THISROW
WHERE     EXISTS (SELECT *
                FROM SUPPLIERS
                WHERE SUPSUPP = THISROW, QUOSUPP
                  AND CODE = 20)
```
A query request to display data in the QUOTATIONS table.

```
QUOPART     PRICE
-------     -------
   124       1.25
   125       0.55
   134       0.04
   135       0.39
   221       0.30
   231       0.10
   105       7.50
   205       0.15
   206       0.15
```
The response to the above query request.

```
UPDATE QUOTATIONS
SET PRICE = 1.30, TIME = 10
WHERE QUOSUPP = 51 AND QUOPART = 124
```
A request to update the data in the QUOTATIONS table.

Figure 10.7   Examples of statements written in SQL.

COMMON USER ACCESS AND DIALOG TYPES

CUA does not directly define all of the dialog types. It employs the menu dialog type for its selection fields and the form-filling dialog type with entry fields. Dialog control uses an action-based dialog, based on the standard dialog actions. Although it does define a command area that can be used to support a command language interface as part of the basic interface, it does not define anything about the structure or syntax of the command language itself. Nor does it define any other type of language dialog.

USE OF SOUND AND GRAPHICS

All of the various types of dialog can be implemented using alphanumeric entry and display capabilities. The interface typically takes the form of data and text displayed on a screen and entered via a keyboard. A pointing device, such as a mouse, can be used to perform selection and other user actions. Although alpha-

```
how many employees in the new york office are male,
administrators, and make over $45,000?

17

for the eastern and western regions, how did actual
sales for last month compare to forecasts?

                 MAY 1990     MAY 1991
                 ACTUAL       FORECAST
REGION           SALES        SALES        CHANGE    %CHANGE

EAST             2820         2000         820       41.00
WEST             3180         2800         380       13.57

show me a ranked percent of total sales by industry.

                              1991
                              SALES
INDUSTRY                      (000'S)      PERCENT

PETROLEUM REFINING    $561,096,647         31.66
MOTOR VEHICLES        $156,021,144          8.80
ELECTRONICS           $137,082,745          7.73
FOOD                  $123,872,646          6.98
CHEMICAL              $106,943,043          6.03
```

Figure 10.8 Examples of natural-language query statements in INTEL-LECT.

numeric dialogs may still be the most commonly used, other forms of interaction can be employed to enrich the user interface.

Graphics can be used in a variety of ways as part of the user interface. The simplest method is to use icons to represent objects and actions. If icons are carefully chosen, the underlying meaning can be directly represented to the user, making the interface easier to learn and use. Icons are also easily manipulated with a pointing device, providing a direct method of user interaction with the computer. Figure 10.9 shows some of the icons displayed by the system software of Apple's Macintosh line of computing equipment. Figure 10.10 shows some of the icons that are used in the workplace extension of CUA to represent various data objects, containers, and devices.

Graphics can also be an effective method of representing data values and

Diskette Icon   Typical Document Icon   File Folder Icon   Typical Application Icon

Figure 10.9 Typical Macintosh icons.

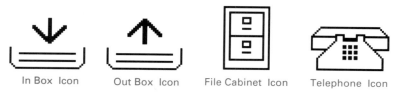

In Box Icon   Out Box Icon   File Cabinet Icon   Telephone Icon

Figure 10.10   Typical CUA icons.

relationships. Sets of data values can be displayed using different forms of charts, graphs, and plots. Diagrams of all types, including engineering drawings, blueprints, flowcharts, and maps, can be a very dense yet easily understandable way of displaying information to the user. In addition to using graphics as part of the display portion of the user interface, it is also possible to develop interaction techniques that allow the user to draw and manipulate graphics. These techniques can include operations that let the user create, copy, or move various graphic elements, such as a points, lines, arcs or other curves, circles, rectangles, or any shape or symbol that are part of the graphic. There can also be operations that operate on the graphic as a whole, such as rotating, zooming, or scaling. The development of high-resolution displays and storage technology like CD-ROM have made it possible to include photographic images that have been scanned and stored in digital form. In robotics, visual images have also served as input to the computer. For example, video has been used to scan parts so that a robotic device can ensure they are positioned correctly for use in assembly operations.

Sound can also be included in the user interface. Beeps and other tones can be used to alert the user to a particular condition. Tones can be combined to play tunes and melodies. The human voice can be part of the interface. Voice answerback systems provide an alternative to displaying data on a screen. They are commonly used for providing information over the telephone, in areas like directory assistance or airline flight information. Voice recognition systems allow users to enter data into the computer by speaking rather than typing the data.

Interactive video disc technology and forms of CD-ROM storage that permit sound and full motion video sequences to be stored allow sound, still-frame pictures, and full-motion video to be combined with computer-generated data and graphics, and for all to be displayed at the user's workstation. This technology has been particularly effective in computer-based training (CBT) applications.

DESIGNING A CUA USER INTERFACE

As noted, the Common User Access interface of SAA defines a set of rules and guidelines that guide the design of the application's user interface. Following these guidelines will help maintain consistency in the user interface, both as the application moves from one computing environment to another and as the user moves from application to application.

Object-Action Principle

The CUA rules and guidelines are based on an underlying principle called the object-action principle. The object-action principle states that the user should first select the *object* to be acted upon and then select the particular *action* to take with respect to that object. To be consistent with this principle, an application should always begin by displaying a panel that allows the user to select an object, and should then follow with a list of possible actions that can be applied to that object. An important benefit of the object-action approach is that the list of actions can always be tailored to the specific object that the user chooses.

Presentation and Interaction

The design of the information that an application displays is an important part of the user interface. CUA defines general panel and window formats, and these definitions be used as the basis for designing application displays. CUA also provides guidelines for the use of color and emphasis within panels.

Because of the differences in capabilities between a nonprogrammable terminal and a programmable workstation, presentation techniques can affect application portability. Formatting decisions, then, may need to reflect the types of workstations supported by the application. CUA also defines standard methods of user interaction. The methods chosen for a particular application may also be determined in part by the hardware upon which the application will run. Certain interaction techniques, such as the use of a mouse or other pointing device, may only be available if the application is run on a programmable workstation. For example, in order for an application to be fully portable, it must not depend on a mouse being available but must also support keyboard interaction for all possible actions.

Message Design

Another part of the design of the user interface involves designing the messages to be displayed when different conditions occur. CUA provides guidelines for formatting and displaying different types of message, including *information, warning,* and *error (action)* messages. The design of the user interface should also address the use of *help* information. CUA includes standards for displaying different levels of help.

Dialog Flow

User interface design concerns include the application's dialog flow. The application designer needs to ask the following questions when choosing the sequence in which to display panels and determining the options the user will have for continuing or terminating the dialog:

- **Normal Workflow.** In what sequence will functions normally occur in the application?
- **Possible Return Sequences.** How will the user terminate a particular function? How will the entire application be terminated? Can the user back up, step by step, within a function? When should the user be prompted to save data?
- **Restart Sequence.** How should a function be restarted if the user is interrupted for a period of time?
- **Help and Message Panels.** In what sequence should message and help panels be displayed? How does the user return to the normal dialog flow?

CUA provides guidelines for developing a dialog flow that will be consistent with the dialog flow of other SAA applications. Consistency in dialog flow is important so that the user learns to expect consistent results when taking similar actions.

REFERENCES

1. Arthur C. Clarke, *2001, A Space Odyssey*. Based on the screenplay by Stanley Kubrick and Arthur C. Clark. Signet Books, New York, 1968.

2. For more information on INTELLECT, contact Artificial Intelligence Corporation, 200 Fifth Avenue, Waltham, MA 02254.

3. INTELLECT is described in James Martin and Joe Leben, *Fourth-Generation Languages, Volume III: 4GLs from IBM*. Prentice Hall, Englewood Cliffs, NJ, 1986.

4. A brief description of SQL can be found in James Martin and Joe Leben, *Fourth-Generation Languages, Volume III: 4GLs from IBM*. Prentice Hall, Englewood Cliffs, NJ, 1986.

5. For an in-depth discussion of SQL, see James Martin and Joe Leben, *DB2: Concepts, Design, and Programming*. Prentice Hall, Englewood Cliffs, NJ, 1989.

11 MITRE CORPORATION DESIGN GUIDELINES

INTRODUCTION   Meeting the design objectives of consistency, efficiency, minimal memory, and flexibility is a difficult task, given the wide range of capabilities possible with current computer technologies. The objectives are very general in nature, and it requires judgment and experience to apply them in a specific situation. The issue of user interface design is of interest to many companies in the computer industry. IBM has addressed it, providing detailed design guidelines and rules for its major computing environments in the Common User Access component of SAA. The MITRE Corporation, working under the sponsorship of the United States Air Force, has also done significant work in this area. As a result of their work they have published a report entitled *Guidelines for Designing User Interface Software* [1]. The report contains 944 guidelines for designing software to support the user interface.

As the report states:

> The design of user interface software will often involve a considerable investment of time and effort. Design guidelines can help ensure the value of that investment.

and

> The design of user interface software is not only expensive and time-consuming, but it is also critical for effective system performance. To be sure, users can sometimes compensate for poor design with extra effort. Probably no single user interface design flaw, in itself, will cause system failure. But there is a limit to how well users can adapt to a poorly designed interface. As one deficiency is added to another, the cumulative negative effects may eventually result in system failure, poor performance, and/or user complaints.

The guidelines included in the Mitre report are intended to help with the task of designing an effective user interface. The guidelines are organized into six areas:

- Data entry
- Data display
- Sequence control
- User guidance
- Data transmission
- Data protection

Examples of the application of the guidelines are included in the report, along with discussion of any contingencies that apply in using the guidelines. The intent of the report is for organizations to use the guidelines to develop specific

BOX 11.1   Data entry functions.

- **Data entry.** Refers to user actions involving input of data to a computer and computer responses to such inputs.
- **Positioning designation.** Refers to user selection and entry of a position on a display or of a displayed item.
- **Direction designation.** Refers to user entry of directional data (azimuth, bearing, heading, etc.) on a display.
- **Text entry.** Refers to the initial entry and subsequent editing of textual material, including messages.
- **Data forms.** Permit entry of predefined items into labeled fields of specially formatted displays.
- **Tables.** Permit data entry and display in row-column format, facilitating comparison of related data sets.
- **Graphics.** Permits entry of data specially formatted to show spatial, temporal, or other relations among data sets. Both the functions of plotting data and drawing are addressed.
- **Data validation.** Refers to checking entries for correct content and/or format, as defined by software logic.
- **Other data processing.** Aids may be provided to facilitate data entry.
- **Design change.** May be needed for software supporting data entry functions to meet changing operational requirements.

design rules to be applied in a given environment. For example, one of the guidelines states that data displays should be formatted consistently. This might be translated by an organization into design rules that identify specific formats to be used for different types of display panels.

The Mitre report guidelines are required reading for anyone who is working on the design of the user interface of a computer application. The remainder of this chapter presents highlights of the six sections of this important report and discusses how CUA guidelines relate to Mitre guidelines in each of the areas.

DATA ENTRY

The data entry section presents guidelines related to user actions in entering data into a computer. Data entry can be done in a variety of ways. It might consist of making a selection; typing in numbers, letters, fields of data, or textual material; spoken input; or drawing or interacting with a graphic. The guidelines for data entry are divided into the subsections listed in Box 11.1. An example of a data entry guideline is shown below.

•9　Explicit ENTER Action

Always require a user to take an explicit ENTER action to initiate processing of entered data; do **not** initiate processing as a side effect of some other action.

　　EXAMPLE: As a negative example, returning to a menu of control options should **not** by itself result in computer processing of data just keyed onto a display.

　　EXCEPTION: In routine, repetitive data entry transactions, successful completion of one entry may automatically lead to initiation of the next, as in keying ZIP codes at an automated post office.

　　COMMENT: Deferring processing until after an explicit ENTER action will permit a user to review data and correct errors before computer processing, particularly helpful when data entry is complex and/or difficult to reverse.

　　REFERENCE: MS 5.15.2.1.4.

　　SEE ALSO: 1.4•1, 1.4•2, 3.0•5, 4.0•2, 6.0•9, 6.3•5.

Key considerations for data entry include context and flexibility. Establishing and maintaining context for the user will allow the user to take advantage of previously entered data, and can make error correction easier. Context can be

BOX 11.2 Data display functions.

- **Data display.** Refers to computer output of data to a user and assimilation of information from such outputs.

- **Text.** Displays provide output of stored textual data, along with messages and other text intended for user guidance.

- **Data forms.** Can display sets of related data items in labeled fields formatted to aid data entry and review.

- **Tables.** Can display data in row-column format to aid detailed comparison of ordered sets of items.

- **Graphics.** Shows spatial, temporal, or other relations among data by special formatting of displayed elements, including the use of

    Scaling
    Scatterplots
    Curves and line graphs
    Bar graphs
    Pie charts
    Pictures and diagrams
    Flowcharts
    Maps and situation displays

- **Format.** Refers to the organization of different types of data in a display to aid assimilation of information.

- **Coding.** Refers to distinctive means for highlighting different categories of displayed data for user attention.

- **Display control.** Refers to procedures by which a user can specify what data are shown, and how. Includes

    Selection
    Framing
    Update
    Suppression
    Window overlays

- **Design change.** May be needed for software supporting data display functions to meet changing operational requirements.

established by saving and making available to the user previously entered values, and by allowing the user to define default values. Flexibility in data entry can be provided by allowing the user to control the pacing and sequence of entering inputs and to define default values.

Common User Access and Data Entry

In the area of data entry, the menu-driven approach of Common User Access helps provide context to the user. Previously entered values are displayed, and the user is prompted to save values when exiting a function. The user does have some control over the sequence of entering inputs, since the object-action approach allows the user either to choose objects and then specify an action or select an action and then choose objects.

CUA leaves some aspects of data entry to the application. For example, context can also be established by including instructions and appropriate information in window and panel titles. This type of content definition is the responsibility of the application developer. Similarly, the choice of default values and whether the user has control over the values used depend on the application.

DATA DISPLAY

The data display section is concerned with computer output of data to a user, and with how the user assimilates information from these outputs. Different forms of presenting outputs are addressed, including visual display, hard-copy printouts, and voice, although the emphasis is on visual display. Box 11.2 lists the subsections for data display. An example of a data display guideline follows.

Data Display Consistent with User Conventions   •4

Display data consistently with standards and conventions familiar to users.

    EXAMPLE: As a negative example, if users work with metric units of measurement, do **not** display data in English units.

    EXAMPLE: Computer time records that are not in directly usable format should be converted for display, to a conventional 12-hour (AM/PM) clock, or a 24-hour clock, in local time or whatever other time standard is appropriate to user needs.

(Continued)

EXAMPLE: Calendar formats should follow user customs.

(American calendar)

S	M	T	W	T	F	S
1	2	3	4	5	6	7
8	9	10	11	12	13	14
15	16	17	18	19	20	21
22	23	24	25	26	27	28
29	30	31				

(European calendar)

S	1	8	15	22	29
M	2	9	16	23	30
T	3	10	17	24	31
W	4	11	18	25	
T	5	12	19	26	
F	6	13	20	27	
S	7	14	21	28	

REFERENCE: BB 3.4; EG 2.2.4.

SEE ALSO: 4.0•16.

For data display, key considerations are context, consistency, and flexibility. Context involves the grouping of items displayed so that interrelated elements can be tied together in a way that provides meaning to the user. Consistency is important because it allows the user to develop an appropriate conceptual model, with correct expectations of where to look for particular information. Flexibility is particularly important when the needs of the user are not predictable and options for tailoring displays must be provided.

Common User Access and Data Display

CUA, with its rules and guidelines for display formatting, helps provide consistency in data display. The user will always find action choices in the action bar and available function key options in the function key area. The standard formats for selection and entry fields also support consistency. Providing context is more an application than a CUA responsibility, since grouping logically related items is based on actual display content and its relationship to application-specific processing.

SEQUENCE CONTROL   Sequence control defines the ways in which the user controls interaction with the computer. This control is based on the notion of a *dialog,* which is defined in the Mitre report as "the sequence of transactions that mediate user-system interaction." Selecting a dialog type is an important design decision, and guidelines for sequence control are provided for different dialog types. The subsections for sequence control are shown in Box 11.3. Following is one of the sequence control guidelines.

BOX 11.3 Sequence control functions.

- **Sequence control.** Refers to user actions and computer logic that initiate, interrupt, or terminate transactions.
- **Dialog types.** Sequence control dialogs must be designed to match the needs of different tasks and different users and can include the following:

  Question and answer
  Form filling
  Menu selection
  Function keys
  Command language
  Query language
  Natural language
  Graphic interaction

- **Transaction selection.** Refers to the control actions and computer logic that initiate transactions.
- **Interrupts.** Capabilities that permit a user to change ongoing transactions allow flexibility in sequence control.
- **Context definition.** The computer can provide context definition to help ensure that control actions are related to a user's current task.
- **Error management.** The computer can provide error management to help prevent user errors and correct those errors that do occur.
- **Alarms.** Alerting signals generated by the computer might be controlled by users in terms of logic and operation.
- **Design change.** May be needed for software supporting control functions to meet changing operational requirements.

Displayed Context   •9

If the consequences of a control entry will differ depending upon context established by a prior action, then display some continuous indication of current context for reference by the user.

EXAMPLE: If activating a DELETE key establishes a **mode,** so that subsequent selection of a PAGE key will erase a page of data rather than simply advancing to display the next page, then some indication of that established DELETE mode should be displayed to the user.

COMMENT: Do not rely on the user always to remember prior actions, nor to understand their current implications.

SEE ALSO: 4.4•13, and Section 3.4.

For sequence control, again, context, consistency, and flexibility are important. Effective user interaction depends on the user clearly understanding the actions available at a given point in time and the results of those actions. Providing appropriate context information is key to that understanding. Effective interaction also depends on the user interface operating consistently. The user should receive a similar response whenever an action is invoked. Flexibility is required to allow the user to initiate, interrupt, or cancel a given function as needed, with appropriate protection against losing data. Flexibility may also be provided in the form of alternate dialog control methods being available to the naive versus the experienced user.

Common User Access and Sequence Control

Providing context in sequence control is a shared responsibility of both CUA and the application. CUA formatting guidelines will ensure that available actions are displayed to the user in a consistent manner. However, the application must ensure that appropriate information is provided to explain possible actions and their results. The standard CUA help facilities can be used to provide the explanations, but the application must define the actual content of the help information.

Consistency in sequence control says that the user should always receive the same response to the same action. CUA rules and guidelines for interaction techniques and for standard dialog actions are based on this principle and are strongly oriented toward consistency. For application-specific actions, the application must ensure this consistency.

Flexibility in sequence control is provided in CUA through the standard dialog actions that allow the user to navigate through the dialog, moving forward, canceling, or exiting from panels as desired. CUA also calls for providing the user with the option to save data when exiting. CUA's support for a command interface also allows for the development of an alternate interface for the experienced user. The application is responsible for determining the appropriate windows or panels to be displayed when navigating through the dialog and for seeing that application-specific actions can be interrupted or canceled.

USER GUIDANCE

User guidance includes the various types of information that help guide the user through interactions with the computer. This can be instructional material, prompts and labels, or messages and alarms. User guidance addresses status information, job aids, routine feedback, and feedback for error correction. Box 11.4 lists the subsections in

BOX 11.4   User guidance functions.

- **User guidance.** Refers to error messages, alarms, prompts, and labels, as well as to more formal instructional material.
- **Status information.** Status information on current data processing should be available at all times, automatically or by request.
- **Routine feedback.** Feedback should be routinely provided by a computer to its users as transactions are processed.
- **Error feedback.** Feedback on errors should be provided if an error or other unexpected event prevents routine processing.
- **Job aids.** Job aids should provide users with specific task-oriented guidance for every transaction sequence.
- **User records.** Permit assessment of performance and improvement of user interface design.
- **Design change.** May be needed for software supporting user guidance functions to meet changing operational requirements.

the user guidance section; following is an example of one of the guidelines on user guidance.

·25   Easy Ways to Get Guidance

Allow users to switch easily between any information-handling transaction and its associated guidance material.

EXAMPLE: Guidance might be displayed as a temporary "window" overlay on the working display, which a user could request or suppress at will.

COMMENT: If user guidance is difficult to obtain, and/or if asking for guidance will disrupt a current transaction (e.g., erase a working display), then users will prefer to guess at proper procedures rather than seeking help.

REFERENCE: Limanowski, 1983.

All elements of the user interface—data entry, data display, sequence control—can provide guidance to the user if they are used properly, and user guidance guidelines should be considered as part of their design. A key consideration for user guidance is consistency. The various forms of help being provided to the user must be immediately usable in order to be effective. The user should not have to learn to deal with new formats or interaction techniques in order to learn about the underlying system.

Common User Access and User Guidance

Several areas within CUA relate to user guidance. The basic display formatting guidelines address the use of instructions, prompts, and headings. CUA defines standard message types and formats and ways of interacting with a message. The CUA help facility provides for different levels of help information, as well as standard interaction techniques for requesting and interacting with help information.

DATA TRANSMISSION

Data transmission, in the context of the Mitre report, is concerned with communication between users. Although this communication can take many forms, the

BOX 11.5   Data transmission functions.

- **Data transmission.** Refers to computer-mediated communication among system users and also with other systems.
- **Preparing messages.** Preparing messages for transmission involves specification of contents, format, and header information.
- **Addressing messages.** May require user action and computer aids to specify the destinations for data transmission.
- **Initiating transmission.** Should usually be under user control, with computer aids for the process.
- **Controlling transmission.** Can often be handled automatically, but users may need information about the process.
- **Receiving messages.** May require computer aids for queuing, reviewing, filing, or otherwise disposing of incoming data.
- **Design change.** May be needed for software supporting data transmission to meet changing operational requirements.

emphasis here is on the use of formatted messages. The data transmission sub-sections are shown in Box 11.5, and a sample guideline is shown below.

System Distribution Lists   •8

Provide formal distribution lists recognized by the system so that users can specify multiple addresses with a single distribution list name.

EXAMPLE: A formal distribution list might be maintained of people who are working on a particular project, or who are members of a particular organizational group.

COMMENT: Recognized system distribution lists need **not** be expanded to the names of individual addressees when a message is transmitted.

COMMENT: The authority to use system distribution lists may be limited in some cases. For example, not everyone might be permitted to send messages to a distribution list of all employees in a large organization.

REFERENCE: Bruder, Moy, Mueller and Danielson, 1981; Deutsch, 1984; Garcia-Luna and Kuo, 1981; Williamson and Rohlfs, 1981.

Data transmission can be viewed as one possible application function; for example, electronic mail is a function in the general group of office system functions, along with text editing and document storage and retrieval. As such, all the guidelines for data entry, data display, and sequence control should be considered in the design of the user interface.

Common User Access and Data Transmission

In the SAA view, the functions addressed by data transmission are either application responsibilities or are addressed in the SAA Common Communications Support (CCS) interface. Actual formatting and processing of the information being communicated are an application responsibility. The way in which communication takes place is the province of the CCS portion of SAA.

DATA PROTECTION

Data protection addresses the issue of security—of protecting data from unauthorized access, computer failure, and damaging user actions, both deliberate tampering and unintended errors. A particular challenge in the area of data protection is finding ways of preventing errors and misuse of the system while keeping the system easy to use

BOX 11.6   Data protection functions.

- **Data protection.** Concerns security from unauthorized use and potential loss from equipment failure and user errors.
- **User identification.** Procedures for user identification should be as simple as possible and consistent with adequate protection.
- **Data access.** Constraints on data access established to exclude unauthorized users should not hinder legitimate use of data.
- **Data entry/change.** Constraints on data entry/change are needed to prevent unauthorized data change as well as data loss from user errors.
- **Data transmission.** Procedures for data transmission should ensure data protection when sending and receiving messages.
- **Design change.** May be needed for software supporting data protection to meet changing operational requirements.

for correct, valid transactions. Thus, data protection must be considered in combination with the other elements of user interface design, and a balance must be struck among competing design objectives. Box 11.6 lists the subsections for data protection; following is one of its guidelines.

Protection from Interrupts   •5

When a proposed user action will interrupt a current transaction sequence, provide automatic means to prevent data loss; if potential data loss cannot be prevented, warn the user and do **not** interrupt without user confirmation.

EXAMPLE: If a user should interrupt a series of changes to a data file, then the computer might automatically save both the original and the changed versions of that file for subsequent user review and disposition.

COMMENT: Some interrupt actions such as BACKUP, CANCEL, or REVIEW, will by their definition cause only limited data change, and so need no special protection. However, if an interrupt action may cause extensive data change (e.g., RESTART, LOG-OFF), then require the user to confirm that action before processing.

REFERENCE: BB 4.7.

SEE ALSO: 3.3•6.

Common User Access
and Data Protection

SAA, at the time of writing, does not address the area of security. IBM has indicated that security will be addressed in the future. In the meantime, security must be dealt with at the application or subsystem level.

REFERENCE

1. *Guidelines for Designing User Interface Software.* Document No. AD A177 198. National Technical Information Service (NTIS), 5285 Port Royal Road, Springfield, VA 22161.

12 APPLE COMPUTER DESIGN GUIDELINES

INTRODUCTION   A popular user interface employed today is that implemented by Apple Computer's Macintosh line of small computers. The design of the Macintosh user interface was heavily influenced by research begun in the 1970s by Alan Kay at the Xerox Palo Alto Research Center (PARC). Kay's vision was a computer he called the *Dynabook,* a computing system with the power and speed of a mainframe in the size and shape of a notebook.

Legend has it that in the late 1970s, about the time that the Lisa project (the Lisa was the commercially unsuccessful forerunner to the Macintosh) was beginning, Steve Jobs, one of the founders of Apple Computer, was touring the PARC development laboratories with a number of other people from Apple. The PARC people demonstrated some prototype equipment that implemented windows and pop-up menus and used a mouse as a pointing device. The machine immediately captivated Jobs, and he is said to have pointed to the machine and declared to the people accompanying him: "I want a machine like that!"

According to the story, that was when the concept of the Lisa, and later the Macintosh, was born. Although many at IBM would be reluctant to admit it, the Advanced Interface of CUA and the workplace extension have their roots in the work done at PARC and in the work done later for the Macintosh by those at Apple Computer.

Much can be learned about dialog design by studying the user-interface guidelines that Apple Computer provides for application developers who work in the Macintosh environment. Many of the same principles also apply to the IBM CUA environment, especially for the CUA Advanced Interface intended for personal computers that implement the OS/2 Presentation Manager. In fact, there are so many similarities between the Macintosh environment and the OS/2 Presentation Management environment that a user familiar with either of the two will find it easy to learn the other. Of course, there are also many subtle and not-so-subtle differences between the two. (Due to the aggressively protective stance that Apple has taken in regard to the user interface it has created for the Macintosh, one wonders how many of the differences between CUA and the Macintosh user interfaces are there because of legal, and not technological, reasons.)

The primary method a Macintosh computer uses for communicating with the user is to display information on a screen that supports relatively high-resolution graphics. The user communicates with the Macintosh via a keyboard and a mouse. (Other pointing devices can also be used, such as trackballs and graphics tablets.) The mouse used with the Macintosh contains a single button; many IBM personal computers use a two-button or a three-button mouse. The user can perform four actions using the Macintosh's single-button mouse: clicking, double clicking, pressing, and dragging. These actions are described in Box 12.1.

POINTER SHAPES   Macintosh application programs use various pointer shapes to give the user a visual cue concerning the type of action that is appropriate in a given situation. For example, a pointer in the shape of an arrowhead indicates that objects can be pointed to and selected, and a pointer in the shape of a wristwatch indicates that the user should wait for some event to complete before initiating any new action.

BOX 12.1   Mouse actions.

- **Clicking.** In performing the *clicking* action, the user points at a screen object and briefly presses and immediately releases the mouse button. Clicking a screen object generally signifies that the user intends to perform some action on that object.

- **Double Clicking.** The user *double-clicks* by clicking on an object twice in rapid succession. Double clicking is normally an enhancement, superset, or extension of the particular feature selected by clicking a screen object.

- **Pressing.** *Pressing* involves holding down the mouse button while keeping the screen pointer positioned over a screen object. Pressing often means the same thing as clicking an object repeatedly.

- **Dragging.** *Dragging* involves moving the mouse while at the same time pressing the mouse button. When an object is dragged, the object, or an outline of it, generally attaches itself to the screen pointer and moves with it as the mouse is moved. When the user releases the mouse button, the object remains at the new location.

THE KEYBOARD

The Macintosh keyboard is used primarily for entering text and numeric data. It can also be used for issuing commands as an alternative to using the standard method, which, as we will see later, consists of using the mouse to select entries in pulldown menus. Various types of keyboard are available for the Macintosh, both from Apple and from other vendors. Some have keys for controlling the cursor and a variety of function keys; others are quite simple and contain little more than the keys required for text entry.

THE GRAPHICS SCREEN

Macintosh computers support graphics displays of various sizes. All information is displayed on the screen in Graphics mode using a system software subsystem called *Quickdraw*. The Macintosh does not support a text mode; text is drawn on the screen using Quickdraw in the same manner as any other type of information.

CONCEPTUAL MODELS

The purpose of a computing system is to manipulate information. The central concepts surrounding the Macintosh user interface all relate to creating, accessing, displaying, moving, duplicating, modifying, and deleting information. There are six conceptual models, described in Box 12.2, that the Macintosh user interface implements to make it easy for users to perform these functions:

- **Desktop.** The working environment
- **Document.** The information itself
- **File.** An entity that *contains* information
- **Application.** A program that *manipulates* information
- **Resource.** An entity that *modifies* the behavior of an application
- **Window.** An area of the screen that *presents* information

OVERLAPPING WINDOWS

The desktop can contain any number of open windows, and windows can overlap one another in any desired way. When windows overlap, there is a simulated front-to-back ordering of the windows. Only one window, called the *active window,* is on top. When the user selects a window by clicking it with the mouse, it becomes the active window and is moved to the front of the simulated stack of overlapping windows. The other windows retain their original front-to-back ordering.

BOX 12.2   Macintosh conceptual models.

- **Desktop.** The *desktop* is the Macintosh's working environment. The user can have any number of objects on the desktop, such as file folders and documents. The user can open these objects, close them, and manipulate the information in them, just as can be done with real file folders and documents on an ordinary desk.

- **Document.** The second conceptual model implemented by the Macintosh user interface is the *document*. A document is an organized collection of information, such as a letter created with a text editor, an illustration created with a graphics editor, or a ledger sheet created with a spreadsheet program. A document as viewed through a window on the display screen generally closely resembles the document as it will appear when printed.

- **File.** A *file* is a container of information. For example, documents are stored in files. Files can also be used to store *applications* and *resources*.

- **Application.** *Applications* are the Macintosh counterparts to application programs. A file that contains an application can be used to access and manipulate the information contained in other files. Each document file is associated with a principal application. When the user opens a text file that was created using a text editor, the text editor that was used to create it is automatically called up and is used to display the document in its window.

- **Resource.** *Resources* are sets of information that application programs use to modify their behavior. For example, a font file is a resource that an application uses to display information using a particular type font. Resource files are created by applications also, but these applications are not normally directly manipulated by the typical user. Resource files are normally created and manipulated by specialized applications called resource editors. For example, there exist font editors that can be used to create and modify font resource files.

- **Window.** The final conceptual model that the Macintosh user interface implements is the *window*. Windows are objects on the desktop that are used to display information.

THE ACTIVE WINDOW

Generally, the last window to be opened or selected is the active window. The active window is always highlighted in some way. For example, in the screen shown in Fig. 12.1, the active window is distinguished from the inactive windows with rows of horizontal highlighting lines in the window's title bar. All

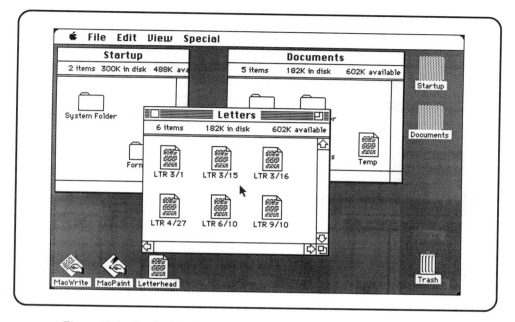

Figure 12.1 On the Macintosh desktop, the active window is distinguished from inactive windows with rows of horizontal highlighting lines.

commands and data that are entered apply to the application that is in control of the active window.

DOCUMENT WINDOWS

Although many specialized windows are displayed by the Macintosh, the most common form of window is that displayed by an application that works with a document. Document display windows and the windows the system software uses to display the contents of disks and folders are generally similar. Figure 12.2 shows an example of the document window displayed by a simple spreadsheet application.

COMMANDS AND MENUS

The primary method of command entry on the Macintosh is through the use of *pulldown menus*. A menu bar is displayed at all times across the top of the screen. The user pulls a window down by pointing at the menu's name and pressing the mouse button. The user issues a command by selecting a menu item. This is done by dragging the pointer to the name of the command to be executed and releasing the mouse button. Figure 12.3 shows an example of a menu bar with one of the menus pulled down.

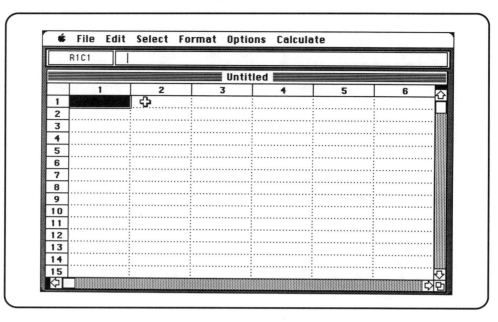

Figure 12.2 A typical Macintosh document window, displayed by a spreadsheet application.

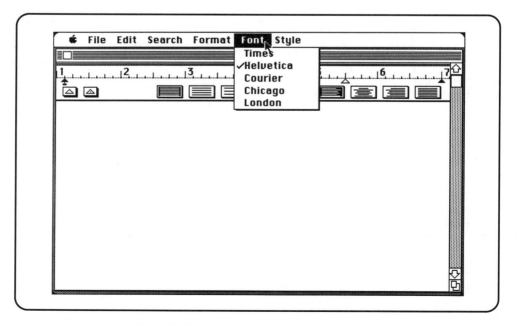

Figure 12.3 A typical Macintosh pulldown menu.

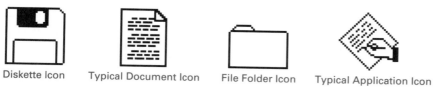

Figure 12.4   Typical Macintosh icons.

ICONS

When possible, most Macintosh applications display information in the form of small pictures called *icons*. An icon is a fundamental object implemented by the Macintosh user interface. Some sample icons, shown earlier, are repeated in Fig. 12.4.

DIALOG AND ALERT BOXES

Dialog boxes and alert boxes are used when the application program needs to inform the user about something, requires information from the user, or when an error or other special event has occurred. A dialog box can be used to prompt the user for information, as shown in Fig. 12.5.

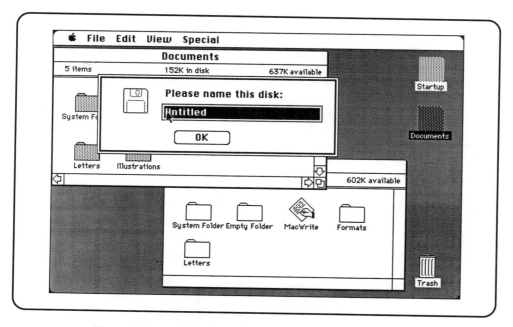

Figure 12.5   A dialog box asking the user to identify a diskette.

MODELESS OPERATION   One of the underlying principles in the Macintosh user interface is that an application program should operate as much as possible in a *modeless fashion*. A *mode* of an interactive system can be defined as the state of the user interface that lasts for some period of time, is not associated with any particular object, and has no role other than to place an interpretation on user input. When a computer system operates in multiple modes, the user often becomes confused, especially when the system changes modes without the user being aware that the change has occurred. Confusion results because the user continually finds the computer in the wrong mode. It is often necessary for a general-purpose computing system to operate in a variety of modes, but mode switching must be completely comprehensible to the user at all times. In general, there are three cases when mode switching is acceptable:

- **Long-term Modes.** When a word processing program is called up, the user expects that the computer will then begin operating in text-editing mode. When the user exits the word processor and calls up the graphics editor, the user expects the computer to switch into graphics-editing mode. This is entirely acceptable and understandable.

- **Short-term Modes.** This type of mode change occurs when the user initiates a short-term event, such as pressing the mouse button and holding it down. This is also desirable. A short-term mode can be referred to as a "spring-loaded" mode. When the user lets go of the button, the mode instantly changes back.

- **Alert Modes.** Alert modes are often used in error situations. When an application program enters an alert mode, it may temporarily stop accepting normal input and accept only a narrow range of inputs relating directly to the error condition. Alert modes are acceptable, but must be implemented in such a way that the user immediately recognizes that something unusual has happened.

Application programs must sometimes change modes for periods of time to implement functions that are not covered by these three situations. When a change in mode occurs, a Macintosh application normally makes the mode change clearly visible and obvious to the user. Acceptable and desirable mode changes within an application program normally meet one or more of the following requirements:

- The mode change is indicative of the normal operation of a simulated real-life object. For example, in drawing lines with a graphics editor, the user is able to change the shape of a simulated paintbrush. Each change of shape causes the editor to change its line-drawing mode.

- The mode change should affect only the attributes of something, and not its operation. For example, when the shape of the paintbrush is changed, the user still draws lines in the same manner; only the shape of the pattern being drawn changes.

- When in the new mode, the software should prevent the user from taking actions not related to the new mode. For example, if the user gets dangerously close to using up all available space on a disk, the program should alert the user and stop accepting normal input until the user has saved the work in progress and has made sufficient space available.

USER INTERFACE HINTS   Apple Computer provides the following advice to application developers grappling with the user interface issues that are part of the development of new applications. These tips reflect many of the design principles and objectives discussed in Chapter 10 and provide sound advice that might be followed for applications for the CUA environment as well.

- A given action should always produce the same sort of result each time the user performs it. Avoid surprising the user.
- Avoid giving the user too many alternatives for performing the same action. For example, a command in a pulldown menu and an alternative command key shortcut are sufficient in most cases. A third or fourth alternative tends to confuse the user.
- Avoid overloading an application with esoteric features. According to Apple, *featurism* is the single major contributor to system complexity and user intimidation.
- Avoid changing the state of the application without making the user aware of it. The environment should be consistent and predictable.
- Avoid a cluttered screen display.
- Avoid the use of multiple modes wherever possible.

COMMON USER ACCESS AND THE MACINTOSH USER INTERFACE   The Macintosh user interface and Common User Access share many concepts in their approach to interface design. Both support the use of overlapping windows with the active window positioned on top, although CUA does allow for implementations that do not support windowing. Both use a horizontal list of actions (menu bar or action bar) with pulldown menus as the primary way of specifying actions, and both use icons. Also, both use pop-up windows (dialog and alert boxes) for displaying information and messages to the user and for extending dialog interactions.

Both CUA and the Macintosh environments provide guidelines for modes of operation, and the CUA emphasis on consistency in interaction techniques and dialog actions helps to prevent unnecessary mode changes. The Apple Computer user interface hints strongly reflect the design objectives of consistency and minimal reliance on user memory, which are also reflected in the CUA rules and guidelines. The Macintosh guidelines also reflect a concern for simplicity that is not directly addressed by CUA.

CUA AND THE COMMON
PROGRAMMING INTERFACE

13 CUA AND THE CPI DIALOG INTERFACE

INTRODUCTION   As we have seen thus far, the SAA Common User Access interface defines the way an application's user interface should appear. It specifies the formats for various types of display and defines standard actions and methods of interaction that form the dialog between the user and the application. The SAA Common User Access interface has close ties to the SAA Common Programming Interface (CPI), as it is the CPI component that allows the application developer to *implement* an application's user interface. Part V explores the relationships that exist between the SAA Common User Access interface and the various parts of the Common Programming Interface.

The CPI portion of SAA defines languages and sets of services that are used to develop SAA-compliant applications. The intent of CPI is for these languages and services to be consistent across the various SAA computing environments. Several of the CPI components address the development of an application's user interface. These components are designed to be consistent across the SAA computing environments and also provide facilities for producing user interfaces that are consistent with CUA principles and guidelines.

CPI components that directly support the user interface include the following:

- The dialog interface
- The presentation interface
- The application generator interface

Although generally CPI components are intended to be implemented in all SAA environments, IBM has stated that it will provide implementations of the dialog interface and the presentation interface only in the OS/2 environment. The CPI dialog interface is discussed in this chapter, the presentation interface is discussed in Chapter 14, and the application generator interface is described in Chapter 15.

THE CPI DIALOG INTERFACE

The CPI dialog interface component provides a set of *dialog services* that an application uses to manage the dialog that takes place between the application and the user. These services provide for displaying information to the user and for accepting requests and data from the user. To use the CPI dialog interface, the application defines certain objects, such as *panels, messages,* and *commands,* using a dialog interface language. Definitions for these objects, formatted according to the rules of the dialog interface language, are then compiled and stored in libraries. When the application is executed, it invokes dialog interface services using subroutine calls. The CPI dialog interface uses the dialog objects that have been stored in libraries as resources in providing the requested services.

The dialog interface specification that is part of the Common Programming Interface defines the general syntax of the language that the application developer uses to define dialog objects and specifies the call statement parameter lists that are used to invoke dialog interface services.

DIALOG ELEMENTS

The dialog interface defines a set of *dialog elements.* These elements are combined, as needed, to define an application's dialog structure. They include the following:

- Function programs
- Variable class tables
- Application command tables
- Key mapping lists
- Panels
- Messages
- Help indexes

FUNCTION PROGRAMS

In SAA dialog interface terminology, an application program is called a *function program.* A function program performs the processing requested by the user by invoking appropriate dialog services. Typical dialog services used by a function program include displaying panels and messages to the user and accepting selections and input data from the user. As discussed, one portion of the dialog interface defines a set of calls that can be used by a function program to invoke dialog services. A function program also performs normal application processing, such as retrieving, manipulating, and storing information in response to user interactions.

DIALOG TAG LANGUAGE

In addition to the function programs that make up an application, there are a number of other dialog elements that an application can use, including:

- Panels and messages that the application displays to the user
- Commands that the user can enter
- Variables that the application uses to pass information back and forth between dialog elements

Dialog elements are defined using the *dialog tag language (DTL)* that the dialog interface of CPI defines. DTL *panel definitions* describe the format of the panels the application displays and define the ways in which the user interacts with the various fields in the panel. DTL panel definitions also specify the details of any field processing that the dialog interface should provide when the panel is displayed. DTL *message definitions* describe the content of messages that the application displays to the user. The DTL panel definition and message definition facilities that are defined by the CPI dialog interface are consistent with the CUA rules and guidelines.

PANELS, WINDOWS, AND MESSAGES

A number of fundamental concepts underlie the CPI dialog interface. Some of these concepts, such as the use of panels, windows, and messages, are much the same as the concepts presented for CUA itself in Part I. With the CPI dialog interface, a *panel* is a particular arrangement of information fields, input fields, and selection fields that are grouped together in a window for presentation to the user. A *window* is a bounded area on the screen that is used to display an entire panel or a portion of a panel to the user. If only a portion of a panel is displayed, the user can use scrolling functions to display the hidden parts of the panel.

Window Types

The dialog interface provides facilities for defining the three types of window supported by the Common User Access interface:

- **Primary Windows.** A primary window is the display area in which the dialog between the user and the application takes place. A dialog application can use only one primary window. According to CUA guidelines, there may be more than one primary window displayed on the screen, one for each application that is currently running, and the user should be able to move or resize primary windows at any time. With the dialog interface, an underlying windowing system may provide these facilities for a dialog interface application. However, the dialog interface itself does not directly provide services for supporting multiple primary windows or for moving or resizing them.

- **Secondary Windows.** An application uses a secondary window to carry on a parallel dialog with the user. With the dialog interface, secondary windows are used to display help information. The user can switch back and forth between the help window and the underlying window from which Help was requested. With the dialog interface, secondary windows are used only for help information and the dialog interface itself does not support moving or resizing them. Again, an underlying window system could be used to provide moving and resizing.

- **Pop-up Windows.** Pop-up windows are used for transient interactions related to the primary window. With the dialog interface, only modal dialogs are supported, where the user must complete the interaction with the pop-up window before being allowed to interact again with the underlying primary window. While the pop-up window is active, the user cannot interact with the underlying primary window. Also, a pop-up window cannot be moved by the user.

Message Types

The dialog interface provides for the definition and display of messages of different urgency. As with CUA, messages fall into three categories:

- Notification (information)
- Warning
- Critical (error/action)

The way in which the message is processed depends on its type.

DIALOG SESSIONS

Another concept important to the dialog interface is the *dialog session*. A dialog session defines the scope of the dialog portion of an application. The session must first be opened, which establishes communication between the function program and the CPI dialog interface and initializes control information and control areas used to process other dialog service requests. When all dialog service requests have been processed, the session can be closed.

A function program can implement multiple dialog sessions, as shown in

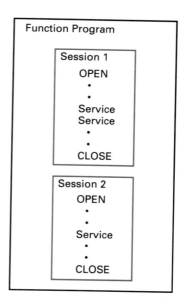

Figure 13.1 Multiple dialog sessions.

Fig. 13.1. Alternatively, a dialog session can involve more than one function program. For example, the Select dialog service can be used to invoke a new function program in an existing dialog session. The new function program must then issue its own Open request if it wishes to use dialog services, but in this case a new session is not established. (See Fig. 13.2).

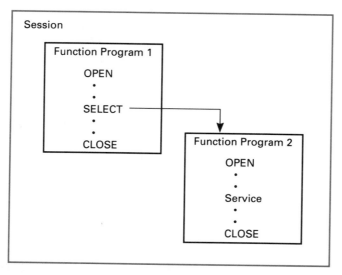

Figure 13.2 Dialog session with multiple function programs.

DIALOG VARIABLES

Dialog variables are used to communicate information among the various elements of a dialog. A dialog variable can be used to pass data from one dialog session to another or to make available to the application system values that the dialog interface provides. These values can then be used by the application in formatting a panel. Also, information that the user enters is stored in dialog variables by the dialog interface. The dialog interface either uses the data stored in these variables directly to control the dialog flow or it passes them to the application. The dialog tag language is used to define dialog variables and to specify the dialog services that are to be used to process them. Dialog variables are stored in *pools*. An application has access to three dialog variable pools:

- Function pool
- Shared pool
- Profile pool

Function Pool

The *function pool* is used to store variables that are accessible only to a given function program. When the function program ends, its function pool is deleted. A function pool contains three types of variables:

- Explicitly defined and currently active variables
- Explicitly defined but not currently active variables
- Implicitly defined variables

Shared Pool

The *shared pool* allows function programs to share dialog variables with one another. When one function program passes control to another function program by invoking the Select service, the new function program has access to variables in the shared pool.

Profile Pool

The *profile pool* provides access to variables that are saved across sessions. This includes application profile variables and system profile variables. An application profile is a set of values that are associated with a particular application; the system profile is a set of values maintained by the system and applicable to all applications. Profiles are stored in profile libraries. There are three levels of profile library:

- **User-Specific Profile Library.** This exists for each user of the dialog interface and contains a copy of the system profile and of the application profile for each application this user has executed.

- **Application Profile Library.** This contains default application profiles, with each application providing its application profile.
- **System Profile Library.** This contains default values for the system profile and for an application profile where the application has not provided its profile.

DIALOG SERVICES   The dialog services that the CPI dialog interface makes available to applications provide three major functions:

- Controlling the display of information on the screen
- Accepting data and processing requests from the user and passing them to the application
- Controlling the flow of the dialog

The CPI dialog interface services can be grouped into the following four categories:

- **Display Services.** These are used to retrieve panel definitions, perform predisplay processing, display panels, and perform postdisplay processing. The display can use either a primary window, pop-up window, or help window. Dialog services that fall into the display services category are described in Box 13.1.

BOX 13.1   Display services.

- **DISPLAY.** Displays a panel and then allows the user to interact with it. If a panel name is specified, that panel is displayed; otherwise, the current panel is refreshed. A message to be displayed on the panel, and the initial cursor position can also be specified. Once the panel is displayed, the user can make selections or enter data into entry fields. The dialog interface validates information as it is entered. When the user's interaction is complete, the dialog interface returns entered data to the application.
- **ADDPOP.** Initiates and positions a pop-up window. Subsequent display service requests display panels in the pop-up window.
- **REMPOP.** Removes a pop-up window. If a series of pop-up windows have been used, either the last window or all windows can be removed.

BOX 13.2   Message services.

- **GETMSG.** Retrieves a message from the message library. Dialog variable names can be specified for storing the message text, the name of the help panel associated with the message, and the message type.
- **SETMSG.** Requests that a message appear on the next panel that the dialog interface displays. The dialog interface retrieves the specified message from the message library and saves it until the next panel is displayed.

BOX 13.3   Dialog session services.

- **DMOPEN.** Initializes communication between the dialog interface and the application so that the application is able to issue dialog service requests.
- **DMCLOSE.** Completes the scope of a DMOPEN call and terminates communication between the application and the dialog interface.
- **SELECT.** Used to invoke a new function program from within a dialog session. Parameters can be passed to the new program as part of the call.

- **Message Services.** These are used to retrieve message texts and to display messages in a panel. Dialog services that are in the message services category are shown in Box 13.2.
- **Dialog Session Control Services.** These are used to control dialog sessions. Dialog session control services are listed in Box 13.3.
- **Variable Services.** These allow a dialog application to communicate with the dialog interface using dialog variables. Function programs, panels, and messages can all access the data values stored in dialog variables. Box 13.4 summarizes variable services that are available.

INVOKING DIALOG SERVICES

The dialog interface specification defines in detail the way in which an application program invokes a dia-

BOX 13.4   Variable services.

- **VCOPY.** Provides the application program with a copy of specified dialog variables.
- **VDEFINE.** Used to define dialog variables for the function pool. It allows the dialog interface to access variables directly within a function program. As part of the call, the format of the variable is specified.
- **VDELETE.** Removes variables previously defined through the VDEFINE service from the function pool.
- **VERASE.** Removes variables from the shared pool or profile pool.
- **VGET.** Copies specified variables from the shared pool or profile pool into the function pool.
- **VPUT.** Copies specified variables from the function pool into the shared pool or profile pool.
- **VREPLACE.** Updates the value of a variable in the function pool.
- **VRESET.** Resets the function pool to empty.

log service. Services are invoked using a call, the format of which is as follows:

CALL ISPCI (dmcomm buflen buffer)

In the ISPCI call, *dmcomm* is the name that has been assigned to a program area called the dialog communication area, *buflen* references a program variable that contains the length of the buffer, and *buffer* references a program variable that contains the name of the service being invoked followed by parameters associated with the service.

Dialog Communication Area

The format of the dialog communication area is shown in Fig. 13.3. The application program defines a storage area having this format and references this area using the dmcomm parameter. The dialog interface uses the return code and reason code fields in the dialog communication area to provide status information to the application program following a service call. The application program can test these codes to determine if the requested service was executed successfully, and if not, the cause of the problem.

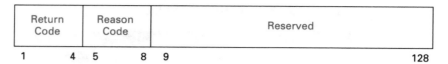

Figure 13.3 Dialog communication area.

Service Name and Parameters

The buffer named in the CALL statement references a storage area that contains the name of the service being invoked and any parameters that are associated with the service request. Figure 13.4 is an excerpt from the *Common Programming Interface Dialog Reference* manual showing the service name and list of parameters for the GETMSG service. This service is used to obtain message text and related information from a message library. The MSG(message-id) parameter is required; the other parameters are optional.

COMMAND PROCESSING   The dialog interface includes built-in facilities for processing commands that are invoked by the user. These built-in facilities support some of the standard dialog actions defined in CUA, including requests to cancel a panel, exit a dialog, and obtain help.

When a user selects one of these commands, the dialog interface performs the necessary actions directly rather than passing the request to the application program for processing. The dialog interface also provides automatic support for scrolling. When the user moves the cursor in a way that triggers scrolling or performs some other scrolling action, the dialog interface changes the portion of the panel being displayed, again without requiring action on the part of the application program.

An application can also define its own commands and specify the action to be taken when each application-defined command is invoked. An application can also change the actions that are associated with any of the standard dialog commands.

HELP FACILITIES   The dialog interface, in its support of standard dialog actions, provides help facilities that conform to CUA guidelines. The Help Manager of the CPI dialog interface responds to all requests for help from the user without requiring intervention by the application program. The Help Manager provides the following types of help information:

- **Field-level Help.** Help for a particular selection or data entry field in an application panel, based on the position of the cursor when help is requested. This is known in CUA as contextual help.

GETMSG

TSO/E	CMS	OS/2
*	*	X

The GETMSG service obtains message text and related information from the message library.

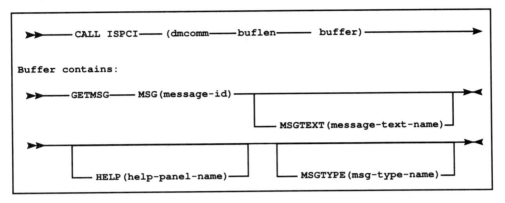

dmcomm
The name of a program variable for the dialog communication area. See "Dialog Communication Area" on page 53 for a description of this parameter.

buflen
A signed 4-byte binary integer containing the character length of the buffer.

buffer
The name of a program variable that contains:

GETMSG
The service name.

MSG (message-id)
The identification of the message and related information that the dialog interface retrieves.

MSGTEXT (message-text-name)
The name of a dialog variable into which the dialog interface stores the message text.

HELP (help-panel-name)
The name of a dialog variable into which the dialog interface stores the help panel name, if any.

MSGTYPE (msg-type-name)
The name of a dialog variable into which the dialog interface stores the message type.

Figure 13.4 The GETMSG service and its parameters.

- **Extended Help.** Help on an application panel as a whole and the task it performs.

- **Reference Phrase Help.** This allows a particular phrase in the text of a help panel to be identified and a help panel to be associated with that phrase. The user can then request help for that phrase, and the associated reference phrase help panel is displayed.

- **Keys Help.** Help that describes the control keys supported by the application and the function of each key.

- **Tutorial Help.** Help that presents a detailed tutorial on how to use the application or a specific function within it. The structure and content of the tutorial are determined by the application.

- **Help Manager Help.** Help on how to use the help facility.

- **Help Index.** Help that provides a list of help topics.

These help facilities conform to the help facilities defined by CUA. In addition, the dialog interface provides facilities not defined in CUA:

- **Message Help.** Help for a particular message.

- **Command Help.** Help for the command area. If no command has been entered, a list of commands is displayed. If a command or partial command has been entered, help that describes the command and its parameters is provided. This is comparable to the command area prompt facility defined by CUA.

- **Search Option for the Help Index.** This allows the user to enter one or more search words. The Help Manager then searches the help index for those words and presents a list that contains only help topics corresponding to these terms.

The dialog tag language contains facilities for defining help panels and for giving them identifying names. Help panels can be associated with objects, such as panels, panel fields, messages, commands, and control keys, as they are defined using the dialog tag language. When a user requests help, the Help Manager retrieves the appropriate help panel and displays it. The Help Manager also controls user interactions with help panels, including switching between an application panel and a help panel, using the interaction techniques defined by CUA.

DIALOG TAG LANGUAGE

As mentioned earlier, the CPI dialog interface includes a dialog tag language that is used to define dialog objects. The language consists of a set of *tags*, or control words, that are used to specify the characteristics of objects. The dialog tag language is based on the *Standard Generalized Markup Language (SGML),* which is an established international standard. Figure 13.5 describes the general syntax used with tags and shows a sample dialog object definition.

```
<tagname attributes>                          <lines>
          •                                   text for line 1
          •                                       indented text for line 2
   text and other content                    more text for line 3
          •                                              text
          •                                              text
</tagname>                                               text
                                              </lines>

        Tag Syntax                                    Tag Example
```

Figure 13.5   Tag syntax and example.

The LINES tag specifies that the text that follows should be displayed as entered and not wrapped around from one line to the next.

In addition to a tagname that identifies the tag, a tag may include attributes that provide information used in processing the tag. The following PANEL tag is used to begin the definition of a panel:

<panel panel-name help-panel key-list-name>

The attributes defined in the tag can be used to provide the following information:

- panel-name. Gives a name to this panel.

- help-panel. Identifies the name of the help panel to be used as extended help for this panel.

- key-list-name. Identifies the name of a list of keys and their corresponding commands. The list is used to determine the content of the function key area in this panel. In a graphics application, the commands are displayed in pushbuttons at the bottom of the panel.

DEFINING A PANEL

The dialog tag language allows the application developer to define panels that conform to the CUA formatting guidelines. Tags can be used to define a panel title, top and bottom instructions, an action bar, panel body areas, information, selection and entry fields, scrollable areas and fields, a message area, a command area, and a pushbutton/function key area. Tags can also associate a help panel with the panel being defined.

The tags that are described in this chapter are taken from the CPI dialog interface specification that is current as of the time of writing. Specific products that implement the dialog tag language may include tags not described here. For example, ISPF, the program product described in Chapter 18, implements the dialog tag language and supports several tags not listed here. This is an example of how SAA is evolving in parallel with IBM's SAA-compliant products. IBM has indicated that as the dialog tag language evolves, new tags will be added to the dialog interface specification. The dialog tag language, as described in the CPI dialog interface specification, will most likely be expanded over time to include the additional ISPF tags, as well as new tags supported by other products.

The various tags that can be used in creating a panel definition are shown in Box 13.5. Figure 13.6 shows a sample panel definition. The tags and panel text are presented in a generalized format; the exact coding that would be used depends on the particular language used to create the application and the specific implementation of the dialog interface used. Figure 13.6 demonstrates how CUA formatting is built into the dialog interface. For example, the application indicates that a particular field is a data entry field. An implementation of the dialog interface then formats the field according to CUA guidelines. Similarly, the application specifies that a field is a particular type of selection field. The dialog interface implementation then automatically provides the appropriate formatting, including selection icons or numbering and emphasis techniques. Scrolling information and interaction are provided by the dialog interface where their use is necessary. Including a key-list-name as part of the PANEL tag results in an appropriately formatted pushbutton/function key area being included as part of the panel.

If a panel definition specifies the use of an action bar or command area,

```
**Specify previously defined function keys in key-list-name

<panel panel-name help-panel key-list-name>Print Options
                                            **Start panel definition
                                            **and specify title
<topinst>Type and select.   Then Enter.     **Define top instruction

<area>                                       **Start scrollable portion

<dtacol column-width>                        **Specify column widths for
                                             **this parameter entry panel
<dtafld variable-name help-panel>File name   **Define first data field

<selfld field-type>Typestyle                 **Specify start of selection
                                             **field definition
<choice help-panel>Prestige elite           **Define selection field
<choice help-panel>Courier                  **choices and specify
<choice help-panel>Essay                    **help panel names
</selfld>                                    **Specify end of selection field

<dtafld variable-name help-panel>Left margin **Define remaining data
<dtafld>1-25                                 **entry fields and
                                             **their descriptive text
<dtafld variable-name help-panel>Number of copies
<dtafld>1-999
<dtafld variable-name help-panel>Starting page number
<dtafld>1-999
</dtacol>                                     **End the data column
</area>                                       **End scrollable portion
</panel>                                      **End panel definition
```

Figure 13.6 Sample panel definition.

BOX 13.5 Panel definition tags.

General Tags

- **PANDEF (Panel Default).** Provides default information for any panel referencing it.
- **PANEL (Panel).** Identifies the beginning of a panel. Can be used to specify an associated help panel, panel depth and width, panel title, initial cursor placement, and a key list for the function key area.
- **TOPINST (Top Instruction).** Specifies instructions to be displayed at the top of the panel.
- **BOTINST (Bottom Instruction).** Specifies instructions to be displayed at the bottom of the panel.
- **CMDAREA (Command Area).** Defines the command area and the text and placement of the command field prompt.

Panel Body Area Tags

- **AREA (Area).** Identifies a scrollable portion of a panel.
- **REGION (Region).** Specifies how fields on a panel are arranged.
- **DIVIDER (Divider).** Provides a separator between panel areas.

Action Bar Tags

- **AB (Action Bar).** Defines an action bar.
- **ABC (Action Bar Choice).** Identifies an action bar choice and its associated pull-down.
- **PDC (Pulldown Choice).** Defines a choice within a pulldown.
- **PDSEP (Pulldown Separator).** Draws a line between choices in a pulldown.
- **M (Mnemonic).** Designates a mnemonic for an action bar or pulldown choice.

Selection and Entry Field Tags

- **DTACOL (Data Column).** Identifies column widths for subsequent entry and selection fields. The dialog interface then vertically aligns the fields and provides dot leaders.
- **DTAFLD (Data Field).** Defines an entry field. Parameters include a dialog variable name, a help panel name, and prompt text to be displayed.

BOX 13.5 *(Continued)*

- **DTAFLDD (Data Field Description).** Provides additional descriptive text for a data field.
- **SELFLD (Selection Field).** Defines a selection field. The particular type of selection field is specified as a parameter.
- **CHOICE (Choice Item).** Identifies a choice within a selection field. A help panel name can be specified.
- **M (Mnemonic).** Designates a mnemonic for a selection field choice.
- **LSTFLD (List Field).** Defines a vertically scrollable list made up of columns of data.
- **LSTCOL (List Column).** Identifies a column within a list field.

Information Tags

- **INFO (Information).** Identifies protected information to be displayed as part of a panel. Other information tags can be used to format the information text.
- **DL (Definition List).** Used along with the DT (Define Term), DD (Define Description), DTHD (Define Term Column Heading), and DDHD (Define Description Column Heading) tags to define a list of terms and their corresponding definitions.
- **FIG (Figure).** Specifies that following text is not to be word-wrapped, and should be set off by a border or spacing. A FIGCAP tag can be used to supply a caption.
- **Hn (Heading Level n).** Identifies main topics and subtopics of information.
- **LINES (Lines).** Specifies that the following text is not to be word-wrapped.
- **LI (List Item).** Identifies an item in a list. The following text is indented from the current level of the list. Used with the OL, SL, and UL tags, which identify the type of list.
- **LP (List Part).** Identifies text that is part of the current list item.
- **NOTE (Single-Paragraph Note).** Identifies following text as a single-paragraph note.
- **NT (Multiple-Paragraph Note).** Identifies following text as a single- or multiple-paragraph note.
- **OL (Ordered List).** Identifies an ordered list of items. The items are formatted as an indented list with order identifiers (1,2,. . .a,b. . .).

BOX 13.5   *(Continued)*

- **P (Paragraph).** Identifies the following text as a paragraph.
- **PARML (Parameter List).** Identifies parameter terms and their descriptions, using the PT (Parameter Tag) and PD (Parameter Description) tags.
- **SL (Simple List).** Identifies a simple list of terms, formatted as an indented list with no item identifiers.
- **UL (Unordered List).** Identifies an unordered list of terms. The items are formatted as an indented list with bullets, hyphens and dashes used as item identifiers.

these are also formatted according to CUA guidelines. Through the use of tags, any type of panel can be generated. The panels conform to CUA both in terms of panel appearance and interaction techniques.

Depending on the environment that a particular implementation runs in, the implementation may generate panels that conform to the entry model, the text subset, or the full graphical model. As you will see later, the Dialog Manager that is part of OS/2 implements the dialog tag language and generates panels consistent with the graphical model in the advanced interface of CUA. The dialog tag language implemented as part of ISPF, on the other hand, generates panels based on the text subset of the graphical model, as described in the basic interface of CUA.

DEFINING MESSAGES

Tags can also be used to define messages, as, for example does the MSG tag. It includes attributes that are used to specify the severity level of the message—notification, warning, or critical—and a help panel to be associated with the message.

DEFINING A COMMAND TABLE

The dialog interface provides the processing necessary to implement certain standard dialog commands, such as HELP, CANCEL, and EXIT. As mentioned earlier, an application can create new commands and specify different actions to take in processing the standard dialog commands. Command processing actions are specified by defining a command table. The CMDTBL tag identifies the beginning of a command table. The CMD tag is then used to define each command in the table. The CMD tag specifies both an external and an internal name for the command and defines the action to be taken when the command is invoked. Commands from the command table can be included as choices in a selection field or action bar pulldown and can be associated with control keys. When the user invokes a command, the dialog interface performs the actions specified for that command in the command table.

DEFINING KEY MAPPING LISTS

A *key mapping list* associates commands with control keys. When a key mapping list is included in a panel definition, it is used to determine what is displayed in the pushbutton/function key area. The following tags are used for a key mapping list:

- **KEYL.** Identifies the beginning of a key list.
- **KEYI.** Associates a command with a control key.
- **LABEL.** Defines the label to be displayed in the pushbutton/function key area to represent a particular control key.

DEFINING VARIABLES

As we introduced earlier in this chapter, variables can be used to communicate values between one dialog element and another. For example, with a data entry field the dialog interface uses a variable to pass to the application the data entered by the user into that data entry field. Variables can also be used to pass values from the application to the dialog interface for display to the user.

The dialog interface provides several processing functions for variables. Sometimes the internal value used for a variable is different from the value that is displayed. The dialog interface provides a mapping function that can be used to translate from internal values to display values. Mapping can also be performed on data entered by the user, in order to convert the data into a format more suitable for processing by the application. Validation checks can be defined that the dialog interface applies to data entered by the user. Assignment lists can also be defined that assign values to one variable that are based on the values of some other variable. Mapping and validation checks can be specified for individual variables or for a variable class. Variable classes and their associated mappings and validation checks are defined in variable class tables. A variable class table applies across an entire application.

Box 13.6 lists the tags that can be used in defining variables. They allow the application developer to supply the characteristics of a specific variable and assign it to a variable class, define an assignment list for a variable, define validation checks for a variable or variable class, and define translation lists for a variable or variable class.

BOX 13.6   Variable tags.

- **VARLIST (Variable List).** Establishes the access technique for specific variables.
- **VARDCL (Variable Declaration).** Establishes characteristics for specific variables.
- **ASSIGNL (Assignment List).** Identifies the beginning of an assignment list.
- **ASSIGNI (Assignment Item).** Defines an entry in an assignment list and provides the association between a value in one variable and the value to be assigned to another.
- **CHECKL (Checklist).** Defines a list of validity checks to be applied to a variable or class of variables. Multiple checklists referencing the same variable or variable class are ANDed together.
- **CHECKI (Check Item).** Defines a single validity check within a checklist. Multiple check items within a checklist are ORed together.
- **XLATL (Translate List).** Identifies the beginning of a translate list used to map between internal dialog variable values and values displayed for the user or entered by the user. A translate list can be defined for a specific variable or a variable class.
- **XLATI (Translate Item).** Defines a single set of mapping values within a translate list.
- **CLSTBL (Variable Class Table).** Defines a variable class table.
- **VARCLASS (Variable Class).** Defines information related to a variable class. CHECKL, CHECKI, XLATL, and XLATI tags can be used within the scope of a VARCLASS tag.

DEFINING HELP PANELS

When a dialog object is defined, such as a panel, a selection or entry field, or a message, a help panel can be associated with the object. The dialog interface then displays the appropriate help panel when the user requests help for that object. Help panels are defined in much the same way as any other type of panel. The tags used to define help panels are shown in Box 13.7. The various information tags shown in Box 13.5 can also be used to format information text in a help panel. The HELP tag defines the beginning of a help panel and gives it a name. The AREA tag can be used to define a scrollable area. An RP tag can be used to identify a reference phrase and to associate a help panel with that

BOX 13.7   Help panel tags.

- **HELP (Help)**. Begins the definition of a help panel.
- **AREA (Area)**. Identifies a scrollable portion of a panel.
- **INFO (Information)**. Identifies protected information to be displayed as part of a panel. Other information tags can be used to format the information text.

phrase. An ICMD tag can be used to associate a help panel with a command. When help is requested for this command, the associated help panel is displayed.

DEFINING A HELP INDEX

A help index is a list of help topics that are available to the user. The dialog interface allows the user to specify search words and then will display help topics associated with the search words. The tags used to define a help index are listed in Box 13.8. The ITOP and ISYN tags are used to build the help index and to provide the information needed to match a search word with certain topics.

The ITOP tag associates a help panel with a topic. When that topic is selected from the help index, the associated help panel is displayed. The ITOP tag also specifies the text that is to be displayed as the index entry for the topic. One or more root words are associated with the topic through the ITOP tag. When the user enters search words, the search words are translated into root words, and the root words are used to identify a topic in the topic index.

The ISYN tag is used to define the mapping from search words entered by the user to root words. The ISYN tag defines one root word and one or more synonyms that are to be mapped to that root word. Figure 13.7 contains an example of the use of the ITOP and ISYN tags. The ITOP tag defines "Copying a File" as an entry in the help index and associates a help panel with the entry. The root words for this entry are "copy file". The ISYN tags define synonyms for copy and file. If the user enters "duplicate data" as search words, they are mapped to "copy file", and the "Copying a File" topic would be included in the resulting help index listing.

CONFORMANCE WITH CUA

The CPI dialog interface provides key user interface services to an application. Dialog interface services

BOX 13.8　Help index tags.

- **ISYN (Index Synonym).** Maps synonyms to search words for index topics.
- **ITOP (Index Topic).** Associates a topic with a help panel.
- **ICMD (Index Command).** Associates a command with a help panel.

can be used to display panels and messages, to accept data entered or actions specified by the user, and to control the flow of the dialog session. An application uses the dialog tag language to define various dialog objects used by the application, including panels, messages, commands, key lists, variables, validation checks, and translations to be performed on variables. The application must also include appropriate calls at points in its logic where it wishes to use particular dialog services and define a dialog communication area for use with the calls. A given implementation of the dialog interface is then used to prepare the application and execute it in a specific SAA computing environment. With this approach, the primary responsibility for seeing that the application's user interface conforms with the CUA rules and guidelines rests with the dialog interface implementation rather than with the application.

Panel Formatting

Through the dialog tag language, an application defines the general contents of the panels it displays. The dialog interface then sees that the content is formatted as described in CUA. As it states in the dialog interface specification, "the dialog tag language provides facilities to specify panel definitions that conform to the Common User Access definitions." For example, the application defines a

```
<help ...>
<itop roots = 'copy file'>Copying a File
    •
    •
</help>

<help>
<isyn root=copy>copy copying duplicate
               duplicating
<isyn root=File>data information file
               document documents
    •
    •
</help>
```

Figure 13.7　Help index example.

particular field as a selection field and indicates the type of the field with a SELFLD tag. The application also defines the text to be displayed for each choice in the selection field with CHOICE tags. The dialog interface is then responsible for the following activities:

- Arranging the text in an appropriate layout
- Including numbers or mnemonics if their use has been specified
- Displaying the appropriate selection icons if the application is a graphics application
- Displaying the selection cursor with appropriate emphasis
- Displaying appropriate selection indicators when a choice is selected
- Displaying a scroll bar or scrolling information for scrollable fields

Similarly, an application defines an entry field with a DTAFLD tag, and names a variable to be used with the field. The dialog interface sees that the entry field is formatted properly, controls the user's interaction with the field, and then provides the data entered to the application in the specified variable.

Through the dialog tag language, the application can specify that standard panel areas such as an action bar, command area, or pushbutton/function key area be included in a panel. For an action bar, the application specifies the actions to be included. For the pushbutton/function key area, the application specifies, via a key list, the actions to be included and their corresponding keys. The application can also specify that a panel body area be scrollable. The dialog interface again is responsible for seeing that the different panel areas that are used are formatted according to the CUA rules and guidelines. The dialog interface is also responsible for the proper use of color and emphasis.

User Interactions

According to the dialog interface specification, "the dialog interface enables the Common User Access rules of user interaction." Thus, the dialog interface implementation is responsible for providing the different interaction techniques defined in CUA. This includes

- Use of a mouse or a keyboard
- Selection techniques such as point-and-select, numbers and mnemonics, or entering a character.
- Insert or replace modes for data entry
- Special field types including autoselect, autoenter, and autotab
- Cursor-driven or cursor-independent scrolling
- Cursor movement techniques for moving from field to field or from one panel area to another

The results of user interactions—selection of a choice or entry of data—are passed to the application via variables. The application is not concerned at all with the way in which the interaction takes place; the interaction is handled by the dialog interface, not by the application.

Dialog Control

The dialog interface provides the standard dialog control actions Enter, Exit, and Cancel. The help facilities that are defined as part of the dialog interface specification are consistent with the CUA help definitions. The dialog interface is responsible for displaying help panels upon request and for controlling user interactions with the different help facilities. The application is responsible for defining the content of the various help panels and specifying which help panel to use for a particular field or panel. The dialog interface also provides facilities for defining and displaying messages. Message definitions include a message type, which can be one of the three message types defined in CUA. The application is responsible for defining the message content and type, and for determining when it should be displayed. The dialog interface sees that the message is formatted properly when it is displayed and controls the user's interaction with the message.

Windowing

The dialog interface does not provide windowing services and restricts a dialog application to a single primary window. However, a dialog application can run in an environment where an underlying system provides windowing capabilities, and these capabilities can then be used with dialog interface windows.

Supporting CUA Models

The services and objects defined as part of the dialog interface provide complete support for both of the basic interface models: the entry model and the text subset of the graphical model. The dialog interface does not support features unique to the full graphical model, such as the use of multiple primary and secondary windows within one application other than for help and the ability to move and resize windows.

14 CUA AND THE CPI PRESENTATION INTERFACE

INTRODUCTION The *presentation interface* is another element in the Common Programming Interface. The presentation interface provides services to an application that concern the display and printing of text, graphics, and image information. Many of the functions that are part of the presentation interface are designed to support the creation, manipulation, display, and storage of graphic pictures. The presentation interface also supports the definition and use of different type fonts, including double-byte character set fonts, and the display of images that are defined pixel by pixel rather than as geometric constructs. The presentation interface includes a general windowing system that supports the display of multiple windows on the display screen and allows users to move and resize windows. In addition, it provides functions that are related to the user interface. The user interface functions are designed to display data using window formats that are consistent with CUA guidelines and to allow the user to interact with the displays using CUA interaction techniques. With its support of graphics and window capabilities, the presentation interface allows the development of a user interface that is fully consistent with the graphical model.

PRESENTATION INTERFACE OUTPUT The presentation interface includes extensive facilities for processing various kinds of output. Presentation interface output can include character data displayed using various fonts, pictures created from primitive elements that include lines, arcs, and areas, and images that are specified pixel by pixel. Output can be presented on different types of devices, including display screens, printers, and plotters. Output can also be directed to picture interchange files, which are used to send graphics objects from one presentation interface environment to another. The graphics and image processing facilities of the presentation interface are beyond the scope of this book. For more information on these facilities, see the companion volume *Systems Application Architecture: Common Programming Interface*.

WINDOWS

Presentation interface processing is based on the use of *windows*. As already described, a window is an area of a display screen used to present information related to a particular application. Multiple windows can be displayed on the screen at the same time, as shown in Fig. 14.1. In Fig. 14.1 all the windows belong to a single application. There can also be windows displayed by multiple applications on the screen, as shown in Fig. 14.2.

Window Hierarchies

Windows are related to one another in a hierarchical manner. The display screen as a whole is called the *desktop*. Each application has at least one *main window,* which is positioned relative to the desktop. A main window can have one or more *child windows,* and a child window can also have its own child windows. A child window is positioned relative to its *parent window*. Child windows that have the same parent window are called *siblings*. Siblings are displayed in a particular visual order, called the *z-order*. When the windows overlap, this determines which sibling is displayed as the topmost window, which is directly underneath it, and so on down the group of windows.

Figure 14.3 shows the hierarchy, or logical relationship, that might exist for a collection of windows. If the z-order is from left to right in the hierarchy, then the windows appear as shown in the bottom of the figure. Main window A

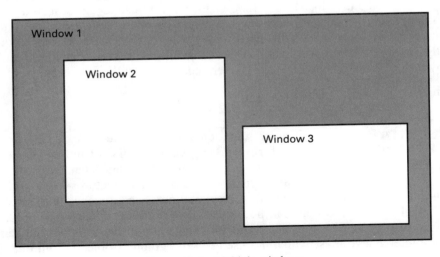

Figure 14.1   Multiple windows.

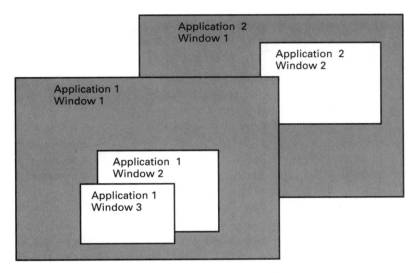

Figure 14.2 Multiple applications.

appears on top of main window B. Child windows A1, A2, and A3 appear on top of each other as specified by the z-order. Child windows B1 and B2 show that windows do not have to overlap if there is space to display them separately.

Window Positioning

When a window is displayed, it will be in a specified position and be a specified size, as determined by the application and the presentation interface. The presentation interface provides facilities that allow the user to alter the position or size of a window on the screen. When one main window is moved or changed, other main windows are unaffected. When a parent window is moved or changed, its children are moved and resized along with it.

The facilities to alter the position or size of a window operate independently of the application. However, the application may choose to be aware of changes and handle any data reformatting or reorganization that may be necessary because of changes to the window. As part of resizing, the user can maximize the window (change it to the application-defined maximum size) or minimize it (change it to the application-defined minimum size).

Window Interactions

Windows are the mechanism used to display information to the user and to accept inputs from the user. The user can interact with a window using either a keyboard or a pointing device. The *cursor* is a symbol on the screen that indicates the position at which the next keyboard interaction will take place. The window that contains the cursor is the *focus window*. The focus window and its

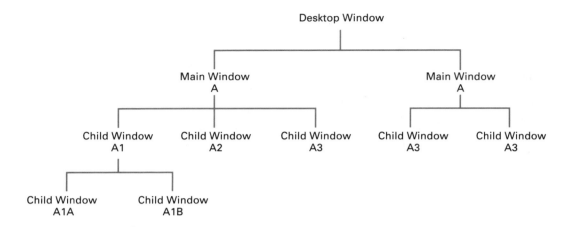

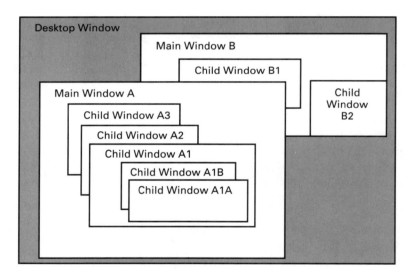

Figure 14.3   Window hierarchy.

children are shown on top of other windows. The main window related hierarchically to the focus window is the *active window*. The active window and its children are shown on top of other main windows.

The *pointer* is a symbol on the screen that indicates where the next pointing device interaction will take place. The position of the pointer on the screen is called the *action point*. The movement of the pointer is under user control, and is not confined to a specific window. It can be used to select an object within a window or to select a window to interact with. When a window is selected, the related main window becomes the active window, and the application establishes the focus window.

Window Characteristics

Each window has associated with it a *window procedure* that is used to process input and output events that are associated with that window. An application can provide its own window procedure, or it can use a standard window procedure that is part of the presentation interface. More than one window can use the same window procedure. The set of windows that share a window procedure is called a *window class*. A window also has a set of *window style* properties. These properties affect the appearance and behavior of a window. For example, one window style attribute can be used to specify that the window be given its maximum size when it is created. A window class can also possess a set of properties, called the *class style*. A particular window class, for example, may have a class style that specifies that a window should be redrawn when its size is changed. Each window in a window class possesses the properties that make up the class style. A window can also have individual window style properties defined for it.

When an application defines a window, it also defines the window's window class, which determines the window procedure and class style that apply to this window. The application can also define the properties that make up the window style for a particular window. In addition to providing standard window procedures, the presentation interface also provides standard window classes that can be used by the application when defining windows.

Messages

The application and the presentation interface work cooperatively to maintain a dialog with the user. To do this, the application requests services from the presentation interface. For example, the application may request that the presentation interface display a window on the screen. At times, the presentation interface may also request services from the application. When the presentation interface is moving a window, for instance, it may need the application to redraw the window in its new position or to redraw other windows that have been uncovered by the move. The partner that is requesting a service is the *service requester* and the other is the *service provider*.

Service requests take the form of messages. Each message is associated with a particular window and is processed by the window procedure associated with that window. Messages have a standard format, and consist of the following:

- **Window Handle.** Identifies the window to which this message relates.
- **Message Identity.** Identifies the type of message.

- **Parameter 1 and Parameter 2.** Contain information related to the specific service request.

Service requests are generated in several different ways. A call to the presentation interface requesting a function to be performed generates a service request message that is either posted to the presentation interface queue or sent directly to a presentation interface window procedure. The presentation interface then processes the message and provides the requested function. As part of its processing, the presentation interface may generate a message that it sends or posts to the application for processing by the application's window procedure. User interactions also generate messages. When a user makes a selection or enters data, the presentation interface generates messages that provide information about the interaction and allow the application to process and respond to it. Service request messages are also generated when certain system events occur.

The window procedure used to process a message may be either a window procedure in an application or the default window procedure in the presentation interface. The window procedure provides a defined response to the message, which might be a change to displayed data or a change to internally or externally stored data. A window class is defined by the responses it provides to the different types of messages that can be sent to a window of that class.

Note that within the presentation interface specification, the term *message* refers to a service request being passed between the presentation interface and an application. This should be distinguished from CUA's use of the term *message,* which relates to status and error information that is displayed to the user.

PRESENTATION INTERFACE DEFINITION

The presentation interface specification is defined primarily in terms of the function calls it supports and the message processing it provides. Figure 14.4 shows the presentation interface function definition for the GpiAssociate function. The three names at the beginning of the definition give the call name used in the C language, in English and in COBOL or FORTRAN. The function definition includes input and output parameters associated with the function and a description of how the function operates. The specification also defines the specific call syntax that is used to invoke the function in the C, COBOL, and FORTRAN languages.

Figure 14.5 illustrates the message definition for the WM_ACTIVATE message. The definition includes a description of the following:

- The parameter values in the message
- Any return values that result from window processing
- General remarks on processing
- The processing performed by the default window procedure for this message

GpiAssociate
AssociATE
GSASS

TSO/E	CMS	OS/400	OS/2
			X

Associate   (hps,hdc,Success)

Function

This call associates or disassociates a graphics presentation space with a device context.

Input parameters

hps *(HPS)*
Presentation-space handle.

hdc *(HDC)*
Device-context handle.

Returns

Success *(BOOL)*
Success Indicator:

TRUE   Successful completion.
FALSE Error occurred.

Remarks

Any type of device context may be used.

Subsequent drawing functions direct output to the associated device context.

If a null handle is supplied for the device context, the presentation space is disassociated from its currently associated device context. An associated presentation space or device context cannot be associated with another device context or presentation space, respectively.

It is an error to try to draw to a presentation space associated with a memory device context that has no bit map selected into it (see GpiSetBitmap).

The processing described for GRES_ATTRS (see GpiResetPS) is performed on the presentation space. Also, the page viewport is reset to its default value (see GpiCreatePS), and any clip region is lost. The save/restore presentation space stack (see GPISavePS) is purged.

Figure 14.4   Associate function definition.

WM_ACTIVATE

This message occurs when an application causes the activation or deactivation of a window.

Parameters

param1

active *(BOOL)*
Active Indicator:

TRUE   The window is being activated.
FALSE The window is being deactivated.

param2

hwnd *(HWND)*
Window handle.

In the case of activation, **hwnd** identifies the window being activated. In the case of deactivation, **hwnd** identifies the window being deactivated.

Returns

reply *(BIT32)*
Reserved.

NULL   Reserved value.

Remarks

A deactivation message (that is, a WM_ACTIVATE message with **active** set to FALSE) is sent first to the window procedure of the main window being deactivated, before an activation message (that is, a WM_ACTIVATE message with **active** set to TRUE) is sent to the window procedure of the main window being activated.

Any WM_SETFOCUS messages with **focus** set to FALSE, are sent before the deactivation message. Any WM_SETFOCUS messages with **focus** set to TRUE, are sent after the activation message.

If WinSetFocus is called during the processing of a WM_ACTIVATE message, a WM_SETFOCUS message with **focus** set to FALSE is not sent, as no window has the focus.

If a window is activated before any of its children have the focus, this message is sent to the frame window or to its FID_CLIENT, if it exists.

Note: Except in the instance of a WM_ACTIVATE message, with **active** set to TRUE, an application processing a WM_ACTIVATE, or a WM_SETFOCUS message should not change the focus window or the active window. If it does, the focus and active windows must be restored before the window procedure returns from processing the message. For this reason, any dialog boxes or windows brought up during the processing of a WM_ACTIVATE, or a WM_SETFOCUS message should be system modal.

Default Processing

The Default Window Procedure takes no action on this message, other than to set **reply** to NULL.

Figure 14.5   WM_ACTIVATE message definition.

SYNCHRONOUS AND ASYNCHRONOUS MESSAGE PROCESSING

Messages, and the services they request, can be processed either synchronously or asynchronously. With *synchronous service provision,* the service requester must wait for the message to be processed and the service to be completed before continuing with processing. When the request is for a synchronous service, the message is *sent* directly to the service provider. With *asynchronous service provision,* the service requester can continue with other processing in parallel with the service provision. When the request is for an asynchronous service, the message is *posted* to a queue associated with the service provider.

APPLICATION STRUCTURE

Each window has a window procedure associated with it. When an application creates a window, it either provides a window procedure for it or specifies that a standard window procedure in the presentation interface be used. The presentation interface can request services from the application either by posting messages to the application's queue or by sending messages directly to window procedures that are part of the application.

An application typically requests services by issuing calls to the presentation interface. The presentation interface then processes the messages generated by the call. A function call may result in a message that is processed by a window procedure in the application. For example, when an application issues a call to create a window, a message is generated and passed to the window procedure in the application allowing the data in the window to be initialized by the application.

Figure 14.6 illustrates the general structure used for an application that uses the presentation interface. The initialization phase is used to establish a connection between the application and the presentation interface. The main processing loop successively accesses the messages in the application's message queue. Each message is sent to a window procedure, based on the class of the window associated with the message. The window procedure processes the message based on its message ID or passes the message back to the presentation interface for processing by the default window procedure.

APPLICATION RELATIONSHIP TO THE PRESENTATION INTERFACE

The general relationship between the application and the presentation interface is shown in Fig. 14.7. The presentation interface acts as an intermediary between the user and the application for both user input and user output.

```
Initialize
    (establish association with presentation interface.)
    (create message queue)
    (identify message IDs to be passed to application)

Process Queue Loop
┌──►(get message)
│   (identify window procedure based on window
│    associated with message)
│   (dispatch message to window procedure
└───────────┘


Terminate
    (disassociate application from presentation interface)

Window Procedure
    IF messgID = value1
        (Process)
    ELSE IF messgID = value2
        (Process)
        •
        •
        •
    ELSE
        (send to default window procedure
         in presentation interface)
```

Figure 14.6 Presentation interface application structure.

User Input

When an input event occurs, such as the user making a selection, entering data, or moving the pointer, the presentation interface generates the messages needed to process the event and either sends them to a window procedure or posts them to the application's message queue. The application retrieves messages from the queue and passes them to a window procedure for processing. An input event is associated with a single window, and the window handle is included as part of the message. This window handle determines the queue in which the message is placed and the window procedure that is used to process it. A given window is associated with only one queue, but more than one window can be associated with the same queue.

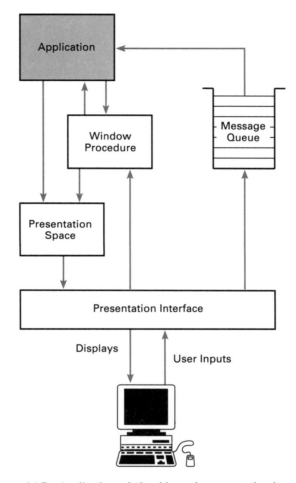

Figure 14.7 Application relationship to the presentation interface.

User input is processed synchronously; processing of one user input message must be completed before the presentation interface allows the next user input message to start processing. This restriction is observed because the processing of one message may affect the way in which the next message is handled. When the application gets messages from the queue, it can use *message filtering* to retrieve only certain types of messages, such as messages associated with a particular window or its children or only those with a message ID in a particular range of IDs.

User Output

When an application has output data to display to the user, the application provides a logical specification of the data in an area called a *presentation space*. The presentation interface then associates the presentation space with a *device context* that contains the device-dependent definitions needed to present, or *draw,* the data in the presentation space on a particular device. This allows an application to define its output data in a device-independent manner and then be executed using different devices by employing different device contexts.

The presentation interface is responsible for actually displaying the data on the screen. The application is responsible for adjusting the data to fit the size of the window. The application does not need to respond to the fact that a window may be partially overlaid by some other window, and is not expected to reformat the data in this case.

MESSAGE PATHS   The presentation interface supports a dialog between an application and an application user. Generally, this dialog takes the form of information flowing between the application and the user, with the presentation interface acting as an intermediary. The normal flow of messages in the dialog is shown in Fig. 14.8.

As we have seen, processing services related to this flow of information are invoked through the passing and processing of messages. The presentation interface includes a standard window procedure that can be used for processing certain types of message. The application can make use of these services by passing certain messages from the queue back to the presentation interface for processing after completing any application-specific processing. The use of the default window procedure is shown in Fig. 14.9.

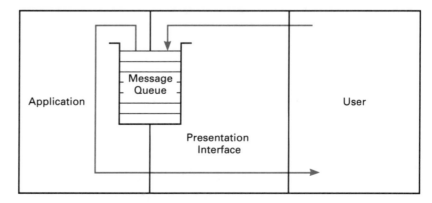

Figure 14.8 Normal message flow.

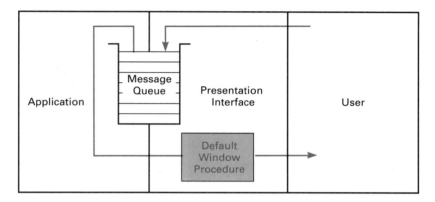

Figure 14.9   Default window procedure.

If there are messages that require only standard processing, the application can allow the presentation interface to process them directly, without first placing them in the application's queue. The delegation of message processing to the presentation interface is shown in Fig. 14.10. This provides for more efficient processing of the messages, since the processing path length is shorter, and the overhead associated with the application processing is removed.

When a system is distributed across processors within a network, there is a potential for realizing even more efficient processing. The elements of the presentation interface can be present on both the processor with the application and the processor that interfaces with the user. Message paths for messages that require only the default window procedure can be "shortcircuited" by processing them on the local processor, as shown in Fig. 14.11. They do not incur the pro-

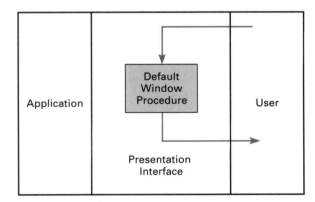

Figure 14.10   Delegating message processing to the presentation interface.

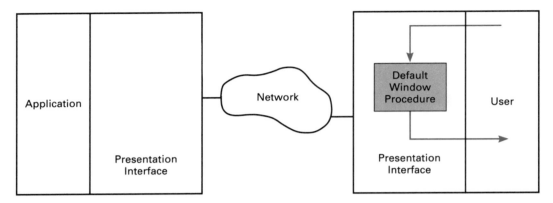

Figure 14.11   Shortcircuiting of message paths.

cessing overhead and time delays associated with routing messages back and forth across the network. This is an example of a form of distributed processing that SAA is designed to support.

USER INTERFACE FUNCTIONS   The presentation interface provides a number of facilities designed to assist an application in implementing a user interface that is consistent with CUA. These facilities include controls, a standard window definition, and a special type of window called a dialog box.

Controls

A control is a special-purpose window with an associated window procedure that reacts to application- or user-generated events in a prescribed manner. Various controls are available to implement CUA-defined methods of data display and user interaction. These controls correspond closely to the controls defined in the graphical model, although not all CUA controls are implemented directly in the presentation interface.

Presentation interface controls are defined to support both selection and data entry actions. Selection controls include the following:

- **Menu.** A series of options from which the user chooses one. Selecting a choice causes its appearance to change, and may cause a submenu to appear. A submenu offers another series of choices. A menu control can be used to define an action bar and its pulldowns.

- **Pushbutton.** A description within a border that is used to represent an action that is performed as soon as the pushbutton is selected. Selection also causes the appearance of the item to change.

- **Radio Button.** Identifies one item in a group of selectable items. When one member of the group is selected, any previously selected item becomes unselected. The selected item is highlighted.

- **Check Box.** Identifies an item within a group of selectable items where more than one item can be selected. When an item is selected, this is indicated by a checkmark within the check box.

- **List Box.** A vertical list of selectable items. If all of the list cannot be displayed at one time, it can be manipulated with a scroll bar. A list box can be defined as either single choice or multiple choice.

The *entry field* control is used for data entry. It is a horizontal area into which the user can type data. A *static control* defines an area that the application can use to display protected data. A scroll bar control identifies a scrollable area. The slider portion of the control indicates the relative position of the currently displayed information, and can be used to change what is displayed.

The Standard Window

Different types of control can be combined to create windows that implement a wide variety of user interface functions, including the interaction techniques defined by CUA. Controls are used in combination to provide the standard window and the dialog box. The *standard window* formats and displays data in a way that is consistent with the general formatting guidelines and window formats in CUA. The presentation interface standard window format is shown in Fig. 14.12. The components that can be included in a standard window are de-

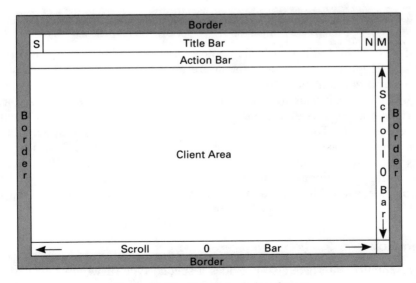

Figure 14.12   Standard window format.

BOX 14.1   Standard window components.

- **Border.** The border of the standard window can have one of four formats:

  Normal border
  Wide border (border is selectable by the user for sizing operations)
  Thin border
  No border

- **System Menu (S).** Selection of the system menu generates a pulldown menu that allows the user to move or resize the window.

- **Title Bar.** Text that identifies the window.

- **Minimize Control (N).** Selecting the minimize control causes the window to assume its minimum size.

- **Maximize Control (M).** Selecting the maximize control causes the window to assume its maximum size.

- **Action Bar.** A menu presented horizontally across the window. Selecting a choice causes either an immediate action to take place or a pulldown menu to appear.

- **Scroll Bar Controls.** Horizontal and vertical scroll bars can be used to identify and control scrollable areas.

- **Client Area.** Contains application data presented in a window defined by the application.

scribed in Box 14.1. Several basic controls are used as part of a standard window. The action bar and system menu are both menu controls. The scroll bars use the scroll bar control.

A window that uses the standard window format is a *frame window,* and the various components that make up a frame window other than the client area are *frame controls.* The client area is a window implemented by the application, and its window class and style are defined by the application. The frame window is responsible for arranging the various frame controls and the client area and for controlling the arrangement if the window is resized or moved. The application is responsible for defining and controlling the content of the client area.

Dialog Box

The presentation interface also provides a special type of window, called a *dialog box,* that can be used to combine various individual controls and to deliver a collection of inputs to the application. The individual controls that make up a dialog box are called *dialog control items*. A dialog box can be used, for example, for bulk data entry. It can also be used to implement pop-up window processing.

There are two types of dialog boxes:

- **Modal.** A modal dialog box requires the user to finish input operations associated with that window or its children before being allowed to interact with another window for that application.

- **Modeless.** A modeless dialog box allows the user to interact with any of the windows of the application.

A standard window procedure is provided for processing a dialog box.

Control Window Messages

Control windows are defined with both a parent and an owner window. The owner window can be, but does not have to be, the parent window. When a significant event occurs, the control sends a message to the window procedure of its owner. The dialog box control receives messages from the individual dialog control items that are part of it and sends messages to its owner. A frame window receives messages from the frame controls that are part of it. It has no owner, but sends messages to the client area.

Control Window Procedures

Each type of control window, including the frame window and dialog box, has a standard window procedure provided as part of the presentation interface that generates and processes messages. The window procedure and its associated window class provide the characteristic processing facilities for that control. The control window procedures provided by the presentation interface for the basic controls are listed in Box 14.2.

In addition to window procedures for the basic controls, there is a window procedure for the standard window, or frame control. The frame control procedure is responsible for arranging the frame controls and client area when the frame window is displayed, sized, or moved and controls user and application interactions with them. An application can use these standard window procedures in addition to or in place of its own window procedures for the controls it uses.

RESOURCES

The presentation interface allows certain kinds of information to be defined and stored and then used by an application. There are different types of information, or resources, that can be used:

BOX 14.2 Control procedures.

- **WC_BUTTON.** Provides the facilities of a pushbutton control, radio button control, and check box control. It allows the user to select a choice represented by a button or box using either a pointing device or the keyboard.

- **WC_ENTRYFIELD.** Provides the facilities of an entry field control. It allows the user to enter and edit a single line of text.

- **WC_LISTBOX.** Provides the facilities of a list box control. It presents a list of items from which the user can make one or more selections.

- **WC_MENU.** Provides the facilities of a menu control. It presents a list of items, displayed either horizontally or vertically, from which the user is allowed to select one. Selection of an item causes the display of an associated pulldown menu, from which further choices can be made.

- **WC_SCROLLBAR.** Provides the facilities of a scroll bar control. It allows the user to scroll the contents of an associated window.

- **WC_STATIC.** Provides the facilities of a static control. It is used to present protected information, which is information that the user cannot change or select.

- **WC_TITLEBAR.** Provides the facilities of a title bar. It is used to display the window title. Highlighting of the title bar indicates the main window with which the user is interacting. The user can move a window by selecting the title bar with the pointer and then moving it.

- **Templates.** Templates are data structures that are used to define certain types of control windows. A *dialog template* is used for a dialog box, and a *menu template* for defining a menu control. The template defines each of the control items that make up the dialog box or menu control and data values associated with each control item. The application then uses the template to display the control and to receive inputs from it.

- **Mnemonics.** Mnemonics can be defined for the choices in a menu control.

- **Accelerators.** An accelerator is a key or key combination that is associated with a particular menu choice. An accelerator table can be defined for an application, showing the correspondence between keys and menu actions. An accelerator can be used to invoke an action even when the menu is not displayed, unlike mnemonics, which can be used only when the menu is visible. Thus, accelerators provide the user with a shortcut for selecting an action.

- **Fonts.** Fonts, which are particular styles used to present characters, can be defined and then used by applications to present text.

USING CONTROLS FOR THE USER INTERFACE

The various controls that are part of the presentation interface can be used to develop a user interface for an application that is compliant with the CUA graphical model with minimal effort on the part of the application developer. The windows required to implement the application's user interface can be defined with a frame window class. They will then be formatted in the presentation interface standard window format, which is consistent with CUA graphical model formatting guidelines. For window formats that vary from the presentation interface standard window format but are still CUA-consistent, windows can be defined using the individual elements of the standard window, such as the title bar, action bar, and scroll bars. Client areas can be defined using individual controls for selection, entry, and display fields to implement the required interface to application objects and actions.

The dialog box can be used to implement pop-up windows. For example, a dialog box can be used to provide a pop-up window that extends the dialog with the user, such as a pop-up window used when a particular pulldown menu choice is selected. A dialog box can also be used to implement help panels or to display messages to the user.

The standard frame and dialog box window procedures can be used by the application to handle the user interactions with the various controls. The presentation interface handles the interactions with individual controls as well as movement from one control to another, or from one window area to another. The presentation interface, in the messages it sends to the application's window procedures, provides the logical results of the user's interactions, identifying choices selected and passing data entered to the application. The application is then responsible for providing the application-specific logic required to process the data or respond to the selection.

CONFORMANCE WITH CUA

As we have seen, the presentation interface provides support for a user interface compliant with the graphical model through the use of controls and their associated window procedures. An application defines windows for displaying information. The application issues service requests to the presentation interface to display windows and accept user interactions with them. Window procedures within the application provide application-specific processing in response to user interactions. A given implementation of the presentation interface is then used to prepare the application and execute it. The presentation interface component in the computing environment is responsible for handling window displays and user interactions in response to the application's service requests. With this approach, the primary responsibility for seeing that the application's user interface conforms with the CUA rules and guidelines rests with the presentation interface implementation rather than with the application.

DISPLAY FORMATTING

An application defines the general content of the information it displays, using the frame control, dialog box, and basic controls as needed. The presentation interface implementation then sees that the content is formatted as described in the presentation interface specification, which is consistent with the formatting guidelines of CUA. For example, the application defines a particular field as a selection field by defining it with a group of radio button controls. The application defines each choice with a radio button control, including the text or graphic to be displayed for that choice. The presentation interface is then responsible for

- Arranging the choices in an appropriate layout
- Including mnemonics if their use has been specified
- Displaying the appropriate selection icons
- Displaying a selection cursor and selected emphasis
- Displaying appropriate selection indicators when a choice is selected
- Displaying a scroll bar or scrolling information if the field is scrollable

Similarly, an application defines an entry field with an entry field control. The presentation interfaces sees that the entry field is formatted properly, controls the user's interaction with the field, and provides the data entered to the application through messages sent to the application's window procedure for that window.

Through the frame control, the application can specify that standard window formats, including a window title bar, border, action bar, and scroll bars, be used. The presentation interface again is responsible for seeing that the different areas that are used are formatted according to the CUA rules and guidelines. Controls can be used to define selection, entry, and display fields in a client area, and the presentation interface is then responsible for formatting the fields correctly. The presentation interface is also responsible for the proper use of color and emphasis.

USER INTERACTIONS

When controls and their associated window procedures are used, the presentation interface is responsible for handling user interactions with a window. Thus, the presentation interface implementation is responsible for providing the different interaction techniques defined in CUA. These techniques include

- Use of a mouse or a keyboard
- Selection techniques such as point-and-select and mnemonics

- Insert or replace modes for data entry
- Special field types, including autoselect, autoenter, and autotab
- Cursor-driven or cursor-independent scrolling
- Cursor movement techniques for moving from field to field or from one window area to another

The results of user interactions—selection of a choice or entry of data—are passed to the application via messages sent to the application's window procedure. The application is not concerned at all with the way in which the interaction takes place; this is the province of the presentation interface.

STANDARD ACTIONS

The presentation interface does not directly support standard actions, such as File, Edit, and Help. The application must provide the logic needed to respond to a user's selection of one of these actions. The application must also determine the actions displayed in pushbuttons and respond appropriately when a pushbutton is selected. A dialog box can be used to display help panels. The presentation interface is responsible for handling the display and removal of the dialog box window and for handling the user's interaction with it. The application is responsible for the logical content of the panels, for determining which panel should be displayed in a particular situation, and for providing the different types of help that CUA defines, such as help index and keys help.

A dialog box can also be used for displaying messages to the user. Again, the presentation interface handles display and removal of the dialog box window and user interaction. The application is responsible for defining both message content and format and for seeing that the user responds in an appropriate way for the message type.

PRESENTATION INTERFACE VS. DIALOG INTERFACE

Both the dialog interface and the presentation interface offer support to an application in terms of developing a user interface that is consistent with CUA rules and guidelines. Both interfaces allow the application to specify the logical content of information to be displayed and then provide the appropriate formatting for the information to make it consistent with CUA in appearance. Both interfaces also handle the way in which the user interacts with panels and are responsible for seeing that interaction techniques are consistent with CUA specifications. The application is concerned only with the result of the interaction, and not the way in which the interaction takes place.

The key differences between the dialog interface and the presentation interface in terms of CUA conformance are in the areas of dialog control and windowing. The dialog interface provides more direct support of dialog control actions through its command processing facility. The dialog interface also provides a full set of help facilities consistent with the CUA specification for help. The dialog interface message facility formats and displays messages based on the message types defined by CUA. With the presentation interface, support for standard actions, help facilities, and message processing is left to the application.

With the presentation interface, a full windowing system is provided. An application can use multiple windows, with the presentation interface handling placement and movement of the windows and switching of control between windows. With the dialog interface, windowing services are more limited. Secondary windows are used only to display help information. Pop-up windows can be used, but are not movable by the user and can support only modal dialogs. The dialog interface does not provide standard window elements such as the title bar and its associated icons, or window borders.

The presentation interface can be used to develop an interface consistent with the graphical model, but with its strong emphasis on the use of graphics and the presentation of information within windows would not be likely to be used to implement a user interface based on the entry model or text subset. The dialog manager, on the other hand, directly supports user interfaces consistent with the entry model or the text subset, but to fully support the graphical model, would have to be used with an underlying windowing system that is also CUA compliant.

15 CUA AND THE CPI APPLICATION GENERATOR INTERFACE

INTRODUCTION   An application generator is a facility designed to make the development of applications easier. Rather than specifying application logic in detail through a series of procedural statements in a programming language, the application developer selects and combines higher-level application functions, and the application generator then translates the functions into a form suitable for execution.

SAA APPLICATION GENERATOR ENVIRONMENTS   As part of SAA, the CPI application generator interface is designed to provide application compatibility and portability across all the SAA computing environments. As currently implemented, the use of an application generator involves three phases:

- **Application Definition.** Application definition includes specifying processing logic, defining data to be used by the application, and defining screen and printer formats to be used for data display.

- **Application Generation.** Application generation uses the various definitions that make up the application and prepares the application for execution in a specific computing environment.

- **Application Execution.** Once the application has been generated, it can be executed repeatedly in a particular environment.

The SAA application generator interface has been implemented through the Cross System Product (CSP) family of products. The intent of the application generator interface is to allow an application to be generated using generator software that operates in any of the supported computing environments and then executed in that same environment or in any of the other supported environments. At the time of writing, not all environments are supported for both generation and execution. Check the specific implementations of CSP to see what restrictions apply.

APPLICATION GENERATOR INTERFACE

The application generator interface that is part of CPI addresses only the application definition phase. It specifies the statements that can be used to define processing logic, to describe data contained in files, databases, or tables, and to format screen and printer displays. An application's user interface is specified using the *map definition facility* to process a set of statements that format screen and printer displays. Map definition consists of two parts: map specification and map structure. *Map specification* defines options related to the map as a whole, such as its size and position on the screen, and *map structure* defines the individual fields that make up the map, along with options related to individual fields.

MAP SPECIFICATION

Map specification statements, shown in Box 15.1, apply to a map as a whole. They can be used to

- Assign a name to a map
- Specify a map's size and position on the screen
- Specify the initial position of the cursor within a map
- Associate a help map with a map
- Specify function key usage
- Specify how certain types of data are displayed
- Specify the device types with which a map can be used

Help Maps

The HELP MAP NAME statement allows one help map to be associated with each application map. The additional help facilities, such as extended help, keys help, help index, and so on, are not directly supported. Help is requested with a PF key. The default for the help PF key is PF1. The HELP PF KEY statement can be used to change this, but F1 should be used to remain consistent with CUA rules and guidelines.

BOX 15.1   Map specification statements.

- **Bypass Edit PF Keys.** Assigns PF keys that allow the user to bypass field edits that have been defined for fields. This statement identifies the PF keys that can be used for this purpose for a map.

- **Cursor Field.** Identifies the map field in which the cursor appears when the map is first displayed.

- **Device Selection.** Specifies the device types on which this map can be displayed or printed.

- **Fold Input.** Specifies whether character data entered into variable fields in this map should be converted to uppercase.

- **Help Map Name.** Identifies the help map to be displayed when help is requested for this map.

- **Help PF Key.** Specifies the PF key that the user can use to request help for this map.

- **Map Name.** Assigns a name to the map. The name consists of a map group name and a map name. The map group name identifies a group of maps used with one application.

- **Position.** Specifies where this map is located when displayed on a terminal screen. The values entered are for the line and column coordinates of the upper left corner of the map.

- **Size.** Specifies the number of lines and columns contained in this map. The map size must be no larger than the screen or page size of the smallest device associated with this map.

- **SO/SI Take Position.** When DBCS data are used in the large-system and midrange environments, special characters (SO and SI) are used to delimit the DBCS data. This statement specifies whether SO/SI characters are to be represented by blanks in printed output.

Map Positioning

Maps can be defined with a size that is smaller than the screen size. Such maps are called *partial maps*. Multiple partial maps can be displayed on the screen at the same time, provided that they

- Do not overlap
- Can be completely contained within the screen area
- Are arranged vertically, and not side by side

MAP STRUCTURE   Map structure statements, shown in Box 15.2, define
                      the individual fields that make up a map. Map struc-
ture statements can be used to

- Define a field as a constant field, variable field, or message field
- Assign attributes, such as color, emphasis, protection, and data type, to a field
- Define edits to be applied to data entered or displayed in a variable field
- Identify a map as a help map

BOX 15.2   Map structure statements.

- **Constant Field.** Used to define a constant field, which is used to display protected information. The following special types of constant fields can also be defined:

    Constant Field—DBCS. Defines a field that contains double-byte character set, or DBCS, data.
    Constant Field—MIX. Defines a field that contains a mixture of single-byte data and DBCS data.

- **Field Attribute.** Used to specify formatting and processing characteristics associated with a field. The different attributes that can be specified are

    Color. Specifies the color used to display a field on a color device.
    Cursor. Identifies this as the field in which the cursor should be positioned when the map is first displayed.
    Data Type. Specifies whether a field will accept any character or only numeric data.
    Extended Highlighting. Used to specify the use of a highlighting technique when the field is displayed. Highlighting techniques include blinking, reverse video, and underlining.
    Light Intensity. Used to specify the brightness used when displaying the field. Possible intensities are normal, bright, and dark (not visible).
    Light Pen Detectable Field. Used to specify that a field can be selected with a light pen.
    Modified Data Tag. Determines how the modified data tag for the field is set when a map is first displayed. The modified data tag indicates whether the contents of a field have been changed.
    Outlining. Used to create lines at the edges of fields on DBCS devices or to define a constant field that is to be displayed with a box around it.
    Protection. Specifies whether data can be entered in a field.

BOX 15.2 *(Continued)*

- **Help Map.** Identifies a map as a help map.
- **Message Field.** Identifies a variable field as the map message field. It is used to display application- and system-defined messages to the user.
- **Variable Field.** Used to define a variable field (one into which a user can enter data). The following types of special variable fields can also be defined:

  Array. Defines a variable field that is part of an array of fields. A map array is specified by giving the same name to each field in the array and following the name with a subscript value.

  DBCS. Defines a variable field that will contain DBCS data.

  MIX. Defines a variable field that can contain a mixture of single-byte and DBCS data.

- **Variable Field Edit.** Used to define different types of edits performed on data entered or displayed. Possible edits include the following:

  Currency Symbol. Specifies that a currency symbol should be inserted when data are displayed in the field and that the user can include a currency symbol when entering data in the field.

  Data Type. Specifies the type of data allowable in the field. Possible types are character, numeric, DBCS, and mixed single-byte and DBCS.

  Date Edit. Specifies the format to be used for a field containing a date. The date is displayed in the format specified and data entered are checked to ensure the correct format.

  Decimal Positions. Specifies the number of positions to the right of the decimal point for numeric fields. For data being displayed, a decimal point symbol is inserted at the appropriate position. For data being entered, a decimal point symbol can be included.

  Description. Provides a text string that describes the variable field. It is used for documentation only.

  Edit Error Message Numbers. Specifies the number of an error message to be displayed when a particular type of error occurs. Different error types for which a message can be displayed are data type error, edit routine error, input required error, minimum input error, and value error.

  Edit Routine. Specifies the name of a processing routine or edit table used to edit the data in this field. Edit tables can be used to match against valid or invalid values or to check against ranges of valid values. The processing routine can be a system-supplied check digit routine or an application-defined routine.

(Continued)

BOX 15.2 *(Continued)*

Fill Character. Specifies the character used to fill unused positions when a field is displayed.

Fold. Specifies whether lowercase alphabetic characters entered by the user should be converted to uppercase.

Hexadecimal. Specifies that only hexadecimal digit values (0–9, A–F) can be entered in the field.

Input Required. Indicates whether data must be entered in this field.

Justify. Specifies whether data are to be left-justified, right-justified, or left as is. Data entered and data displayed are aligned within the field as specified here.

Maximum Value. Specifies the largest value that can be entered into a numeric field.

Minimum Input. Specifies the minimum number of characters that must be entered in a field.

Minimum Value. Specifies the smallest value that can be entered in a numeric field.

Numeric Separator. Specifies whether a numeric field contains separator characters, such as commas. If separator characters are used, they are inserted in data being displayed and allowed in data entered by the user.

Sign. Specifies whether a sign is used with a numeric field, and if so, where it appears. It is inserted for displayed data and allowed for entered data.

Zero Edit. Specifies the display format for numeric fields with a zero value. The format depends on values specified for decimal positions, currency symbol, numeric separators, and the fill character.

- **Variable Field Edit Order.** Specifies the order in which fields on a map are edited.

- **Variable Field Name.** Assigns a name to a variable field. The application can refer the field for processing by this name.

Constant fields are used to display protected information; variable fields allow the user to enter data into the field. The application generator interface provides extensive editing capabilities for the data entered in a variable field. Editing options can also be used to format data before they are displayed.

A map is created by "painting" it directly on the terminal screen. The application developer determines the map layout by entering each field in the position where it should appear when the map is displayed on a screen or printer. Constant fields are defined by typing the appropriate information at the desired position. Variable fields are defined by using special character codes. As fields are being defined, or "painted," formatting characteristics and editing checks can be assigned to them.

MESSAGES

As part of application development, a message file can be created and messages defined and stored in it. Each message is identified by a message number. When the application processing logic detects an error condition, it specifies the number of a message to be displayed. That message is then retrieved from the message file and displayed. If the MESSAGE FIELD map structure statement has been used to define a message field, the message is displayed in the message field. If no message field has been defined, the screen is erased and the message displayed. System-defined messages are similarly displayed.

RELATIONSHIP TO COMMON USER ACCESS

The initial version of the application generator interface is based on the existing family of CSP products, which were designed to operate in the large-system environment. As a result of this, the user interface facilities are oriented toward the use of a nonprogrammable terminal rather than a programmable workstation. The panel formatting and interaction techniques supported in the application generator interface are those that have been defined in CUA for the entry model, although even here, at the time of writing, compliance with CUA is not complete. IBM has stated that the interface specification is evolving and will be enhanced over time, so later versions of the interface may well provide more built-in support for CUA facilities and make it easier to develop applications that are compliant with the text subset and, eventually, the full graphical model.

PANEL FORMATTING

The application generator interface provides little in the way of direct support for CUA-consistent panel formatting. The application is responsible for arranging the choices in a selection field and for including numbers or mnemonics as part of the choices in a single-choice field. The application is also responsible for defining and arranging descriptive information associated with an entry field or selection field.

Panel Areas

Unlike the dialog interface and the presentation interface, the application generator interface does not provide directly for the various panel elements that make up the standard CUA panel format. If an application is to provide maps that contain a command area or function key area, all the formatting and interactions that are needed to produce them must be defined by the application itself. A message area can be defined by using the MESSAGE FIELD map structure statement and messages defined and displayed using the application generator interface message facilities. Complying with CUA guidelines for message format is the application developer's responsibility.

Color and Emphasis

The application generator interface supports a wide range of color and emphasis techniques through the specification of field attributes for color, extended highlighting, light intensity, and outlining. Emphasis techniques include high-intensity display, blinking, reverse video, and underlining. However, it is up to the application developer to see that the color and emphasis techniques are used in ways that are consistent with CUA guidelines.

INTERACTION TECHNIQUES   The selection, entry, and cursor movement techniques provided are those defined in CUA for a nonprogrammable terminal. Selections are made by entering a character in an entry field associated with the selection field as a whole (single-choice) or with an individual choice (multiple-choice). The standard cursor movement keys are used to move around a map. The application generator interface does not support scrolling, either for individual fields or for the map as a whole.

DIALOG CONTROL   The application generator interface does not provide support for the CUA-defined dialog control actions, other than Help. The application generator interface allows help maps to be defined and one help map associated with a given application map. Implementation of other help facilities, as well as other dialog control actions, is the application developer's responsibility.

PART **VI**   CUA IMPLEMENTATIONS

16 THE OS/2 OPERATING SYSTEM

INTRODUCTION   As we have seen, SAA is an architecture that is implemented by various hardware and software products that are part of the different SAA computing environments. At the time of writing, implementation of SAA is somewhat of a patchwork affair. Not all elements of the architecture have been implemented in all the SAA computing environments, and when a particular element has been implemented, there are differences between environments in terms of how closely the implementation complies with the SAA rules and guidelines. Implementations vary considerably in completeness as well.

Implementations of the Common User Access component of SAA vary from one environment to another. Some implementations implement only the entry model of CUA for nonprogrammable terminals, and others implement the graphical model for programmable workstations. IBM's *Operating System/2 (OS/2)* is a key implementation of the graphical model of CUA for programmable workstations and is the only environment for which IBM has committed to implement the CPI dialog interface and presentation interface.

OS/2 runs on various models of personal computer and provides basic operating system functions, including executing programs, providing multitasking facilities, handling file and directory management, and controlling hardware resources, such as memory and peripherals. There are various versions of the OS/2 operating system. The versions that contain a component called the *Presentation Manager (PM)* provide support for a CUA user interface based on the graphical model. The Presentation Manager provides an interface to the operating system itself and a set of facilities that can be used by an application developer to develop the user interface for an application.

We will look first at how the Presentation Manager implements CUA rules and guidelines in providing the user interface to OS/2 itself.

PRESENTATION MANAGER: AN INTERFACE TO OS/2

The Presentation Manager provides a menu-driven, window-based interface to OS/2 facilities, which is the default for system operation. However, the user can switch to a command line interface, such as that used for the DOS operating system. With the command line interface, the user enters system commands directly. In this chapter we are concerned only with the Presentation Manager interface. The Presentation Manager is a faithful and complete implementation of the CPI presentation interface in terms of the user interface facilities that it offers to the application developer. It is based on the same basic windowing concepts and offers the same facilities for developing the user interface. As such, it is also a strongly compliant implementation of the CUA graphical model. A key reason for this strong compliance is that the OS/2 Presentation Manager and the CUA architecture itself have been developed in parallel, evolving together over time.

DISPLAY FORMATTING

All OS/2 Presentation Manager displays follow CUA formatting conventions. In the following sections, we will examine a number of the windows that are displayed by OS/2 and a typical OS/2 application program.

The Start Programs Menu

Figure 16.1 shows the primary OS/2 menus displayed when the operating system is first started. These menus are used to execute programs. There is a window title bar at the top of each window with system menu and window sizing icons. Below that is an action bar, with mnemonics indicated for the different choices. The client area contains a single-choice selection field, which can be used to select the program to be started. It also contains a vertical scroll bar, formatted in the CUA-specified manner.

Pulldown Menu

When a choice is selected from the action bar, a pulldown menu appears, as shown in Fig. 16.2. The pulldown contains a series of choices with mnemonics identified. Ellipses are used to indicate that a further dialog is required for a choice; a pop-up window continues the dialog. Some choices have accelerator keys (ENTER and DELETE).

Pop-Up Window

Figure 16.3 shows the pop-up window that appears if New is selected from the pulldown menu. The window title bar contains the system menu icon, and the border can be used to move the window but not resize it. This pop-up window

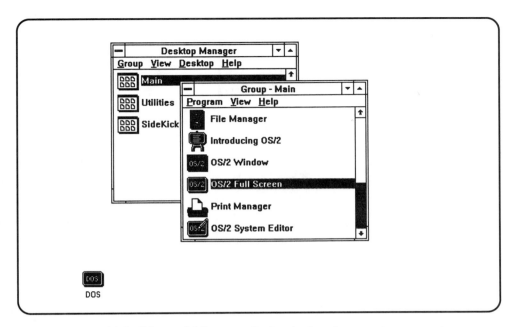

Figure 16.1 Primary OS/2 menus displayed when the operating system is first started.

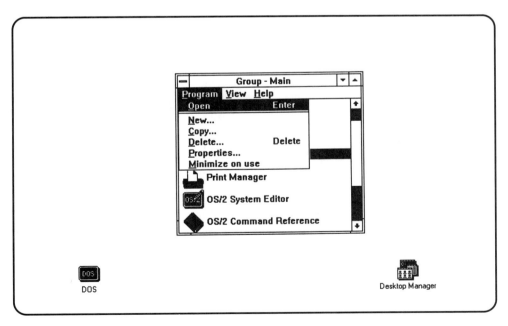

Figure 16.2 When a choice is selected from the action bar, a pulldown menu appears.

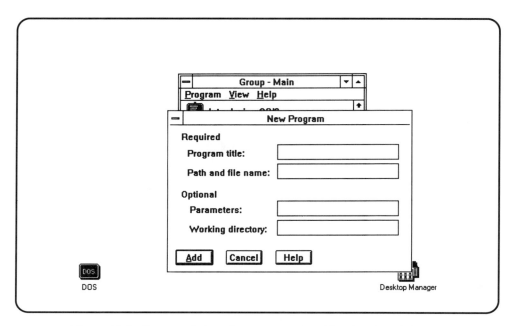

Figure 16.3 Pop-up window that appears when New is selected from the pulldown menu.

demonstrates the use of an entry field. It also contains pushbuttons showing the actions that are available from this window.

Formatting of Controls

Figure 16.4 contains a window that illustrates the use of several types of controls, including an entry field, radio button controls, and check box controls. All these controls are consistent with the CUA formatting guidelines. The window also demonstrates the use of field prompts, column headings, and group boxes for displaying descriptive information.

**USER
INTERACTIONS**   Either the keyboard or a mouse can be used to interact with OS/2 through the Presentation Manager interface. The interaction techniques supported are consistent with CUA.

Using the Keyboard

To use the keyboard for interaction, the user moves the cursor with the arrow keys or the tab key. Selections can be made by entering a mnemonic when mnemonics have been defined for choices, or by using the point-and-select tech-

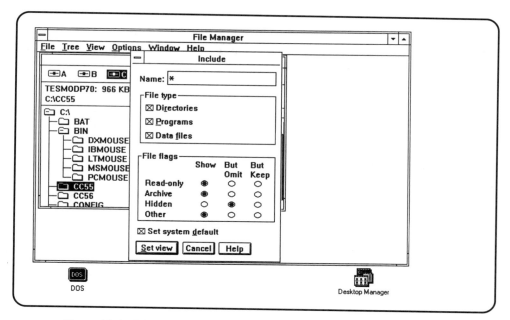

Figure 16.4　Window illustrating the use of an entry field, radio button controls, and check box controls.

nique with either explicit or implicit selection. Data entry can be done in either insert or replace mode.

Special keys can be used to move from one window area to another. For example, F10 is used as the switch-to-action-bar key, which is the standard CUA key assignment. Scrolling can be accomplished either by moving the cursor or with special scrolling keys like F7 (Backward) and F8 (Forward) or PgUp and PgDn.

Using a Mouse

For a mouse, clicking is used for selection. A double click can be used to make a selection and specify a default action for processing. Dragging is used for direct manipulation operations, like using the window border to move or resize a window. It can also be used to mark a text segment. Scrolling can be accomplished by clicking on one of the arrows within the scroll bar, by clicking on an area between an arrow and the slide box, or by moving the slider box within the scroll bar.

Action Bar and Pulldown Interactions

When an action bar choice is selected, using either the keyboard or a mouse, its associated pulldown appears. The user interacts with the pulldown using standard interaction techniques. If accelerator keys have been defined for pulldown choices, they can be used to select a choice. When the interaction with the pulldown is complete, and no further information is needed, the user's request is submitted to the application for processing. If the dialog needs to be continued, a pop-up window appears.

The user interacts with the pop-up window using standard interaction techniques. Selecting a pushbutton completes the interaction with the dialog box. If the dialog needs to continue further, another dialog box appears, overlapping the previous one. When the dialog is complete, the user's request is submitted for processing and the dialog boxes are removed from the screen.

STANDARD ACTIONS

The Presentation Manager interface to OS/2 provides support for standard actions where they are appropriate (see Fig. 16.4). The standard actions File, View, Options, Window, and Help are included in the action bar, and the actions Cancel and Help are available as pushbuttons. There are also application-specific actions, like Tree and Set view, that are made available to the user. Standard window actions are available through the system menu icon in the window title bar.

HELP FACILITIES

Many of the windows displayed by the Presentation Manager have help information available, which is accessible through the standard methods: selecting the Help action in the action bar or pushbutton or pressing F1. Figure 16.5 shows an OS/2 Help window. Help for Help, Extended Help, Keys Help, and Help Index are available through the Help action in the Help window action bar. Figure 16.6 shows a portion of the OS/2 Help index. Standard scrolling techniques can be used to scroll through the Help index. Help windows may also be provided for a particular field within a display.

MESSAGES

The system displays messages to confirm actions, to warn of possible problems, and to identify error conditions. Messages generally are displayed in a window, and Help for the message may be available as a pushbutton option. Some messages are displayed directly. Help can be requested for these messages by specifying the message number. Figure 16.7 contains an example of a message displayed in a window with Help as an option.

WINDOWING

The Presentation Manager interface is a windowing system and is consistent with both the CUA graphical model and the CPI presentation interface specifications for windowing. Multiple

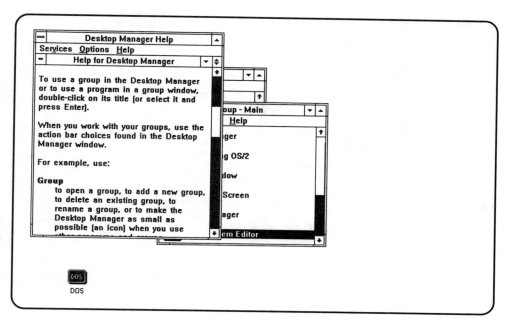

Figure 16.5 OS/2 Help window.

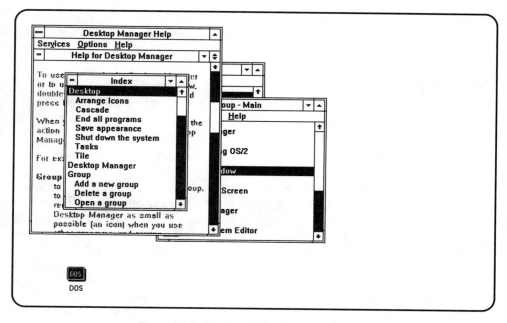

Figure 16.6 Portion of the OS/2 Help index.

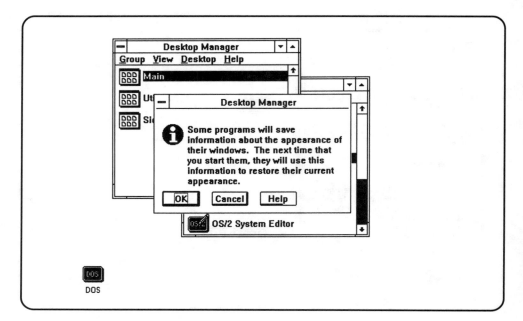

Figure 16.7   A message displayed in a window with Help as an option.

windows can be displayed on the screen at the same time. A single application, or program, can use multiple windows, and windows can be present for more than one application.

Multiple Windows

OS/2 multitasking facilities allow multiple programs to be run concurrently, with windows for each program displayed on the screen. An example of multiple applications is shown in Fig. 16.8.

Window Controls

Users are allowed to move and resize windows. The window title bar contains icons that are consistent with the standard window described by the CPI presentation interface. Figure 16.9 illustrates these icons. The figure also shows the system menu pulldown that appears when the system menu icon is selected. The options in the pulldown can then be used to move or resize the window.

The window sizing icons in the window title bar can also be used to resize the window. The up arrow in the title bar is the Maximize window control that causes the window to expand to its full size, which typically causes it to fill the screen. The down arrow is the Minimize control that can be used to reduce the window to a small icon that is displayed at the bottom of the screen. The two

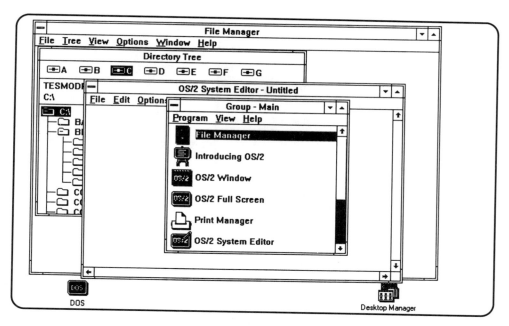

Figure 16.8   Multiple applications.

small icons at the bottom of the screen in Fig. 16.9 are examples of windows that have been minimized.

A mouse can also be used to manipulate a window directly. Dragging the title bar with the mouse pointer moves the window; dragging a window border or corner resizes the window.

DEVELOPING OS/2 APPLICATIONS

Applications developed to run under the Presentation Manager can take advantage of the windowing environment it provides. Application screens are presented within a window. Standard window controls, including those in the system menu, allow the user to move and resize the application window. When a window is minimized, it is represented by an icon placed along the bottom of the screen.

The Presentation Manager uses the same window conventions as those described for the CPI presentation interface in Chapter 14. Windows are arranged in a parent/child hierarchy. The topmost window is the full display screen—the desktop window. Windows immediately below the desktop window are main or top-level windows. Child windows with the same parent are siblings. Child windows appear on top of their parent window on the screen, and the order in

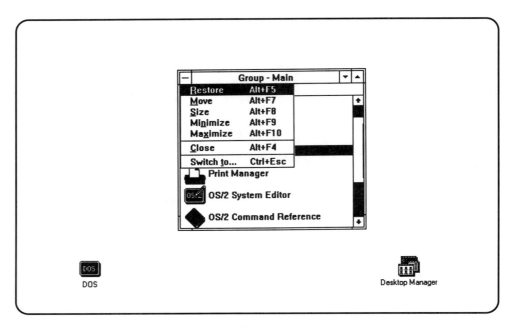

Figure 16.9   Window title bar icons.

which siblings appear is specified by the z-order. Windows have an initial position and size, but the user is able to move or resize them. The window that will receive the next keyboard input is the input focus window. The main window that is the input focus window or whose child is the input focus window is the active window. The user is able to change which window is the active window, using either the mouse or keyboard. The new active window is then displayed as the top main window on the screen.

WINDOW
PROCESSING

As with the standard CPI presentation interface, each window has a window procedure that processes messages associated with that window. The set of windows that share the same window procedure is a window class, which has a class style associated with it that determines how the windows in that window class behave. An individual window can also have its window style.

Messages are used to request services related to windows. A window procedure provides the services in response to the message. When the service is to be provided synchronously, the message is sent directly to the window procedure. When the service is to be provided asynchronously, the message is posted to an input queue associated with the window procedure. A Presentation Manager application can define window procedures to provide application-specific processing, but the Presentation Manager provides a default window procedure that can be used to process messages in a standard manner.

Messages can be generated in several ways. Messages are generated when an application requests a service of the Presentation Manager. For example, when the application requests that a window be created or drawn on the screen, messages are generated that cause the appropriate processing to take place. User interactions generate messages, and messages are used as the method of passing user inputs to the application. Messages may also be generated in response to certain system conditions. For example, when one window is moved, other windows may need to be redrawn. Messages trigger the processing needed to redisplay these windows.

DEVELOPING CUA-COMPLIANT APPLICATIONS

The Presentation Manager component provides an application program interface (API) that can be used in developing applications that run under OS/2. The Presentation Manager's application programming interface is an implementation of the presentation interface defined by CPI. The approach taken in the Presentation Manager is to supply defaults that provide consistency with CUA but to allow the developer to define an interface that does not conform to CUA if desired.

The standard window provides a standard window layout containing elements consistent with the window definition in CUA. These elements include

- Window title bar
- System menu icon
- Window sizing icons
- Sizable border
- Action bar and pulldown menus
- Vertical and horizontal scroll bars
- Client area

When an application uses the standard window, the Presentation Manager is responsible for the formatting of the various window elements, as well as the user interactions with the window.

The application is responsible for formatting the client area. A number of controls are available that are consistent with CUA. The controls are

- Pushbutton
- Check box
- Radio button
- List box

- Combination box
- Entry field, single line or multiline
- Scroll bar
- Menu

Both mnemonics and accelerator keys can be defined and used as part of a menu control. With these controls, the Presentation Manager again is responsible for formatting and interaction.

Pop-up window processing can be accomplished using dialog boxes and message boxes. Any of the controls can be used within a dialog box, and the interaction with the dialog box can be either modal or modeless. A message box contains a text display and a set of pushbuttons.

The Presentation Manager also provides support for various types of help information. An application can define help panels using a set of help tags that are part of the Information Presentation Facility (IPF) Tag Language. The panels are compiled and stored in a library and are displayed by the application as needed. A help table and subtables are defined to link specific help panels to application windows and entry and selection fields within a window. The Presentation Manager provides a main Help window within which different help panels can be displayed. When the user requests help, the Presentation Manager sends a message to the application identifying the type of help requested. The application then provides the appropriate help panel for display. Help panels can be displayed for

- Field-level help
- Extended help
- Help index
- Keys help
- Tutorial help

Standard Help for Help information is provided by the Presentation Manager, but can be replaced by help information from the application. System help topics and their associated help panels are supplied as part of the help index. Additional index topics can be defined by the application. The application is responsible for providing extended help, keys help, and tutorial help.

IPF TAG LANGUAGE

The IPF tag language provides facilities for defining help panels that are essentially comparable to those defined as part of the dialog tag language defined by the dialog interface and implemented as part of the Dialog Manager in OS/2. Box 16.1 lists the IPF tags particularly useful for implementing CUA-defined

BOX 16.1   IPF help tags.

- **:h.** Defines the beginning of a panel.
- **:i1,:i2.** Define index entries and associate a panel with each entry.
- **:isyn.** Maps synonyms to search words for index topics.
- **:icmd.** Associates a panel with a command.
- **:link.** Links a phrase in one panel to another panel. Can be used to implement reference phrase help.

types of help. In addition, the IPF tag language provides tags that can be used to format information in the help panels. The IPF tags provide all the formatting facilities offered by the information tags in the dialog interface, as well as additional facilities, such as the use of color, highlighting, character graphics, and bit-mapped graphics.

A SAMPLE PRESENTATION MANAGER APPLICATION

Applications developed to run under a Presentation Manager typically provide a user interface similar to the Presentation Manager interface. In general, most applications will be consistent with CUA rules and guidelines.

Application Window

Figure 16.10 shows a window from a Presentation Manager application called Sidekick from Borland International. The window contains window control icons, a title bar, an action bar, and a client area that displays a phone book entry. The action bar uses mnemonics and provides the standard actions File, Edit, and Help. Textual scrolling information (Card 1 of 5) is provided that indicates the relative position of the selected entry within the phone book.

Action Bar Pulldown

Figure 16.11 shows an action bar pulldown menu. It contains a selection field where choices can be made using either mnemonics or the point-and-select technique. Control key combinations, or accelerators, are available for fast path selection of certain options. Ellipses indicate where a pop-up window will continue the dialog.

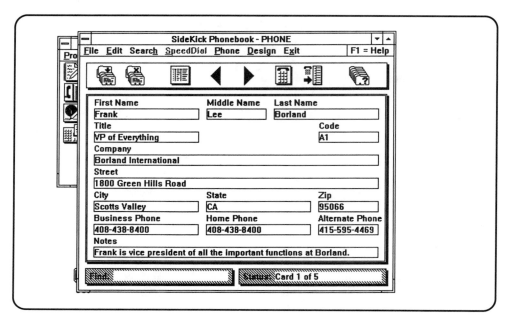

Figure 16.10   Window from the Presentation Manager application Sidekick from Borland International.

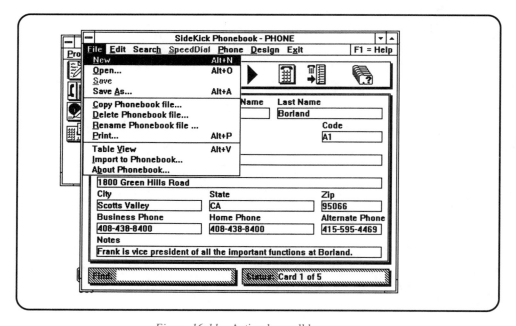

Figure 16.11   Action bar pulldown menu.

Pop-Up Window

Figure 16.12 shows a pop-up window used to continue the dialog for a particular pulldown selection. It contains a list box control, entry fields, and a check box. The window contains pushbuttons for the actions available. Figure 16.13 contains a pop-up window with radio button and check box controls.

Help Window

Help windows are available in the standard way. Figure 16.14 shows a Help window for a choice in one of the action bar pulldown menus. As can be seen from the pushbuttons in this Help window, Extended Help, Help Index, and Keys Help are also available. Since the Presentation Manager does not directly support the different types of help facilities, these have been developed as part of the application.

Message Window

Messages generally appear in pop-up windows, as shown in Fig. 16.15.

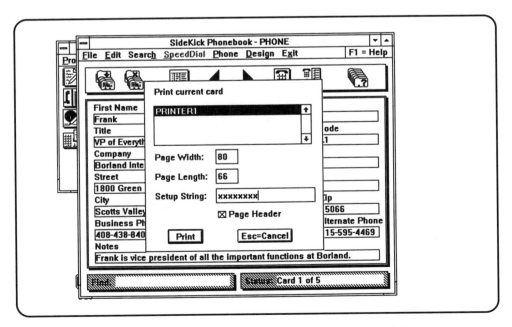

Figure 16.12 Pop-up window used to continue the dialog for a pulldown selection.

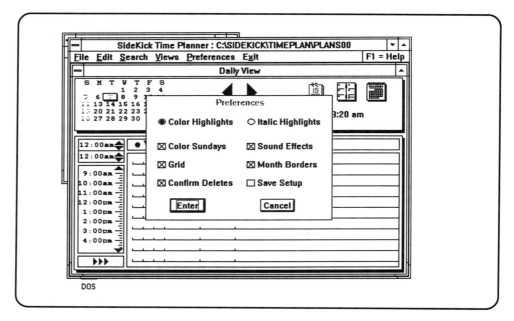

Figure 16.13 Pop-up window with radio button and check box controls

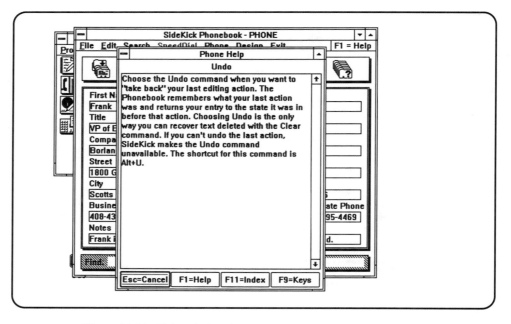

Figure 16.14 Help window for an action bar pulldown menu choice.

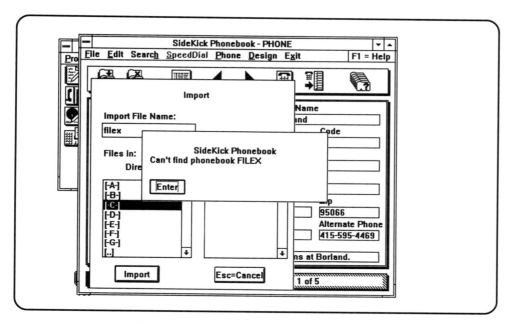

Figure 16.15   A message in a pop-up window.

DIALOG MANAGER

OS/2 offers another facility for developing CUA-compliant applications, called the *Dialog Manager*. The Dialog Manager is an implementation of the CPI dialog interface described in Chapter 13. As described, the Dialog Manager controls the dialog or conversational activity between a user and an application, using a display screen and keyboard or pointing device. An application makes calls to the Dialog Manager in order to invoke its services.

DIALOG MANAGER WINDOWING

With the Dialog Manager, application panels are displayed in windows. The main window used to display application panels is called the primary window. Only one application panel can be displayed in the primary window, and when a new panel is displayed, it replaces the previous one. A primary window can be moved and resized by the user.

Panels can be displayed in pop-up windows. Multiple pop-up windows can be displayed at one time. A pop-up window can be moved by the user, but not resized. The application controls when pop-up windows are displayed and removed. Pop-up windows are commonly used to extend the dialog with the user and to display messages.

DIALOG MANAGER PANEL ELEMENTS

Figure 16.16 illustrates a main window that is part of a Dialog Manager application. In addition to the elements shown, a Dialog Manager panel can be defined containing top and bottom instructions, a command area, or a function key area. When panels are defined for an application, it is up to the application designer to select the appropriate elements. For example, an action bar and a function key area would not normally be used in the same panel. However, the Dialog Manager ensures that the different elements are formatted according to CUA guidelines, and that user interactions with panels are consistent with CUA. The Dialog Manager also provides window controls, including the system menu icon, window sizing icons, and a sizable or nonsizable window border.

The panel body area can contain single-choice (radio button) or multiple-choice (check box) selection fields, list boxes, entry fields, pushbuttons, and formatted information, as needed for the application. Figure 16.17 shows a Dialog Manager panel that contains single- and multiple-choice selection fields and a function key area. This panel is displayed in a pop-up window.

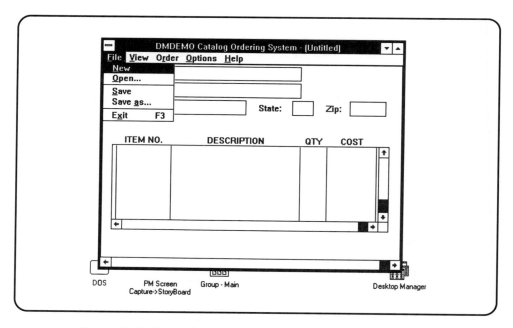

Figure 16.16 Main window displayed by a Dialog Manager application.

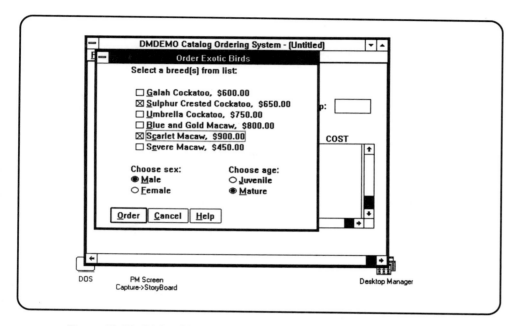

Figure 16.17 Dialog Manager panel containing single- and multiple-choice selection fields and a function key area.

DIALOG ELEMENTS

A dialog is made up of dialog elements, which include the following:

- **Function Programs.** An application program that uses dialog services.

- **Variables.** Used to communicate information between an application and the Dialog Manager. Function programs, panels, and messages use variables to reference data.

- **Panel Definitions.** Used to define the content and processing characteristics of a panel. Panel formatting and interaction techniques provided by the Dialog Manager are CUA-compliant.

- **Message Definitions.** Used to provide the text of messages to be displayed to the user. Messages are used to confirm user-request actions, warn of possible problems, and report errors.

- **Key Mapping Lists.** Used to associate commands with control keys. They are used to determine the contents of pushbutton/function key areas.

- **Command Tables.** Used to define the actions to be performed in response to a particular command. They can be used to define application-specific commands or change standard dialog commands.

DIALOG SERVICES   The Dialog Manager provides services that an application can use to implement its user interface. These services fall into three categories:

- **Display Services.** Used to provide support for the display of panels. Either a new panel is displayed or the current panel redisplayed. Panels may be displayed in the primary window or a pop-up window. Display services include functions like performing validations on input entered by the user and translating between internal and external forms of data entered or displayed in the panel. Display services can also be used to retrieve message texts from a library and display them to the user. Messages are displayed in pop-up windows using a modal dialog.

- **Variable Services.** Used to pass information among the Dialog Manager, applications, panels, and messages.

- **Dialog Control Services.** Used to control the execution of a dialog application.

BOX 16.2   Dialog Manager services.

Display Services

- **DISPLAY.** Displays an application panel in a primary window and can include field validation and translation of values.
- **ADDPOP.** Displays an application panel in a pop-up window.
- **REMPOP.** Removes specified or all pop-up windows.

Variable Services

- **VDEFINE.** Defines a program variable in the function pool.
- **VDELETE.** Deletes a program variable from the function pool.
- **VCOPY.** Obtains a copy of a dialog variable.
- **VREPLACE.** Updates the value of a variable.
- **VRESET.** Sets the function pool to empty.

Dialog Control Services

- **DMOPEN.** Initializes a Dialog Manager application and establishes communication between the application and the Dialog Manager.
- **DMCLOSE.** Terminates a Dialog Manager application and ends communication with the Dialog Manager.

Available service calls are listed in Box 16.2. They are a subset of the function calls defined for the dialog interface.

DIALOG TAG LANGUAGE
The dialog tag language is used to define panels and other dialog elements. Using the techniques described in Chapter 13, an application developer can use the dialog tag language to identify the individual components that make up a panel and their content without being concerned about the formatting or interaction techniques to be used.

Box 16.3 lists the tags that are part of the dialog tag language for the Dialog Manager. They correspond closely to the tags defined in the dialog interface. Figure 16.18 shows the tags used to define the Dialog Manager application panel in Figure 16.17.

BOX 16.3   Dialog tag language tags.

General Tags

- **PANDEF (Panel Default).** Provides default information for any panel referencing it.
- **PANEL (Panel).** Identifies the beginning of a panel. Can be used to specify an associated help panel, panel depth and width, panel title, and a key list for the function key area.
- **TOPINST (Top Instruction).** Specifies instructions to be displayed at the top of the panel.
- **BOTINST (Bottom Instruction).** Specifies instructions to be displayed at the bottom of the panel.
- **CMDAREA (Command Area).** Defines the command area and the text and placement of the command field prompt.

Panel Body Area Tags

- **AREA (Area).** Identifies a scrollable portion of a panel.
- **REGION (Region).** Specifies how fields on a panel are arranged.
- **DIVIDER (Divider).** Provides a separator between panel areas.
- **UC (User Control).** Defines a field on the panel that is directly controlled by the application.
- **ICON (Icon).** References an icon.

(Continued)

BOX 16.3 (Continued)

Action Bar Tags

- **AB (Action Bar).** Defines an action bar.
- **ABC (Action Bar Choice).** Identifies an action bar choice and its associated pulldown.
- **PDC (Pulldown Choice).** Defines a choice within a pulldown.
- **ACTION (Action).** Defines the action to be taken when a pulldown choice is selected.
- **PDSEP (Pulldown Separator).** Draws a line between choices in a pulldown.
- **M (Mnemonic).** Designates a mnemonic for an action bar or pulldown choice.

Selection, Entry, and Display Field Tags

- **DTACOL (Data Column).** Identifies column widths for subsequent entry and selection fields. The dialog interface then vertically aligns the fields and provides dot leaders.
- **DTAFLD (Data Field).** Defines an entry field. Parameters include a dialog variable name, a help panel name, and prompt text to be displayed.
- **DTAFLDD (Data Field Description).** Provides additional descriptive text for a data field.
- **SELFLD (Selection Field).** Defines a selection field. The particular type of selection field is specified as a parameter.
- **CHOICE (Choice Item).** Identifies a choice within a selection field. A help panel name can be specified.
- **ACTION (Action).** Identifies the action to be taken when a particular choice is selected.
- **M (Mnemonic).** Designates a mnemonic for a selection field choice.
- **SELFLD (Selection Field).** Defines a selection field that consists of a scrollable list of choices.
- **SELCOL (Selection Column).** Defines the data that make up the list of choices in a selection field.
- **LSTFLD (List Field).** Defines a vertically scrollable list made up of columns of data.
- **LSTCOL (List Column).** Identifies a column within a list field. A column can be defined for displaying data, entering data, or both.

BOX 16.3 *(Continued)*

Information Tags

- **INFO (Information).** Identifies protected information to be displayed as part of a panel. Other information tags can be used to format the information text.

- **CAUTION (Caution).** Alerts the user of a possible risk.

- **DL (Definition List).** Used along with the DT (Define Term), DD (Define Description), DTHD (Define Term Column Heading), and DDHD (Define Description Column Heading) tags to define a list of terms and their corresponding definitions.

- **FIG (Figure).** Specifies that the following text is not to be word-wrapped and should be set off by a border or spacing. A FIGCAP tag can be used to supply a caption.

- **Hn (Heading Level n).** Identifies main topics and subtopics of information.

- **LINES (Lines).** Specifies that the following text is not to be word-wrapped.

- **LI (List Item).** Identifies an item in a list. The following text is indented from the current level of the list. Used with the OL, SL, and UL tags, which identify the type of list.

- **LP (List Part).** Identifies text that is part of the current list item.

- **NOTE (Single-Paragraph Note).** Identifies following text as a single-paragraph note.

- **NT (Multiple-Paragraph Note).** Identifies following text as a single- or multiple-paragraph note.

- **OL (Ordered List).** Identifies an ordered list of items. The items are formatted as an indented list with order identifiers (1,2,. . .a,b. . .).

- **P (Paragraph).** Identifies the following text as a paragraph.

- **PARML (Parameter List).** Identifies parameter terms and their descriptions, using the PT (Parameter Tag) and PD (Parameter Description) tags.

- **SL (Simple List).** Identifies a simple list of terms, formatted as an indented list with no item identifiers.

- **UL (Unordered List).** Identifies an unordered list of terms. The items are formatted as an indented list with bullets, hyphens, and dashes used as item identifiers.

- **WARNING (Warning).** Alerts the user of possible error conditions.

- **XMP (Example).** Identifies an example of system input or output.

(Continued)

BOX 16.3 *(Continued)*

Variable Tags

- **VARLIST (Variable List).** Establishes the access technique for specific variables.

- **VARDCL (Variable Declaration).** Establishes characteristics for specific variables.

- **ASSIGNL (Assignment List).** Identifies the beginning of an assignment list.

- **ASSIGNI (Assignment Item).** Defines an entry in an assignment list and provides the association between a value in one variable and the value to be assigned to another.

- **CHECKL (Checklist).** Defines a list of validity checks to be applied to a variable or class of variables. Multiple checklists referencing the same variable or variable class are ANDed together.

- **CHECKI (Check Item).** Defines a single validity check within a checklist. Multiple check items within a checklist are ORed together.

- **XLATL (Translate List).** Identifies the beginning of a translate list used to map between internal dialog variable values and values displayed for the user or entered by the user. A translate list can be defined for a specific variable or a variable class.

- **XLATI (Translate Item).** Defines a single set of mapping values within a translate list.

- **LIT (Literal).** Identifies a string where all blanks are significant and are included in the value.

- **VARCLASS (Variable Class).** Defines information related to a variable class. CHECKL, CHECKI, XLATL, and XLATI tags can be used within the scope of a VARCLASS tag.

Command Table Tags

- **CMD (Command Definition).** Defines a command in the application command table.

- **CMDACT (Command Action).** Defines the action to be taken when an associated command is issued.

- **CMDTBL (Command Table).** Begins the definition of an application command table.

- **T (Truncation).** Designates the minimum command name that must be entered in order to issue a command.

BOX 16.3   *(Continued)*

Message Tags

- **MSG (Message).** Defines a message.
- **MSGMBR (Message Member).** Defines a member of a message library.
- **VARSUB (Variable Substitution).** Includes variables in a message definition. When the message is displayed, the current value of the variable is shown.

Key Mapping List Tags

- **KEYI (Key Item).** Associates a command with a key.
- **KEYL (Key List).** Defines a key list for one or more panels.

Help Tags

- **HELP (Help).** Begins the definition of a help panel.
- **ISYN (Index Synonym).** Maps synonyms to search words for index topics.
- **ITOP (Index Topic).** Associates a topic with a help panel.
- **ICMD (Index Command).** Associates a command with a help panel.
- **RP (Reference Phrase).** Specifies a word or phrase in help text that has additional help information associated with it.
- **SORTKEY (Sort Key).** Defines a sort key used instead of the actual command or index topic when creating an index.

HELP PANELS   Help panels can be associated with different application panel elements, and are then displayed by the Dialog Manager when help is requested for a panel or a particular element. An extended help panel can be associated with a particular application panel by specifying the help panel name as part of the PANEL tag. A help panel can also be associated with each of the following:

- Action bar choice
- Pulldown choice
- Function key
- Command

```
<!-- ****************************************************** -->
<!--              F I R S T   P A N E L                    -->
<!--              DMP101 - Order Exotic Birds              -->
<!-- ****************************************************** -->

<panel name=DMP101 help=chp002 width=44 depth=17 keylist=kylst1>Order Exotic Birds
  <!--                                                    -->
  <!--              TOP INSTRUCTION TAG                   -->
  <!--                                                    -->
  <topinst>           Select a breed(s) from list:
  <!--                                                    -->
  <!--              AREA AND REGION STARTS HERE           -->
  <!--                                                    -->
  <region dir=horiz>
    <divider type=none gutter=7>
    <region>
    <!--                                                  -->
    <!--               SELECTION INSTRUCTION TAGS         -->
    <!--                                                  -->
      <selfld type=multi>
        <choice help=chp010 checkvar=pbird1><m>Galah Cockatoo,  $600.00
        <choice help=chp011 checkvar=pbird2><m>Sulphur Crested Cockatoo,  $650.00
        <choice help=chp012 checkvar=pbird3><m>Umbrella Cockatoo,  $750.00
        <choice help=chp007 checkvar=pbird4><m>Blue and Gold Macaw,  $800.00
        <choice help=chp008 checkvar=pbird5>S<m>carlet Macaw,  $900.00
        <choice help=chp009 checkvar=pbird6>S<m>evere Macaw,  $450.00
      </selfld>
    </region>
  </region>
  <!--                                                    -->
  <!--               SELECTION INSTRUCTION TAGS           -->
  <!--                                                    -->
    <divider type=none gutter=1>
  <region dir=horiz>
    <divider type=none gutter=6>
    <region>
      <selfld help=chp021 type=single>Choose sex:
        <choice checkvar=ptype1 match=1><m>Male
        <choice checkvar=ptype1 match=2><m>Female
      </selfld>
    </region>
    <divider type=none gutter=8>
    <region>
      <selfld help=chp021 type=single>Choose age:
        <choice checkvar=ptype2 match=1><m>Juvenile
        <choice checkvar=ptype2 match=2><m>Mature
      </selfld>
    </region>
  </region>
    <divider type=none gutter=1>
  <region dir=horiz>
    <divider type=none gutter=2>
    <selfld help=KEYSHELP type=action dir=horiz>
      <choice checkvar=fkaType match=1><m>Order
        <action setvar=fkaType value=1>
        <action run=ENTER>
      <choice checkvar=fkaType match=2><m>Cancel
        <action setvar=fkaType value=2>
        <action run=CANCEL>
      <choice checkvar=fkaType match=3><m>Help
        <action run=EXHELP>
    </selfld>
  </region>
</panel>
```

Figure 16.18 Tags used to define the Dialog Manager application panel from Fig. 16.17.

274

- Message
- Reference phrase in a help panel

Help panels are defined using the help tags that are part of the dialog tag language.

RELATIONSHIP OF DIALOG MANAGER TO PRESENTATION MANAGER

Both the Dialog Manager and the Presentation Manager support the development of applications with a CUA-consistent user interface based on the graphical model. Action bars and pulldown menus are supported, and control fields such as radio buttons, check boxes, list boxes, entry fields, and scroll bars are formatted according to the graphical model. Various window elements, such as the window title and window icons, are provided and are positioned according to the standard window layout in CUA.

The primary differences between the Presentation Manager and the Dialog Manager are that the Presentation Manager provides additional capabilities to the application developer, but is more complex to use. The Presentation Manager, for example, allows an application to display multiple primary and secondary windows at the same time, whereas a Dialog Manager application can use only one primary window. Also, the Presentation Manager has extensive support for graphic input and output. The Presentation Manager is more complex to use because of its event-driven and message-oriented application structure and the large number of messages and function calls (approximately 950) that are part of it. With the Dialog Manager, a more traditional procedural application structure is used, and only 12 service calls are used. One other difference is that the Dialog Manager enforces CUA conformance, whereas the Presentation Manager implements it through defaults, which can be overridden by the application developer.

The Dialog Manager is actually a Presentation Manager application. The services the Dialog Manager provides are based on the use of underlying Presentation Manager functions. Thus, a Dialog Manager application actually runs under the Presentation Manager windowing environment, and will have the same appearance and interactions as a Presentation Manager application, within the constraints of the windowing facilities supported by the Dialog Manager.

Generally, the Presentation Manager would be used when graphics are required, when the user interface must be tailored, or performance is a key consideration. The Dialog Manager would be used when application development productivity is critical and the more restricted facilities of the Dialog Manager are adequate for the application.

17 THE OFFICEVISION PRODUCT FAMILY

INTRODUCTION   The OfficeVision family of products is IBM's first major SAA-compliant application. It supports office requirements in a consistent manner across the various SAA computing system and operating system environments. The products that make up the family and the environments in which they operate include

- **OfficeVision/2 LAN Series.** For personal computers running the OS/2 Extended Edition operating system in a local area network environment.
- **OfficeVision/400 Series.** For AS/400 midrange processors running the OS/400 operating system.
- **OfficeVision/MVS Series.** For large-system processors running the MVS operating system.
- **OfficeVision/VM Series.** For large-system processors running the VM system software.

The OfficeVision products provide a consistent set of office services across the different environments, a user interface that is consistent in appearance across the products, and the ability to interconnect the products with full sharing and interchange of all types of information. Providing complete support for office services in all the environments, with consistency in both function and appearance and full interconnection and interchange capabilities, is a difficult goal. Initial releases of the OfficeVision products represent a first step toward that goal, with an understanding that the products will continue to evolve over time until full consistency and a full range of functions have been implemented.

Initial releases of the various OfficeVision products differ in function and appearance because of a need to maintain compatibility with earlier office products that IBM offered. With this compatibility, an installation is able to convert to OfficeVision products without having to retrain users familiar with the IBM office system product that is currently used. The OfficeVision/400 Series is based on the AS/400 Office product, and the first release of the OfficeVision/400 Series product is considered and treated as a new release of AS/400 Office. Similarly, the OfficeVision/VM Series is based on the PROFS product, and was made available as a new release of PROFS. The OfficeVision/MVS Series product combines the functions previously offered in the MVS environment by Personal Services/CICS, Application Support Facility, and Personal Manager.

In this chapter we examine the OfficeVision products in terms of their overall design, with emphasis on consistency and integration, rather than focusing on the status of the implementations that exist at any given point in time, or on the limitations or differences that may still be present as you read this.

OFFICEVISION FUNCTIONS

The sets of services that are part of the OfficeVision family of products have support for the following categories of function:

- Document processing
- Electronic mail
- Calendar management
- Library services
- Decision support

The following sections discuss each of the above categories.

Document Processing

Document processing in OfficeVision is provided by the *Correspondence Processor,* which supports creating, viewing, revising, and printing notes and documents. The correspondence processor operates in a what-you-see-is-what-you-get (WYSIWYG) style and supports basic functions such as block operations and search-and-replace processing. Style templates can be defined and used to handle the standard formatting of similar documents. Typographical-style fonts can be used for text documents. Spelling checks and synonym searches are available, with a wide range of dictionaries supporting spell checking for documents in various languages. Composite documents that contain text, graphics, and images can be processed. Document interchange between the different OfficeVision products and other IBM office products is also supported.

Electronic Mail

Electronic mail facilities allow users to send, reply to, and forward notes, documents, and data files. When sending information, multiple copies can be sent and acknowledgments can be requested. OfficeVision provides in-basket and out-basket facilities for tracking the status of mail that is sent and received. Other users can be granted access to a particular user's mail baskets. Both public and personal address books can be used to keep track of the names and addresses of other users on the office system. The address book facilities provide for the use of distribution lists, nicknames, and dynamically generated distribution lists called *search lists*. Address books can also maintain phone numbers, and if the proper hardware is available, telephone numbers can be automatically dialed.

Calendar Management

OfficeVision supports the use of a personal calendar for each user. Entries can be made, and the calendar can be viewed showing a daily, weekly, monthly, or six-month time span. As with mail baskets, other users can be granted access to any user's personal calendar. Both single and recurring meetings can be scheduled, and the system has the ability to check for schedule conflicts and to send automatic notifications to meeting participants.

Library Services

Library services provide for storing, retrieving, updating, copying, and deleting documents and data files. Both personal and shared libraries can be used. Other users can be granted access to a personal library. Various parameters can be defined when an object is stored in a library, and searches can be done based on sets of parameter values.

Decision Support

The decision support capabilities allow a user to query, extract, and analyze data. Reports can be generated in various formats using the data, and charts can be prepared to reflect the data in graphical form. Report and chart formats can be predefined to allow users to employ the facilities with little training.

Function Availability

Not all of the functions that we have described were included in the initial releases of all of the OfficeVision products, but IBM's stated design goal is to have the products evolve to support a common set of functions, where each OfficeVision product provides the same set of integrated office services. The OfficeVision products are also designed to allow add-on products to be integrated into them that provide additional office or application functions. Such add-on products will be built by IBM as well as other software vendors. Facilities provided by add-on products include interfaces designed for executive-level access to data, facsimile processing, document editors other than the included Correspondence Processor, statistical analysis packages, project management systems, and a wide range of business applications that can be made accessible through the OfficeVision interface.

User Access

For a user to gain access to OfficeVision functions, the user must be registered at an office node that provides the various office services. For the OfficeVision/2 LAN Series, a personal computer operating as a LAN server that runs the OfficeVision software acts as the office node. For the products that run on the midrange and large-system processors (OfficeVision/400 Series, OfficeVision/VM Series, and OfficeVision/MVS Series), the host processor is the office node.

There are different ways that a user can be attached to an office node, depending on the type of workstation the user has and the particular OfficeVision product that is installed. The next sections discuss these various connection methods.

OFFICEVISION/2
LAN SERIES
ACCESS

With the OfficeVision/2 LAN Series product, users access the office node (LAN office server) using a programmable workstation on a local area network. The workstation can be running either the DOS or the OS/2 Extended Edition operating system, as illustrated in Fig. 17.1. The OfficeVision/2 LAN Series consists of two programs:

- **OS/2 Office.** This program provides office services and supports the OfficeVision interface for workstations running OS/2 Extended Edition. A user running the OS/2 Office program works with the common graphical user interface implemented by all OfficeVision products.

- **OS/2 DOS Requester.** The OS/2 Office DOS Requester program provides the interface to OS/2 Office services for workstations running DOS. A user running the OS/2 DOS Requester program works with a user interface that is similar in appearance to that implemented by the OS/2 Office program.

The interface to OS/2 Office complies with the rules and guidelines defined by the CUA graphical model and is an implementation of the Workplace Environment. Figure 17.2 shows the main menu from this interface and includes many of the icons used for the various office functions.

The OS/2 Office program is the basis by which consistency in function and appearance is made available across the different OfficeVision platforms. OS/2 Office is not only included with the OfficeVision/2 LAN Series product but is also used by the other three OfficeVision products—the OfficeVision/400 Series, OfficeVision/MVS Series, and OfficeVision/VM Series—to implement a consistent user interface and to provide a common set of services.

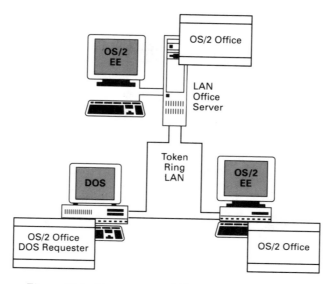

Figure 17.1   User access to OfficeVision/2 LAN Series.

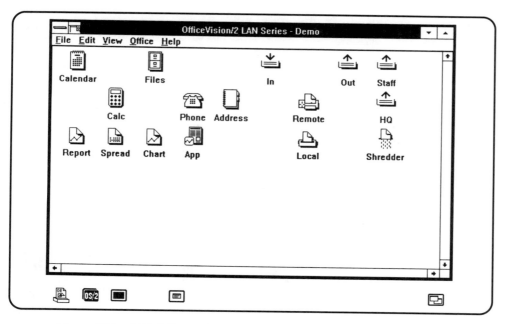

Figure 17.2   OS/2 Office main menu including many of the icons used for office functions.

OFFICEVISION/400 SERIES ACCESS

Figure 17.3 illustrates the different ways in which users can access an OfficeVision/400 Series office node. These connection methods are as follows:

- **Nonprogrammable Terminals.** When users are directly attached using a nonprogrammable terminal, a menu- and function key–driven interface is provided that, in the first product releases, is compatible with the interface used in the original AS/400 Office product.

- **Personal Computers Running DOS.** The Personal Computer Support program allows a personal computer running the DOS operating system to be directly attached to an AS/400 office node. With this option, a single menu gives the user access to both host-based office services through OfficeVision/400 and personal computer–based applications. When the user accesses OfficeVision/400 in this manner, the personal computer operates in terminal emulation mode and the nonprogrammable terminal interface is used. The Personal Computer Support program automatically handles the switching between terminal emulation mode and normal DOS operating mode and also helps in handling data transfer between the AS/400 host processor and the personal computer.

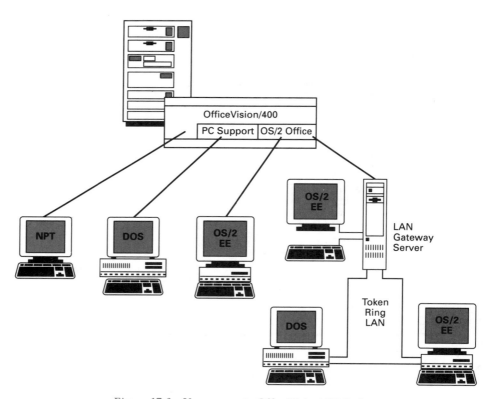

Figure 17.3   User access to OfficeVision/400 Series.

- **Personal Computers Running OS/2 Extended Edition.** The OS/2 Office program allows a user at a personal computer running the OS/2 Extended Edition operating system to be directly attached to the host processor. With this method, the user employs the graphical user interface that is consistent across all four OfficeVision platforms.

- **LAN Gateway Server.** A LAN gateway server can be attached to the AS/400 host processor. The LAN Gateway server runs the OfficeVision/2 LAN Series software and allows both DOS and OS/2 Extended Edition workstations to be attached to the LAN gateway server. OS/2 Extended Edition users employ the same graphical interface that is supported for the previous connection option. DOS users that are attached to a LAN Gateway server communicate with the server using the OS/2 DOS Requester program described earlier and work with a user interface that is similar to that implemented by the OS/2 Office program.

OFFICEVISION/VM SERIES AND OFFICEVISION/MVS SERIES ACCESS

The ways in which users can access an OfficeVision/MVS Series and OfficeVision/VM Series host processor are shown in Fig. 17.4. These connection methods are similar to those for the OfficeVision/400 Series:

- **Nonprogrammable Terminals.** Users with nonprogrammable terminals can be directly attached to an OfficeVision host processor. The interface used is based on menus and function keys, and resembles the original office products from which these versions of OfficeVision evolved: PROFS and Personal Services/CICS.

- **Personal Computers Running DOS.** The DOS Office Direct Connect program allows personal computers running DOS to be directly attached to the host processor. A single menu provides access to OfficeVision–based office services in terminal emulation mode and to personal computer applications in normal DOS operating mode. As with the Personal Computer Support program, switching between modes is handled automatically and data transfer is facilitated. The same user interface as for nonprogrammable terminals is used.

- **Personal Computers Running OS/2 Extended Edition.** An OS/2 Extended Edition workstation can be directly attached to the large-system host allowing the user to employ the common graphical user interface.

- **LAN Gateway Server.** The OS/2 Office program also provides for connecting a LAN gateway server that runs the OfficeVision/2 LAN Series product. As with OS/2 Office in the other environments, OS/2 users see the same iconic interface, have access to the same office services, and have the same online help and tutorial facilities available. DOS users that are attached to a LAN Gateway server communicate with the server using the OS/2 DOS Requester program described earlier and work with a user interface that is similar to that implemented by the OS/2 Office program.

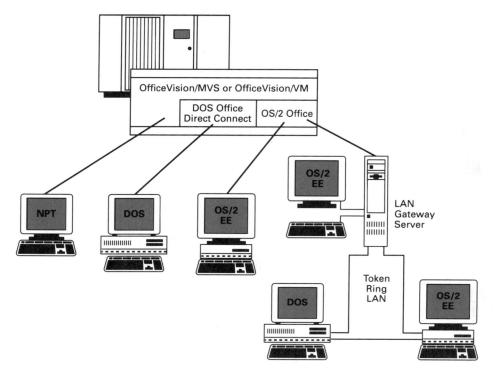

Figure 17.4   User access to OfficeVision/MVS and OfficeVision/VM Series.

OFFICEVISION NETWORKS

The OfficeVision family of products has been designed to allow an installation to build office networks that implement multiple office nodes on different types of processor. This is illustrated in Fig. 17.5. As shown at the bottom of the illustration, local area networks can be interconnected, and an OfficeVision/2 LAN Series office node can support users from an interconnected local area network. The various OfficeVision products can also be interconnected with one another. A user is registered with one particular office node and receives office services from that node. The user is also able to communicate across the network with users at other office nodes. Users can send and receive all types of information across the network, including notes, documents, calendars, and data files. Users can also access libraries at other office nodes, assuming they have the proper authorization. This full set of interconnection and intercommunication facilities was not supported in initial releases of the OfficeVision products but is the goal toward which the products will evolve. Also, device limitations may restrict a particular user's ability to process certain types of data, such as graphics and images.

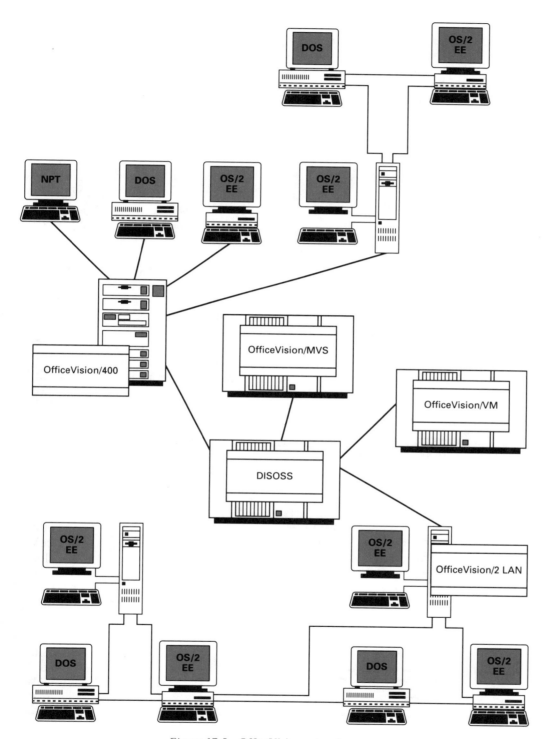

Figure 17.5 OfficeVision network.

THE OS/2 OFFICE INTERFACE AND CUA

The OS/2 Office interface that is part of OfficeVision is designed to be consistent with the graphical model of CUA, and also the Workplace Environment that is part of the advanced interface. As with the user interface to the OS/2 operating system, the OfficeVision user interface and the CUA architecture itself are evolving in parallel.

IMPLEMENTING THE GRAPHICAL MODEL

The OS/2 Office interface is window-based. Figure 17.2 showed the main menu, or workplace window. As shown, the windows contain a window title bar, with the system menu icon and window sizing icons. An action bar provides access to the primary actions for the application. Standard scroll bars allow the window client area to be scrolled. The action bar includes standard actions defined as part of the graphical model of CUA. Figure 17.6 shows the pulldown for the File action. The choices in the pulldown correspond to the Workplace Environment definition for File in a list handler window. The pulldown for Edit is shown in Fig. 17.7. For Edit, the Workplace Environment uses the standard CUA graphical model choices. Figure 17.8 shows the pulldown for View, with its application-specific choices.

Full help facilities are available. Contextual help screens provide informa-

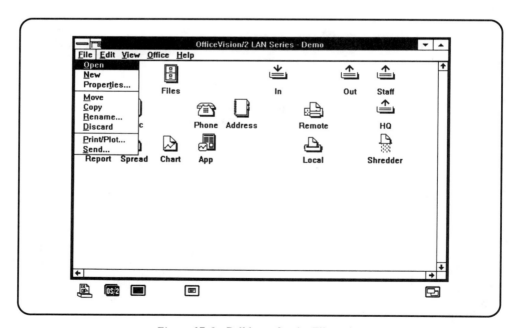

Figure 17.6 Pulldown for the File action.

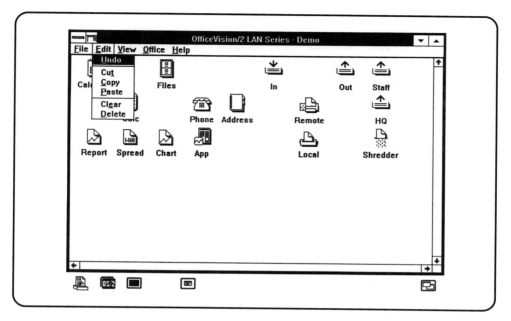

Figure 17.7 Pulldown for the Edit action.

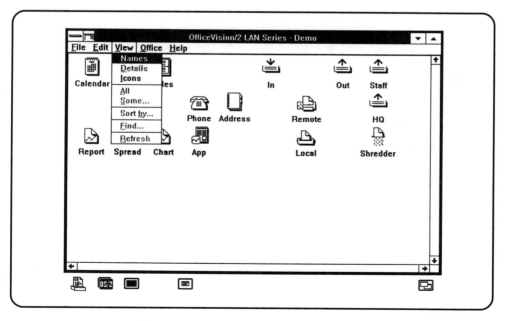

Figure 17.8 Pulldown for the View action.

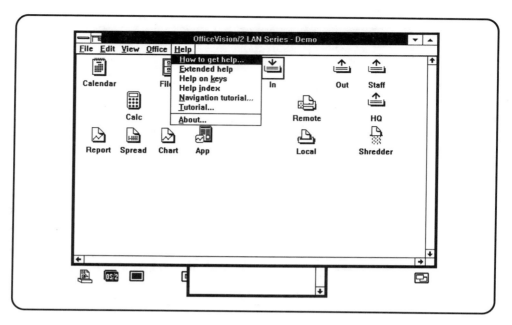

Figure 17.9 Help pulldown.

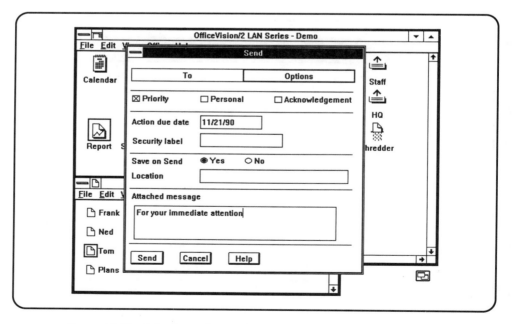

Figure 17.10 Selection and entry fields implemented using the controls defined in the graphical model.

tion related to the task in progress and the point that has been reached in performing the task. Extended help panels provide more general explanations. Certain phrases in a help panel may be highlighted, and reference phrase help is available for these phrases. Figure 17.9 shows the Help pulldown. As shown, Help for Help, Extended Help, Keys Help, Help Index, and Tutorials are available.

Selection and entry fields are implemented using the controls defined in the graphical model. This is illustrated in Fig. 17.10.

IMPLEMENTING THE WORKPLACE ENVIRONMENT

The Workplace Environment is icon-oriented. The OfficeVision workplace window illustrates various types of icon (see Fig. 17.2). Data objects include calendars and documents; container objects include file cabinets, in-basket, and out-basket; and device objects include printers, a shredder, and a telephone. Direct manipulation of the icons can be used to invoke various kinds of processing. Figure 17.11 shows the results of selecting the in-basket. Since the in-basket is a container, a list handler window is used to display its contents. Selecting one of the documents in the in-basket results in the window shown in Fig. 17.12, which is an object handler window.

Icons can be copied and moved as well as selected. Dragging a document

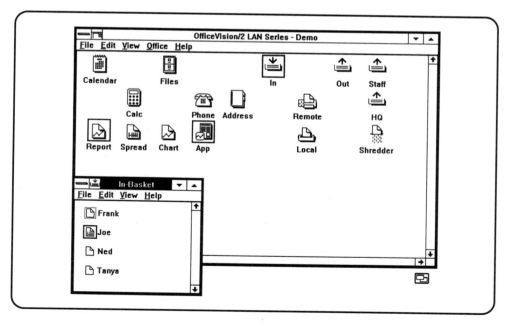

Figure 17.11   Result of selecting the in-basket.

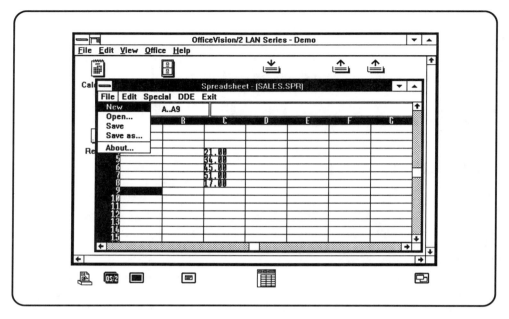

Figure 17.12 Window resulting from selecting a document in the in-basket.

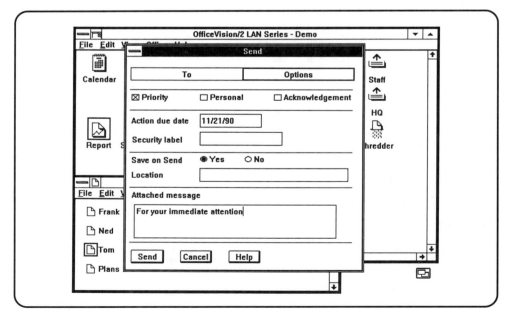

Figure 17.13 Title bar mini-icon.

icon to the printer causes the document to be printed. Dragging the document to the file cabinet causes it to be stored. When an object is dragged to a container, such as the file cabinet, it is moved, which causes its icon to be removed from the in-basket. The title bar mini-icon, as shown in Fig. 17.13, can be used for direct manipulation operations on a selected object. Here the selected document can be printed, sent, or stored using the title bar mini-icon.

OTHER OFFICEVISION INTERFACES

Other interfaces to OfficeVision are available, but are not based on the Workplace Environment. When a PC DOS computer is used to access OfficeVision, the interface is menu-driven and follows the CUA guidelines for the basic interface. Selection fields use numbering for choices, and the panel contains a function key area.

The nonprogrammable terminal interfaces to OfficeVision reflect the earlier products from which OfficeVision evolved, such as PROFS, AS/400 Office, and Personal Services/CICS. Each of these interfaces is different in appearance, and since the products were designed prior to the development of SAA, generally do not reflect CUA formatting and interaction guidelines.

18 ISPF

INTRODUCTION

The *Interactive System Productivity System* (ISPF) is an IBM program product that provides services to interactive applications. There are versions of ISPF for both the MVS and the VM environments. ISPF services assist the application in displaying panels, tailoring files, and using variables and tables. An application that runs under control of ISPF is a *dialog*. ISPF dialog management services can be used to develop and control the execution of dialogs. These services include an implementation of the dialog tag language that we introduced in Chapter 13, which can be used to define panels consistent with CUA guidelines. The services also support CUA-defined processing options such as pop-up windows and standard actions, such as Exit and Cancel.

DEFINING THE USER INTERFACE IN ISPF

ISPF provides facilities that allow dialog interfaces to be developed that are consistent with the text subset of the graphical model. The primary development tool is the dialog tag language (DTL), which can be used to define panels containing action bars and pulldowns, single- and multiple-choice selection fields, entry fields, scrollable display fields, a message area, a command area, and a function key area—all in CUA format. The dialog tag language can also be used to define messages and help panels.

In addition to the dialog tag language, general ISPF facilities provide for

- Displaying the function key area, command area, and message area in CUA-defined locations within a panel

- Controlling how the function key area is displayed
- Using pop-up windows
- Providing the standard actions Exit, Cancel, Display panel IDs, and Display keys
- Controlling cursor movement in CUA-defined ways

DIALOG TAG
LANGUAGE
FACILITIES

As discussed in Chapter 13, the dialog tag language can be used to define panels, messages, command tables, and key lists. Items defined with the dialog tag language are then run through an ISPF conversion utility that converts the tag language into the ISPF source language. The ISPF source language is then used to generate a dialog application that runs under the control of ISPF. The ISPF dialog tag language is based on the ISO Standard Generalized Markup Language (SGML). Although IBM has not committed to implementing the dialog interface outside of the OS/2 environment, the ISPF dialog tag language is consistent with the dialog interface defined as part of the Common Programming Interface of SAA (see Chapter 13).

Many of the tags listed in this chapter are identical to those in Chapter 13. They are listed here again because ISPF supports several tags that are not defined in the dialog interface specification, and does not support some of the tags that are in the specification.

PANEL TAGS

Box 18.1 lists the tags that can be used to define application and help panels. The general panel tags provide information about the panel as a whole, including its dimensions, and can be used to specify the overall format of the panel. The panel body area tags define general formatting for the panel body area. The action bar tags are used to define the action bar and its associated action bar and pulldown choices. There are tags for defining selection and entry fields, and selection fields can be specified as either single choice or multiple choice. The display field tags can be used to define displayed information. The associated information region tags shown in Box 18.2 can be used following an INFO tag to specify a number of different formats for the displayed information. The help tags are used specifically for help panels. In addition, the AREA, INFO, REGION, and information region tags can be used to format the information displayed in a help panel.

BOX 18.1 Application panel tags.

General Tags

- **PANDEF (Panel Default).** Provides default information for any panel referencing it.

- **PANEL (Panel).** Identifies the beginning of a panel. Can be used to specify an associated help panel, panel depth and width, panel title, and a key list for the function key area.

- **TOPINST (Top Instruction).** Specifies instructions to be displayed at the top of the panel.

- **BOTINST (Bottom Instruction).** Specifies instructions to be displayed at the bottom of the panel.

- **CMDAREA (Command Area).** Defines the command area and the text and placement of the command field prompt.

Panel Body Area Tags

- **AREA (Area).** Identifies the text area on a panel body.

- **REGION (Region).** Specifies how fields on a panel are arranged.

- **DIVIDER (Divider).** Creates a blank or solid divider line within the text portion of the panel body.

Action Bar Tags

- **AB (Action Bar).** Defines an action bar.

- **ABC (Action Bar Choice).** Identifies an action bar choice and its associated pulldown.

- **PDC (Pulldown Choice).** Defines a choice within a pulldown.

- **ACTION (Action).** Specifies an action to be taken for an action bar pulldown choice.

- **M (Mnemonic).** Designates a mnemonic for an action bar or pulldown choice.

Selection and Entry Field Tags

- **DTACOL (Data Column).** Identifies column widths for subsequent entry and selection fields. The dialog interface then vertically aligns the fields and provides dot leaders.

- **DTAFLD (Data Field).** Defines an entry field. Parameters include a dialog variable name, a help panel name, and prompt text to be displayed.

(Continued)

BOX 18.1 *(Continued)*

- **DTAFLDD (Data Field Description).** Provides additional descriptive text for a data field.
- **SELFLD (Selection Field).** Defines a selection field. The particular type of selection field is specified as a parameter.
- **CHOICE (Choice Item).** Identifies a choice within a selection field. A help panel name can be specified.
- **ACTION (Action).** Specifies an action to be taken for a selection field choice.
- **M (Mnemonic).** Designates a mnemonic for a selection field choice.

Display Field Tags

- **LSTFLD (List Field).** Defines a vertically scrollable list made up of columns of data used for a table display.
- **LSTCOL (List Column).** Identifies a column within a list field.
- **INFO (Information).** Identifies protected information to be displayed as part of a panel. Other information region tags can be used to format the information text.

Help Panel Tags

- **HELP (Help Panel).** Begins the definition of a help panel.
- **HELPDEF (Help Default).** Defines default information that is common to different help panels displayed by an application.
- **RP (Reference Phrase).** Specifies a word or phrase that has help text associated with it.

Tag Syntax

The general syntax for tags is

- A less than sign ($<$)
- The tag name
- Optionally one or more parameters
- A greater than sign ($>$)
- Optionally text to be displayed as part of the panel

BOX 18.2   Information region tags.

- **CAUTION (Caution).** Alerts the user of a possible risk.

- **DL (Definition List).** Used along with the DT (Define Term), DD (Define Description), DTHD (Define Term Column Heading), and DDHD (Define Description Column Heading) tags to define a list of terms and their corresponding definitions.

- **FIG (Figure).** Specifies that the following text is not to be word-wrapped, and should be set off by a border or spacing. A FIGCAP tag can be used to supply a caption.

- **Hn (Heading Level n).** Identifies main topics and subtopics of information.

- **LINES (Lines).** Specifies that the following text is not to be word-wrapped.

- **LI (List Item).** Identifies an item in a list. The following text is indented from the current level of the list. Used with the OL, SL, and UL tags, which identify the type of list as ordered, simple or unordered.

- **LP (List Part).** Identifies text that is part of the current list item.

- **NOTE (Single-Paragraph Note).** Identifies following text as a single-paragraph note.

- **OL (Ordered List).** Identifies an ordered list of items.

- **P (Paragraph).** Identifies the following text as a paragraph.

- **PARML (Parameter List).** Identifies parameter terms and their descriptions, using the PT (Parameter Tag) and PD (Parameter Description) tags.

- **SL (Simple List).** Identifies a simple list of terms.

- **UL (Unordered List).** Identifies an unordered list of terms.

- **WARNING (Warning).** Alerts the user of possible error conditions.

- **XMP (Example).** Identifies an example of system input or output.

For example, the following tag defines an entry field and the prompt text (Name) to be displayed for the field:

```
<DTAFLD  DATAVAR  =  name
         REQUIRED  =  no
         DISPLAY  =  yes>
         Name
```

If one tag contains other tags nested within it, the end of the tag is indicated by repeating the tag name with a slash preceding it. Here a selection field is defined by a SELFLD tag followed by a series of CHOICE tags:

<SELFLD . . . .
                  .
                  .
<CHOICE . . . .
                  .
                  .
<CHOICE . . . .
                  .
                  .
</SELFLD>

Sample Panel Definition

Figure 18.1 shows a sample panel. Figure 18.2 shows the panel definition code that would be used to generate the panel in Fig. 18.1. The PANEL tag provides basic information about the panel, including the help panel associated with this panel and the key list that is used to define the contents of the function key area. The action bar contains three choices, defined with the three ABC tags. Each ABC tag has nested within it a set of PDC tags defining the pulldown choices

```
   File   Search   Help
                            Library Card Registration
   Type in patron's name and card number (if applicable)

   Date . . . . 89/02/28
   Card No. . .  _____    (A seven digit number)
   Name . . . .  _____    (Last, First, M.I.)

   Choose one of the following. . __   1.  New
                                       2.  Renewal
                                       3.  Replacement
   Check valid branches.
   _   North Branch
   _   South Branch
   _   East Branch
   _   West Branch



   Enter a command ===> _____
    F1=Help      F3=Exit      F4=Actions   F5=Display   F12=Cancel
```

Figure 18.1   Sample panel.

```
<PANEL NAME     = ab
       HELP     = cnvhhlp
       KEYLIST  = convkeys
       DEPTH    = 24
       WIDTH    = 80  >
       Library Card Registration

<!-- ACTION BAR DEFINITION -->
<AB>

<ABC>File
     <PDC NAME=addent>Add Entry
         <ACTION RUN=add>

     <PDC NAME=addent>Delete Entry
         <ACTION RUN=delete>

     <PDC NAME=addent>Update Entry
         <ACTION RUN=update>

<ABC>Search
     <PDC NAME=srchnm CHECKVAR=whchsrch MATCH=1>Search on name
         <ACTION SETVAR=whchsrch VALUE=1>
         <ACTION RUN=Search>

     <PDC NAME=srchid CHECKVAR=whchsrch MATCH=2>Search on Card Number
         <ACTION SETVAR=whchsrch VALUE=2>
         <ACTION RUN=Search>

<ABC>Help
     <PDC NAME=cnvhlp>Help...
         <ACTION RUN=cnvhhlp>
     <PDC NAME=exthlp>Extended Help...
         <ACTION RUN=cnvxhlp>

     <PDC NAME=keyhlp>Keys Help...
         <ACTION RUN=cnvkhlp>
</ABC>

</AB>

<!-- TOP INSTRUCTION -->
<TOPINST>
Type in patron's name and card number (if applicable)
<AREA>
<DTACOL PMTWIDTH=12
        ENTWIDTH=30
        DESWIDTH=25
        SELWIDTH=30>

<DTAFLD DATAVAR  = curdate
        PMTWIDTH = 10
        ENTWIDTH = 10
        PMTLOC   = BEFORE
        USAGE    = OUT>
        Date

<DTAFLD DATAVAR  = cardno
        VARCLASS = number
        ENTWIDTH = 7
        DESWIDTH = 25
        ALIGN    = END
        PMTLOC   = BEFORE
        HELP     = crdhlp
        USAGE    = BOTH>
        Card No.
<DTAFLDD>(A seven digit number)

<DTAFLD DATAVAR  = name
        REQUIRED = NO
        DISPLAY  = YES>
```

Figure 18.2 Dialog tag language.

(Continued)

```
     Name
<DTAFLDD>(Last, First, M.I.)

<DIVIDER>

<!-- SINGLE CHOICE SELECTION FIELD -->
<SELFLD NAME    = select
        PMTWIDTH = 30
        TYPE     = single
        PMTLOC   = BEFORE
        Choose one of the following.

<CHOICE CHECKVAR = card
        MATCH    = 'NEW'>
        New
        <ACTION SETVAR=card VALUE='NEW'>

<CHOICE CHECKVAR = card
        MATCH    = 'RENEW'>
        Renewal
        <ACTION SETVAR=card VALUE='RENEW'>

<CHOICE CHECKVAR = card
        MATCH    = 'REPLACE'>
        Replacement
        <ACTION SETVAR=card VALUE='REPLACE'>

</SELFLD>
</DTACOL>

<!-- MULTI CHOICE SELECTION FIELD -->
<SELFLD TYPE    = multi
        PMTWIDTH = 30
        SELWIDTH = 25>
        Check valid branches.

<CHOICE NAME    = no
        HELP    = nthhlp
        CHECKVAR = north>
        North Branch
        <ACTION SETVAR=north VALUE=1>

<CHOICE NAME    = so
        HELP    = sthhlp
        CHECKVAR = south>
        South Branch
        <ACTION SETVAR=south VALUE=1>

<CHOICE NAME    = ea
        HELP    = esthlp
        CHECKVAR = east>
        East Branch
        <ACTION SETVAR=east VALUE=1>

<CHOICE NAME    = we
        HELP    = wsthlp
        CHECKVAR = west>
        West Branch
        <ACTION SETVAR=west VALUE=1>

</SELFLD>
</AREA>
<CMDAREA>Enter a command
</PANEL>
```

Figure 18.2   (Continued)

for that action bar choice. ACTION tags are used within the PDC tag to define actions to be taken when that choice is selected.

The DTACOL tag is used to align subsequent entry and selection fields. The three entry fields in the panel are defined with DTAFLD tags. The two selection fields are defined with the SELFLD tag and a set of nested CHOICE and ACTION tags. The first field is a single-choice field (TYPE = single), and the second field is multiple-choice (TYPE = multi). Single-choice fields are automatically formatted with numbers and a single-choice entry field. Multiple-choice fields are formatted with a choice entry field for each choice. The dialog tag language defines a mnemonics tag (M), but mnemonics are not currently supported by ISPF. Thus, the M tag can be coded to identify mnemonics, but the mnemonics will not be identified on the resulting screen and will not be available as a selection method.

The CMDAREA tag defines a command area and its associated prompt.

VARIABLE PROCESSING

Variables can be defined and used with entry fields to check values that are entered for validity, to set one variable to a particular value based on the value of another variable, and to translate between a value that is displayed and a value that is used for internal processing. The tags used for defining and processing variables are shown in Box 18.3.

```
                 Hotel Register


     Type in the following information for the hotel
     register.
     Name. .  .  .  .  .   _____
     Length of stay.  _____
     Room type  .  .  .   _____
     Payment Method.  _____

     Press Enter to Continue
```

Figure 18.3 Data entry panel.

Figure 18.3 contains an example of a data entry panel. Figure 18.4 shows the dialog tag language definitions that would be used to generate the panel in Fig. 18.3. A variable class table is defined preceding the PANEL definition. The variable class table defines checking of input values that should be done for the different types of variables, using CHECKI and CHECKL tags. For one variable class, a translation of values is also specified. Here a single-digit numerical value is used internally, while a descriptive name for the payment method is used on screen.

Within the DTAFLD tags, each entry field is associated with a variable class and the checking and translation associated with that class. This association is defined using the VARCLASS parameter. Within the DTAFLD tag defining the room type, ASSIGNL and ASSIGNI are used to set the variable xrm to a numerical value of 1 or 2 based on the value entered in the data entry field.

BOX 18.3   Variable definition tags.

- **VARLIST (Variable List).** Establishes the access technique for specific variables.

- **ASSIGNL (Assignment List).** Identifies the beginning of an assignment list.

- **ASSIGNI (Assignment Item).** Defines an entry in an assignment list and provides the association between a value in one variable and the value to be assigned to another.

- **CHECKL (Checklist).** Defines a list of validity checks to be applied to values that the user enters for variables.

- **CHECKI (Check Item).** Defines a single validity check within a checklist.

- **XLATL (Translate List).** Identifies the beginning of a translate list used to map between internal dialog variable values and values displayed for the user or entered by the user.

- **XLATI (Translate Item).** Defines a single set of mapping values within a translate list.

- **CLSTBL (Variable Class Table).** Defines a variable class table.

- **VARCLASS (Variable Class).** Defines information related to a variable class.

- **LIT (Literal).** Identifies a string where all blanks are significant and are included in the value.

```
<!-- CLASSTABLE for PANEL ASSIGNI -->
<CLSTBL>

<VARCLASS NAME=aa>
<CHECKL MSG=cara001>
<CHECKI TYPE=ALPHA>
</CHECKL>
</VARCLASS>

<VARCLASS NAME=bb>
<CHECKL MSG=cara002>
<CHECKI TYPE=NUMERIC>
</CHECKL>
</VARCLASS>

<VARCLASS NAME=cc>
<CHECKL MSG=cara003>
<CHECKI TYPE=VALUES
        PARM1=EQ
        PARM2='SINGLE DOUBLE'>
</CHECKL>
</VARCLASS>

<VARCLASS NAME=dd>
<XLATL USAGE=BOTH
<XLATI VALUE=1>MASTERCARD
<XLATI VALUE=2>VISA
<XLATI VALUE=3>AMERICAN
<XLATI VALUE=4>CHECK
<XLATI VALUE=5>CASH
</XLATL>
<CHECKL MSG=cara004>
<CHECKI TYPE=VALUES
        PARM1=EQ
        PARM2='1 2 3 4 5'>
</CHECKL>
</VARCLASS>
</CLSTBL>

<!-- PANEL DEFINITION FOR ASSIGNI -->
<PANEL NAME=assigni
       DEPTH=12
       WIDTH=50>
       Hotel Register

<INFO>
<P>
Type in the following information for the hotel register.

</P>
</INFO>

<VARLIST>
<VARDCL NAME=xname
        VARNAME=xn>
</VARDCL>
<VARDCL NAME=xlos
        VARNAME=xl>
</VARDCL>
</VARLIST>

<AREA>

<!-- DATA ENTRY FIELD FOR NAME -->
<DTAFLD DATAVAR=xname
        USAGE=IN
        VARCLASS=aa
        REQUIRED=YES
        ENTWIDTH=23
        PMTWIDTH=15
        MSG=cara005>
        Name
</DTAFLD>
```

Figure 18.4   Panel definition code for the data entry panel in Fig. 18.3.

(Continued)

```
<!-- DATA ENTRY FIELD FOR LENGTH OF STAY -->
<DTAFLD DATAVAR=xlos
        VARCLASS=bb
        ENTWIDTH=23
        PMTWIDTH=15>
        Length of stay
</DTAFLD>

<!-- DATA ENTRY FIELD FOR ROOM TYPE -->
<DTAFLD DATAVAR=xroom
        VARCLASS=cc
        ENTWIDTH=23
        PMTWIDTH=15>
        Room type

<!-- SET xrm BASED ON xroom -->
        <ASSIGNL DESTVAR=xrm>
        <ASSIGNL VALUE='SINGLE' RESULT=1>
        <ASSIGNL VALUE='DOUBLE' RESULT=2>
        </ASSIGNL>

</DTAFLD>

<!-- DATA ENTRY FIELD FOR PAYMENT METHOD -->
<DTAFLD DATAVAR=xpaym
        VARCLASS=dd
        ENTWIDTH=23
        PMTWIDTH=15>
        Payment method

</DTAFLD>
</AREA>
<BOTINST>Press Enter to Continue.
</PANEL>
```

Figure 18.4   (Continued)

KEY LISTS

Key list tags, shown in Box 18.4, can be used to define key lists, which determine the content of the function key area. Figure 18.5 contains a key list definition for the panel in Fig 18.1. The KEYI tag associates an action with a function key. When the function key is pressed, that action is performed. The action can be a system action, such as Help, Exit, Actions, or Cancel. It can also be an application-defined action. In the example in Fig. 18.5, Search is an application-defined action.

BOX 18.4   Key mapping list tags.

- **KEYI (Key Item).** Associates a command with a key.
- **KEYL (Key List).** Defines a key list for one or more panels.

```
<KEYL NAME=convkeys>
    <KEYI KEY=f1   CMD=help    FKA=short>Help
    <KEYI KEY=f3   CMD=exit    FKA=short>Exit
    <KEYI KEY=f4   CMD=actions FKA=short>Actions
    <KEYI KEY=f5   CMD=search  FKA=long >Display
    <KEYI KEY=f12  CMD=cancel  FKA=no   >Cancel
</KEYL>


<PANEL NAME    = ab
       HELP    = cnvhhlp
       KEYLIST = convkeys
       DEPTH   = 24
       WIDTH   = 80 >
       Library Card Registration
            .
            .
            .
```

Figure 18.5 Panel definition code for a key list.

DIALOG ACTIONS   The dialog user can invoke various dialog actions in a number of ways. One is through pressing a currently active function key. Another way is through entering a command via the command area. Actions can be associated with pulldown choices and selection field choices, and invoked by selecting that choice. Dialog actions can be based on either an ISPF system command or an application-defined command.

ISPF SYSTEM   ISPF system commands are provided as part of the
COMMANDS   ISPF dialog manager and can be included as part of a dialog application. System commands that correspond to CUA standard actions are shown in Box 18.5. There are both dialog actions and scrolling and cursor movement actions. These commands can be associated with function keys in a key list, as shown in Fig. 18.5. A default key list is available that assigns the actions to the CUA-recommended keys. This key list is given in Box 18.6. Some of the key assignments correspond to ISPF functions that are not part of CUA. The user can also invoke these functions by entering the ISPF system command name via the command area.

APPLICATION-   Actions can also be defined as part of a dialog appli-
DEFINED ACTIONS cation. An application command table can be used to define actions invoked via a function key or the command area. Box 18.7 lists the tags that are used to define an application command table.

Figure 18.6 contains an example of an application command table. The search command is referenced in the key list as the action for F5. The other commands are associated with action bar pulldown choices. Within the PDC tag that defines a pulldown choice, an ACTION tag with a RUN parameter is used

**BOX 18.5   ISPF system commands
for CUA-defined actions**

Standard Dialog Action

ISPF Command	CUA Action
CANCEL	Cancel
EXIT	Exit
FKA	Display keys
HELP	Help
PANELID	Display panel IDs
RETRIEVE	Retrieve

Scrolling and Cursor Movement

ISPF Command	CUA Action
ACTIONS	Switch to action bar
BACKWARD	Scroll backward
DOWN	Scroll forward
FORWARD	Scroll forward
LEFT	Scroll left
RIGHT	Scroll right
UP	Scroll backward

to specify a command to execute when that pulldown choice is selected. The ACTION tag can also be used within a selection field CHOICE definition to associate a command with a selection field choice.

In the command table, the CMDACT tag is used to define the action executed for a particular command. Depending on the ACTION parameter value, either a command name is passed to the application via a system variable for application processing or the ISPF SELECT service is invoked. The SELECT service can be used to display a panel via ISPTUTOR or to invoke an ISPF function.

BOX 18.6   ISPF default key list

Key	Action
F1	Help
F2	Split
F3	Exit
F9	Swap
F12	Cancel
F13	Help
F14	Split
F15	Exit
F21	Swap
F24	Cancel

HELP FACILITIES   Help panels are defined using the HELP tag. The AREA, REGION, INFO, and information region tags can be used as part of the help panel to format the information being displayed. Figure 18.7 shows an example of a help panel. Figure 18.8 shows the panel definition code for the help panel in Fig. 18.7.

A help panel can be associated with a particular entry field, selection field, or selection field choice by defining the help panel name with the HELP param-

BOX 18.7   Application command table tags.

- **CMDTBL (Command Table).** Begins the definition of an application command table.
- **CMD (Command Definition).** Defines a command in the application command table.
- **CMDACT (Command Action).** Defines the action to be taken when an associated command is issued.
- **T (Truncation).** Designates the minimum command name that must be entered in order to issue a command.

```
<KEYL NAME=convkeys>
    <KEYI KEY=f1  CMD=help    FKA=short>Help
    <KEYI KEY=f3  CMD=exit    FKA=short>Exit
    <KEYI KEY=f4  CMD=actions FKA=short>Actions
    <KEYI KEY=f5  CMD=search  FKA=long >Display
    <KEYI KEY=f12 CMD=cancel  FKA=no   >Cancel

<CMDTBL APPLID=conv>

<!-- COMMAND DEFINITION FOR ADD -->
<CMD NAME=add>Add
<CMDACT ACTION=setverb>
</CMD>

<!-- COMMAND DEFINITION FOR DELETE -->
<CMD NAME=delete>Del<T>ete
<CMDACT ACTION=passthru>
</CMD>

<!-- COMMAND DEFINITION FOR UPDATE -->
<CMD NAME=update>Up<T>date
<CMDACT ACTION='alias add'>
</CMD>

<!-- COMMAND DEFINITION FOR SEARCH -->
<CMD NAME=search>Search
<CMDACT ACTION='SELECT PGM(LIBCARD) PARM(name cardno whchsrch)'>
</CMD>

<!-- COMMAND DEFINITION FOR CNVHHLP -->
<CMD NAME=cnvhhlp>
<CMDACT ACTION='SELECT PGM(ISPTUTOR) PARM(CNVHHLP)'>
</CMD>

<!-- COMMAND DEFINITION FOR CNVXHLP -->
<CMD NAME=cnvxhlp>
<CMDACT ACTION='SELECT PGM(ISPTUTOR) PARM(CNVXHLP)'>
</CMD>

<!-- COMMAND DEFINITION FOR CNVKHLP -->
<CMD NAME=cnvkhlp>
<CMDACT ACTION='SELECT PGM(ISPTUTOR) PARM(CNVKHLP)'>
</CMD>

</CMDTBL>

<CLSTBL>
<VARCLASS NAME=number>
    <CHECKL  MSG = CARA007>
    <CHECKI TYPE = numeric>
    </CHECKL>
</VARCLASS>
</CLSTBL>

<PANEL NAME   = ab
       HELP   = cnvhhlp
       KEYLIST = convkeys
       DEPTH  = 24
       WIDTH  = 80 >
       Library Card Registration

<!-- ACTION BAR DEFINITION -->
<AB>

<ABC>File
    <PDC NAME=addent>Add Entry
       <ACTION RUN=add>

    <PDC NAME=delent>Delete Entry
       <ACTION RUN=delete>

    <PDC NAME=addent>Update Entry
       <ACTION RUN=update>
```

Figure 18.6   Panel definition code for a command table.

```
<ABC>Search
    <PDC NAME=srchnm CHECKVAR=whchsrch MATCH=1>Search on name
        <ACTION SETVAR=whchsrch VALUE=1>
        <ACTION RUN=Search>

    <PDC NAME=srchid CHECKVAR=whchsrch MATCH=2>Search on Card Number
        <ACTION SETVAR=whchsrch VALUE=2>
        <ACTION RUN=Search>

<ABC>Help
    <PDC NAME=cnvhlp>Help...
        <ACTION RUN=cnvhhlp>

    <PDC NAME=exthlp>Extended Help...
        <ACTION RUN=cnvxhlp>

    <PDC NAME=keyhlp>Keys Help...
        <ACTION RUN=cnvkhlp>
</ABC>

</ABC>
                    .
                    .
                    .
```

Figure 18.6   (Continued)

eter in the DTAFLD, SELFLD, or CHOICE tag. The help panel will be displayed if the help action is invoked while the cursor is positioned on the field, thus providing a contextual help facility. A help panel can also be associated with an application panel through the HELP parameter in the PANEL tag. This panel is displayed if help is invoked and there is no field help panel to display, thus providing an extended help facility.

```
              Keys Help

These are the key assignments for this
program.

F1   Help on the current panel.

F3   Exit current level of program.

F4   Move selection cursor between
     panel body and action bar.

F5   Display the card information
     based on card number.

F12  Cancel current panel.  (back one
     panel)
```

Figure 18.7   Help panel.

```
<HELP NAME=cnvkhlp WIDTH=40 DEPTH=22>Keys Help
<AREA>
<INFO>
<P>
These are the key assignments for
this program.
<PARML BREAK=none TSIZE=5>
<PT>F1
<PD>Help on the current panel.
<PT>F3
<PD>Exit current level of program.
<PT>F4
<PD>Move selection cursor between
panel body and action bar.
<PT>F5
<PD>Display the card information
based on card number.
<PT>F12
<PD>Cancel current panel. (back
one panel)
</PARML>
</INFO>
</AREA>
</HELP>
```

Figure 18.8　Panel definition code for the help panel in Fig. 18.7.

Other CUA-defined help facilities, such as Keys Help, Help Index, Help for Help, and Tutorial Help, are the responsibility of the application. Appropriate panels must be defined by the application and function keys must be assigned to the actions for displaying the panels. Help panels do not have key lists associated with them, and thus do not have function key areas. The function keys used to invoke secondary help facilities would have to be included in the function key definitions for regular application panels.

A reference phrase help tag (RP) has been defined as part of the dialog tag language and can be included within a help panel definition. However, the RP tag is not currently supported by ISPF, and reference phrase help is not provided when the RP tags are coded.

MESSAGE DEFINITION

Messages can be defined with the message tags shown in Box 18.8. Figure 18.9 shows examples of

BOX 18.8　Message tags.

- **MSG (Message).** Defines a message.
- **MSGMBR (Message Member).** Defines a member of a message library.
- **VARSUB (Variable Substitution).** Includes variables in a message definition. When the message is displayed, the current value of the variable is shown.

```
<MSGMBR NAME=CARA00>

<MSG SUFFIX=1
     MSGTYPE=notify>Name must be alphabetic.
<MSG SUFFIX=2
     MSGTYPE=notify>Enter only number of days.
<MSG SUFFIX=3
     MSGTYPE=critical>The only rooms we have available,
     <VARSUB VAR=lname> are either SINGLE or DOUBLE.
<MSG SUFFIX=4
     MSGTYPE=warning>Please enter either
     MASTERCARD, VISA, AMERICAN, CHECK, or CASH.
<MSG SUFFIX=5
     MSGTYPE=warning>Please enter your name.
<MSG SUFFIX=6
     MSGTYPE=notify>Please enter Y or N.
<MSG SUFFIX=7
     MSGTYPE=notify>Card number is a seven digit number.

<!-- CLASSTABLE for PANEL ASSIGNI -->
<CLSTBL>

<VARCLASS NAME=aa>
<CHECKL MSG=cara001>
<CHECKI TYPE=ALPHA>
</CHECKL>
</VARCLASS>

<VARCLASS NAME=bb>
<CHECKL MSH=cara002
<CEHCKI TYPE=NUMERIC>
</CHECKL>
</VARCLASS>

<VARCLASS NAME=cc>
<CHECKL MSH=cara003
<CEHCKI TYPE=VALUES
        PARM1=EQ
        PARM2='SINGLE DOUBLE'>
</CHECKL>
</VARCLASS>

<VARCLASS NAME=dd>
<XLATL USAGE=BOTH>
<XLATI VALUE=1>MASTERCARD
<XLATI VALUE=2>VISA        <LIT>        </LIT>
<XLATI VALUE=3>AMERICAN    <LIT>  </LIT>
<XLATI VALUE=4>CHECK       <LIT>        </LIT>
<XLATI VALUE=5>CASH        <LIT>        </LIT>
</XLATL>
<CHECKL MSG=cara004
<CHECKI TYPE=VALUES
        PARM1=EQ
        PARM2='1 2 3 4 5'>
</CHECKL>
</VARCLASS>
</CLSTBL>
```

Figure 18.9   Message definition.

message tags and references to the messages as part of a variable class table. A message will be displayed automatically as part of variable validation when an invalid value is detected. Messages can also be displayed directly as part of application processing using ISPF message display services. A message can be defined as a notify, warning, or critical message. The message type then determines the physical display characteristics for the message, as shown in Box 18.9.

BOX 18.9   **Message display characteristics.**

Type	Color	Intensity	Alarm	Placement
Notify	White	High	No	Message area or pop-up window
Warning	Yellow	High	Yes	Message area or pop-up window
Critical	Red	High	Yes	Pop-up window

CUA FORMATTING AND INTERACTION   When panels are defined using DTL tags, the basic format of the panel follows CUA guidelines. This includes placement of the panel ID, panel title, message area, command area, and function key area, and the formatting of selection and entry fields and the function key area. When a panel contains an action bar and pulldowns, ISPF displays the pulldowns automatically in the proper format and in the appropriate position. Figure 18.10 shows an example of a panel with an action bar with one of the pulldowns displayed.

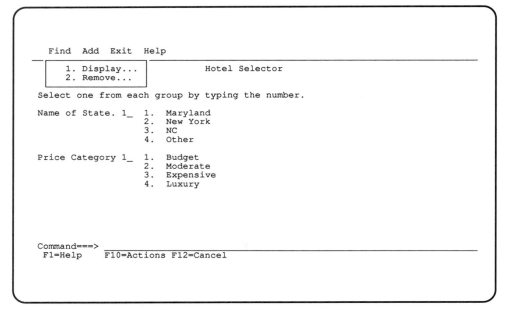

Figure 18.10   Panel with action bar and pulldown.

POP-UP WINDOWS   Pop-up windows are available but are primarily under application control. The application can specify that a panel be displayed in a pop-up window, and can define the location of the pop-up. Figure 18.11 shows an example of the dialog from Fig. 18.10 being continued in a pop-up window. If pop-up windows are used to continue a dialog, it is up to the application to position them according to the CUA guidelines. Help panels can also be displayed in pop-up windows, again with the application controlling the window location. An application can directly use ISPF services to display messages in pop-up windows and can control whether the window is modal or modeless. When messages are defined with the dialog tag language, the application has less control over the use of pop-up windows versus the message area.

SCROLLING   Scrolling is supported only to a limited extent in the dialog tag language. Fields defined with the LSTFLD and LSTCOL tags are vertically scrollable. The CUADIS panel in the pop-up window in Fig. 18.11 contains an example of a LSTFLD field. The scrolling indicator used is of the form ROW X OF Y, where X refers to the top row shown on the screen. If a help panel is defined with more information than will fit on the screen at one time, the information is broken down into multiple pan-

```
   Find   Add   Exit   Help
 _____
  CUASELC                         Hotel Selector

  Select o   ┌───────────────────────────────────────────────────┐
  Then sel   │ CUADIS          MARYLAND Hotels in BUDGET Category    ROW 1 OF 3 │
             │                                                   │
  Name of    │ Hotel Name             Address            Phone  │
             │ Bethesda Ramada        8400 Wisconsin Av  301-897-9400 │
             │ Hilton                 1750 Pike Ave      301-555-1212 │
             │ Holiday Inn Gaithers   2 Montgomary Vill  301-948-8900 │
  Price Ca   │ Command===>                                       │
             │  F7=Bkwd        F8=Fwd        F12=Cancel          │
             └───────────────────────────────────────────────────┘
                      4.   Luxury



  Command===> _____
   F1=Help     F10=Actions F12=Cancel
```

Figure 18.11   Using a pop-up window to continue a dialog.

```
              Extended Help
                         More:    - +
F3=Exit
              Leave help

F9=Keys help
              A list of key assignments
              for the program

F11=Help Index
              An alphabetical list of help
              panels

The actions in the help pull-down on
the action bar are

1.  How to get help (this panel)
```

Figure 18.12   Multiscreen help panel with scrolling indicators.

els and the user is able scroll back and forth through the panels. Figure 18.12 shows a help panel that is the middle panel in a series. Scrolling is indicated by the More: − + shown at the top of the screen. The breaking into multiple panels and subsequent scrolling is handled automatically by ISPF. Scrolling can be performed by entering the ISPF system commands (FORWARD/BACKWARD or DOWN/UP) or by using function keys associated with these functions.

19 THE OS/400 OPERATING SYSTEM

INTRODUCTION   The IBM Application System/400 (AS/400) is IBM's designated SAA computing environment for mid-range systems. An outgrowth of the earlier System/36 and System/38 families of computers, the AS/400 and its operating system, OS/400, implement many of the interfaces defined by SAA. For the Common Programming Interface, the COBOL, RPG, and SQL interfaces are supported. Support for other interfaces, including C, FORTRAN, and the application generator, dialog, presentation, procedure language, communications, and query interfaces, are planned enhancements. For Common Communications Support, the AS/400 system supports the 3270, DCA, and IPDS data streams, distributed data management, SNADS, DIA, SNA network management, LU 6.2, APPN, X.25, SDLC, and token ring communications.

THE AS/400 AND COMMON USER ACCESS   The user interface that is part of OS/400 has been designed to conform to CUA principles. However, because of the nature of the AS/400 and the types of display device typically used with it, its CUA implementation is based on the guidelines for the CUA entry model, used with non-programmable terminals. Thus, action bars and pulldown menus are not used. Also, cursor-based selection and pop-up windows are not supported. Information is displayed using full-screen panels.

GENERAL PANEL FORMATTING   A typical OS/400 screen is shown in Fig. 19.1. A panel title appears at the top of the panel. Panel IDs are not generally used, but may appear on some panels. The work area, which in this case is in parameter format, follows the CUA

```
                    Specify Members to Work With
        Type choices, press Enter.

           File  . . . . . . . . .   grpgsrc      Name

             Library . . . . . . .   example      *LIBL, *CURLIB, name

           Member:
             Name  . . . . . . . .   *ALL         *ALL, generic*, name
             Type  . . . . . . . .   *ALL         *ALL, *BLANK, type




        F3=Exit      F5=Refresh      F12=Previous
```

Figure 19.1   AS/400 panel format.

guidelines for formatting instructions and entry fields. A function key area in standard CUA format appears at the bottom of the panel.

Command Area

The OS/400 interfaces include the use of system commands. The panel shown in Fig. 19.2 shows a command area, located just above the function key area. Because pop-up windows are not used, commands are always entered via a command line that is part of the panel. The basic format for this command area is consistent with the CUA guidelines.

Message Area

Messages are displayed in a message area that is part of the panel rather than in a pop-up window (see Fig. 19.3). Rather than being located above the command area, as specified in CUA, the OS/400 message area is normally the last line on the screen.

Multiple Panel Body Areas

An OS/400 panel may contain multiple panel body areas, although only horizontally divided panels are supported. Figure 19.4 illustrates a panel with multiple panel body areas.

```
                    Work with Members Using PDM

File  . . . . . .  QDDSSRC              Position to . . . . .
  Library . . . .  EXAMPLE

Type options, press Enter.
  2=Edit          3=Copy      4=Delete       5=Display       6=Print
  7=Rename        8=Display description    9=Save          13=Change text

Opt   Member      Type        Text
____   AREA        PF          Area_File
____   DISPLAY     DSPF        Display File for Sale Application
____   PERSON      PF          Salesperson File
____   PRODUCT     PF          Product File
____   RESULT      PF          Results_File
____   SALEREF     PF          Field Reference File
____   SELLS       PF          Sells File

                                                          Bottom
Parameters or command
===>_____
F3=Exit          F4=Prompt        F5=Refresh          F6=Create
F9=Retrieve      F12=Previous     F23=More options    F24=More keys
```

Figure 19.2 Use of command area.

```
                    Work with Members Using PDM

File  . . . . . .  QDDSSRC              Position to . . . . .
  Library . . . .  EXAMPLE

Type options, press Enter.
  2=Edit          3=Copy      4=Delete       5=Display       6=Print
  7=Rename        8=Display description    9=Save          13=Change text

Opt   Member      Type        Text
____   AREA        PF          Area_File
____   DISPLAY     DSPF        Display File for Sale Application
____   PERSON      PF          Salesperson File
____   PRODUCT     PF          Product File
____   RESULT      PF          Results_File
____   SALEREF     PF          Field Reference File
____   SELLS       PF          Sells File

                                                          Bottom
Parameters or command
===> call areapli
F3=Exit          F4=Prompt        F5=Refresh          F6=Create
F9=Retrieve      F12=Previous     F23=More options    F24=More keys
Run-unit ended at 0 in AREAPLI.
```

Figure 19.3 Use of message area.

```
Columns . . . .:   1 71              Edit              EXAMPLE/QDDSSRC
Find  . . .                                                    SALEREF
FMT PF  .....A..........T.Name+++++RLen++TDpB......Functions+++++++++++++++++
         ************* Beginning of data ************************************
0001.00    A         R REFREC                    TEXT('SALE REFERENCE')
0002.00    A           NAME          20           TEXT('NAME OF AN ENTITY')
0003.00    A           ADDRESS       30           TEXT('ADDRESS')
0004.00    A           OLD           6P           TEXT('NUMBER OF OLD_TITLES'
0005.00    A           NEW           6P           TEXT('NUMBER OF NEW_TITLES'
0006.00    A           SALES         8P           TEXT('CURRENT SALES')
0007.00    A           QUOTA         8P           TEXT('CURRENT QUOTA')

Columns . . . .:   1 71              Browse        Pending . . . . . .:  CC
Find  . . .
         ************* Beginning of data ************************************
CC         A         R REFREC                    TEXT('SALE REFERENCE')
0002.00    A           NAME          20           TEXT('NAME OF AN ENTITY')
0003.00    A           ADDRESS       30           TEXT('ADDRESS')
0004.00    A           OLD           6P           TEXT('NUMBER OF OLD_TITLES'
0005.00    A           NEW           6P           TEXT('NUMBER OF NEW_TITLES'

F3=Exit                  F5=Refresh              F6=Move split line
F10=Top                  F11=Bottom              F24=More keys
Specify a target for the include.
```

Figure 19.4   Multiple panel body areas.

```
HELP                    Work with Members Using PDM

Library

    This prompt initially contains the value you entered in the Library
    prompt on the SPecify Members to Work With display.  It is the name
    of the library that contains the file containing the members
    displayed in the list.  You can display a file containing the
    members in a different library by changing this value.  This prompt
    works in conjunction with the File prompt.  Choose from the
    following:

    *CURLIB
        Type *CURLIB to specify that the file containing the members you
        want to work with is in the current library.  If no current
        library is defined, QGPL is assumed.

    *LIBL
        Type *LIBL to specify that the file containing the members you
        want to work with is in one of the libraries in the library
                                                              More...
F2=Extended help   F3=Exit help   F11=Search index   F12=Previous
F24=More keys
```

Figure 19.5   Scrolling indicator.

SCROLLING   The OS/400 user interface supports scrolling, using the text scrolling indicators More . . . and Bottom. Figure 19.5 illustrates a screen with a scrollable work area. Scrolling is indicated by the symbol "More . . ." that appears in the lower right corner of the panel. When the end of the scrollable information has been reached, the indicator changes to "Bottom", as shown in Fig. 19.3.

SINGLE-CHOICE SELECTION FIELDS   Single-choice selection fields are generally consistent with CUA guidelines, as shown in Fig. 19.6. Choices are arranged vertically, and are numbered. A choice is selected by entering its number in the selection entry field. The entry field appears just above the function key area rather than in the CUA standard location, to the left of the first choice. Mnemonics are not used in the AS/400 environment.

MULTIPLE-CHOICE SELECTION FIELDS   Multiple-choice fields are typically implemented using an action list approach, as illustrated in Fig. 19.7. Rather than a slash in the entry field for a particular choice, the user enters the action code associated with the select action (1 = Select).

```
                AS/400 Programming Development Manager (PDM)

   Select one of the following:

        1. Work with libraries
        2. Work with oblects
        3. Work with members

        9. Work with user-defined options




   Selection or command
   ===> 1_____

   F3=Exit       F4=Prompt      F9=Retrieve      F12=Previous
   F18=Change defaults
```

Figure 19.6   Single-choice selection field.

```
                              Select Member

  File . . . . . . . :   QDDSSRC                Library . . . :   EXAMPLE

  Type information, press Enter.
    Position to . . . . . . . . . . . . . . . . . . . . . .

  Type Choice, press Enter.
    1=Select
 Opt  Member       Date         Text
 ____   AREA         03/22/89     Area_File
 ____   DISPLAY      12/02/88     Display File for Sale Application
 ____   PERSON       12/02/88     Salesperson File
 ____   PRODUCT      12/02/88     Product File
 ____   RESULT       12/02/88     Results_File
 ____   SALEREF      12/02/88     Field Reference File
 ____   SELLS        12/02/88     Sells File


                                                               Bottom
  F3=Exit        F5=Refresh        F12=Previous        F14=Display type
  F15=Sort date
```

Figure 19.7   Multiple-choice selection field.

```
                        Work with Members Using PDM

  File . . . . .  QDDSSRC              Position to . . . . .
    Library . . . .  EXAMPLE

  Type options, press Enter.
    2=Edit          3=Copy        4=Delete        5=Display      6=Print
    7=Rename        8=Display description    9=Save        13=Change text

 Opt  Member     Type      Text
 5__   AREA       PF        Area_File
 5__   DISPLAY    DSPF      Display File for Sale Application
 5__   PERSON     PF        Salesperson File
 5__   PRODUCT    PF        Product File
 ___   RESULT     PF        Results_File
 ___   SALEREF    PF        Field Reference File
 ___   SELLS      PF        Sells File
                                                               Bottom
 Parameters or command
 ===>
 F3=Exit           F4=Prompt          F5=Refresh          F6=Create
 F9=Retrieve       F12=Previous       F23=More options    F24=More keys
```

Figure 19.8   Action list.

ACTION LIST FIELDS

Action list fields are also used in their standard CUA format, where there are multiple actions and multiple action codes. This is illustrated in Fig. 19.8.

ENTRY FIELDS

Entry fields also reflect CUA formatting guidelines. An example of a group of entry and selection fields in parameter format is shown in Fig. 19.9. Although not always visible in the screen prints shown in the figures, entry fields appear on the screen as under-lined. Prompts and possible values associated with each field follow the CUA formatting rules. If a field requires more space than is available on a single line, the entry field can be defined to include multiple lines.

All three panel formats are used: Figure 19.9 illustrates the parameter panel format, Fig. 19.10 the form fill-in format, and Fig. 19.11 the tabular format.

INTERACTION TECHNIQUES

The standard CUA interaction techniques for nonprogrammable terminals are used with the AS/400. Cursor-based selection is not supported; selections are made by entering a character value. The arrow keys are used for cursor move-

```
                        Browse/Copy Services
    Type Choice, press Enter.

        Selection . . . . . . . . . . .    1         1=Member
                                                     2=Spool file
                                                     3=Output queue
        Copy all records . . . . . . .    N          Y=Yes, N=No
        Browse/copy member . . . . . .    SAMPLE     Name, F4 for list
          File . . . . . . . . . . . .    QDDSSRC    Name
            Library . . . . . . . . . .    WENZEL    Name, *CURLIB, *LIBL

        Browse/copy spool file . . . .    SAMPLE     Name
          Job . . . . . . . . . . . . .   SAMPLE     Name
            User . . . . . . . . . . .    WENZEL     Name
              Job number . . . . . . . .  *LAST      Number, *LAST
          Spool number . . . . . . . .    *LAST      Number, *LAST, *ONLY

        Display output queue . . . . .    QPRINT     Name, *ALL
          Library . . . . . . . . . . .   *LIBL      Name, *CURLIB, *LIBL

    F3=Exit              F5=Refresh          F12=Previous
    F13=Edit Services                        F14=Find/Change Services
```

Figure 19.9 Parameter entry.

```
QUERY1                                    Mode . . . . :    ENTRY
Format . . . . :    SELLSR              File . . . . :    SELLSF

SALESPERSON NAME:
PRODUCT NAME:
PRODUCT SALES:
PRODUCT QUOTA:




F3=Exit                  F5=Refresh             F6=Select format
F9=Insert                F10=Entry              F11=Change
```

Figure 19.10 Form fill-in entry panel.

```
Columns . . . .:    1 71              Edit                EXAMPLE/QDDSSRC
Find  . . .                                                     SALEREF
FMT PF .....A..........T.Name++++++RLen++TDpB......Functions+++++++++++++++++++
       *************** Beginning of data ************************************
0001.00      A                                        REF(SALE/SALEREF)
0002.00      A         R SELLSR                        TEXT('SELLS RECORD')
0003.00      A           PERSON      R                 COLHDG('SALESPERSON' 'NAME'
0004.00      A                                         REFFLD(NAME)
0005.00      A           PRODUCT     R                 COLHDG('PRODUCT' 'NAME')
0006.00      A                                         REFFLD(NAME)
0007.00      A           SALES       R                 COLHDG('PRODUCT' 'SALES')
0008.00      A           QUOTA       R                 COLHDG('PRODUCT' 'QUOTA')
0009.00      A         K PERSON
0010.00      A         K PRODUCT
''''''''
''''''''
''''''''
''''''''
''''''''

       *************** End of Data ************************************

F3=Exit                  F4=Prompt              F5=Refresh
F10=Top                  F11=Bottom             F24=More keys
```

Figure 19.11 Tabular entry panel.

ment and can be used to move the cursor to any panel area. The TAB/BACK-TAB and NEW LINE keys can also be used to move the cursor. Scrolling backward and forward is performed using the PGUP and PGDN keys. For horizontal scrolling, left and right movement is performed using function keys F19 and F20, respectively.

STANDARD ACTIONS

The function key actions defined by CUA are included as part of the AS/400 user interface, and they have generally been implemented in conformance with CUA guidelines. The display panel IDs and display keys actions are not supported, and the user does not have control over whether or how these areas are displayed. Also, Undo, Mark, and Unmark are not provided.

NAVIGATION ACTIONS

The standard dialog navigation actions of Enter, Exit, and Cancel are provided to the user as ways of moving through a dialog. The standard CUA key assignments, F3 for Exit and F12 for Cancel, are used with the AS/400 interface. Figure 19.1 includes these actions. In Fig. 19.1, the Cancel action is represented with the word Previous. However, this wording is being changed to the more standard designation, Cancel. Cancel, or Previous, causes the previously displayed screen to be redisplayed. Exit returns the user to the point from which the current unit of work was requested.

COMMAND ACTIONS

When command entry is supported, a command area will be included as part of the panel body, as shown in Fig. 19.12. The area is always visible, and the user can move to it with the arrow keys, so the Command action is not necessary and is not supported as an action. When commands can be entered, the Retrieve action may be supported, also shown in Fig. 19.12. The Retrieve action is invoked with F9, as defined in CUA.

REFRESH AND PROMPT ACTIONS

The AS/400 supports both the Refresh and Prompt actions.

The Refresh Action

When values are being entered into entry fields, the AS/400 interface supports the Refresh action, using the standard CUA key assignment of F5. This is shown in Fig. 19.13.

```
MAIN                        AS/400 Main Menu
                                                        System:    SYS400C6
Select one of the following:

     1. User tasks
     2. Office tasks
     3. General system tasks
     4. Files, libraries, and folders
     5. Programming
     6. Communications
     7. Define or change the system
     8. Problem handling
     9. Display a menu

    90. Sign off



Selection or command
===> go program

F3=Exit   F4-Prompt   F9=Retrieve   F12=Previous   F13=User support
F23=Set initial menu
                               (C) COPYRIGHT IBM CORP. 1980, 1988.
```

Figure 19.12   Command entry and the Retrieve action.

Prompt with Entry Fields

The Prompt action is also supported, using F4. The descriptive text for the
Member entry field in Figure 19.13 shows that the Prompt action is supported
for this field. If the cursor is positioned on the field and F4 is pressed, a selection panel with a list of possible member names, like that shown in Fig. 19.14,
is displayed. Selecting one of the names from the list causes it to be inserted in
the entry field.

Prompt in the Function Key Area

Figure 19.15 shows a panel where Prompt is available in the function key area.

Prompt after Command Entry

Prompt can also be used with commands. If F4 is pressed after entering a command, a panel is displayed that prompts for the associated command parameter
values. This is shown in Fig. 19.16.

HELP FACILITIES   The AS/400 help facilities conform in large part to
                          the CUA guidelines. Help panels are available for in-
dividual choices and for entry fields in a panel.

```
                            Exit
Type choices, press Enter

    Change/create member  . . . . . . .   N            Y=Yes, N=No
       Member . . . . . . . . . . . . .                Name, F4 for list
       File  . . . . . . . . . . . . .   QDDSSRC       Name
          Library . . . . . . . . . . .   EXAMPLE      Name
       Text  . . . . . . . . . . . . .   Field Reference File

    Resequence member . . . . . . . .   Y            Y=Yes, N=No
       Start . . . . . . . . . . . .   0001.00      0000.01 - 9999.99
       Increment . . . . . . . . . .   00.01        00.01 - 99.99

    Print Member  . . . . . . . . . .   N            Y=Yes, N=No

    Return to Editing . . . . . . . .   N            Y=Yes, N=No

    Go to member list . . . . . . . .   N            Y=Yes, N=No


F3=Exit      F5=Refresh      F12=Previous
```

Figure 19.13   The Refresh action.

```
                        Select Member
  File  . . . . . . . :  QDDSSRC              Library . . . :   EXAMPLE

  Type information, press Enter.
    Position to . . . . . . . . . . . . . . . . . . . . . . . . . .

  Type choice, press Enter.
    1=Select
Opt Member      Date        Text
___ AREA        03/22/89    Area_File
___ DISPLAY     12/02/88    Display File for Sale Application
___ PERSON      12/02/88    Salesperson File
___ PRODUCT     12/02/88    Product File
___ RESULT      12/02/88    Results_File
___ SALEREF     12/02/88    Field Reference File
___ SELLS       12/02/88    Sells File


                                                            Bottom
F3=Exit      F5=Refresh      F12=Previous      F14=Display type
F15=Sort date                 F17=Subset
```

Figure 19.14   Prompt values.

```
PROGRAM                        Programming
                                                       System:   SYS400C6
Select one of the following:

     1. Programmer menu
     2. Programming Development Manager (PDM)
     3. Utilities
     4. Programming language debug
     5. Structured Query Language (SQL) pre-compiler
     6. Question and answer
     7. IBM product information
     8. Copy screen image

    50. System/36 programming

    70. Related commands


Selection or command
===> dsplib_____

F3=Exit   F4=Prompt   F9=Retrieve   F12=Previous   F13=User support
F16=System main menu
```

Figure 19.15 Prompt for commands.

```
DSPLIB                      Display Library

Type choices, press Enter.

Library . . . . . . . . . . . .   *LIBL____    'Name, *LIBL, *USRLIBL...
                + for more values
Output . . . . . . . . . . . .   *_____    *, *PRINT




                                                              Bottom
F3=Exit    F4=List   F5=Refresh   F11=Keywords   F12=Previous
F13=How to use this display
```

Figure 19.16 Prompt for parameter values.

Help Panel

Figure 19.17 shows a help panel for a specific selection choice. As seen in this panel, extended help and a help index are available.

Extended Help Panel

Figure 19.18 contains an extended help panel that describes a display in general terms. It also contains descriptions of the individual choices in the display.

Help Index Panel

Figure 19.19 illustrates a portion of the help index.

Function Key Help

The AS/400 does not provide a separate Keys Help option. However, information about active functions keys is included as part of the general help information. This is shown in Fig. 19.20.

Help on Help

The AS/400 also provides help information on the Help function itself, as shown in Fig. 19.21.

```
HELP              AS/400 Programming Development Manager (PDM)

9. Work with user-defined options

    Choose this selection to perform operations such as create, change,
    delete, or display user-defined options.  When you press Enter, the
    Specify Option File to Work With display appears.




                                                              Bottom
F2=Extended help    F3=Exit help    F11=Search index    F12=Previous
F24=More keys
```

Figure 19.17   Selection choice help panel.

```
HELP                AS/400 Programming Development Manager (PDM)

   Use this display to select the type of list you want to work with.

   To choose a selection, type the selection number on the command line
   and press Enter.  For more information about a selection, move the
   cursor to the selection number and press Help.

   To run a command, type the command and press Enter.  For help in
   entering a command, type the command name and press F4 (Prompt).
   For assistance in selecting a command, press F4 (prompt) without
   typing anything.  A display appears listing all the possible types
   of commands.

1. Work with libraries

   Choose this selection to perform operations such as delete, display,
   copy, rename, add, save, and restore libraries and to display such
   information as the library description.  When you press Enter, the
   Specify Libraries to Work With display appears.
                                                            More...
F3=Exit help   F10=Move to top   F11=Search index   F12=Previous
F24=More keys
```

Figure 19.18 Extended help panel.

```
Index Search for ADT

Type options, press Enter.
   5=Display topic    6=Print topic

Option Topic
        Active User-Defined Options (PDM)
        Application Development Tools (ADT)
        Browse.Copy services display
        Creating a DFU program in a Syst/36 environment
        Creating a DFU program in an AS/400 environment
        DBCS Codes and Numbers (CGU)
        DCBS Matrix sizes and Font tables (CGU)
        DCBS Sort Tables (CGU)
        Examples of User-Defined Options (PDM)
        File definitions used by DFU
        Find/Change Services display (SEU)
        Four modes of using a DFU program
                                                            More...
Or to search again, type new words and press Enter.
   edit

F3=Exit help   F5=All topics   F12=Previous   F13=User support
```

Figure 19.19 Help index search results.

```
HELP                          Programming
          see the last command you ran.  By pressing this key twice, you
          will see the next-to-last command that you ran, and so on.

      F12=Previous
          Returns to the previous menu or display.

      F13=User Support
          Shows a menu with several types of assistance available.

      F16=System Main menu
          Goes to the System Main menu.

      F23=Set initial menu
          Changes the initial menu (the first menu you see after you sign
          on) in your user profile.  When you press this key, the menu
          currently being displayed is set as the initial menu in your
          user profile.

                                                             More...
F3=Exit help    F10=Move to top    F11=Search index    F12=Previous
F24=More keys
```

Figure 19.20   Help information on keys.

```
                          How to use Help
Online help information is provided for all system displays. The type
of help provided depends on the location of the cursor and on the type
of information displayed.
o    For all displays, the following information is provided:
     -   What the display is used for
     -   How to use the display
         --  How to use the command line if there is one
         --  How to use the entry fields and parameter line if any
         --  What function keys are active and what they do
o    The following information is also provided for specific fields or
     areas on the display:
     -   Menus:  What you can do with each option
     -   Entry (prompting) displays: Meanings and use of all values for
         each input field.
     -   List displays:  Meaning and use of each column

If you press the help key when the cursor is in an area where item
specific online help information is available, the text for that area of
the display is shown.  Press F2 to view online help information for the
                                                             More...
F3=Exit    F12=Previous
                          (C) COPYRIGHT IBM CORP. 1980, 1988.
```

Figure 19.21   Help on help.

Help for Messages

Special help information is also provided for messages. If the cursor is positioned on a message and the HELP key is pressed, a panel containing additional message information is displayed, as shown in Fig. 19.22.

**DEVELOPING
CUA-COMPLIANT
APPLICATIONS**

In the AS/400 application development environment, application displays are defined using an RPG-like language called the *Data Description Specification (DDS)*. The DDS language is used to describe various types of file, including display files. File descriptions are then associated with a device description for a particular device. For display files, the combination of file description and device description determines the actual appearance of a panel on the screen. An application program uses display file descriptions for displaying screens and accepting inputs entered by the user. Variables are used to pass specific data values from the application to be displayed as part of the panel, and to pass values entered by the user to the application.

USING DDS

With DDS, a panel is defined by specifying the various fields that make it up. An example of a DDS

```
                        Additional Message Information

 Message ID  . . . . . . :   PLI9001          Severity . . . . . . :   40
 Mesage type . . . . . . :   INFO
 Date sent . . . . . . . :   03/22/89         Time sent  . . . . . :   14:38:40
 From program  . . . . . :   QUOCMD           Instruction  . . . . :   0000
 To program  . . . . . . :   QUOMAIN          Instruction  . . . . :   0000

 Message . . . . :   Run-unit ended at 0 in AREAPLI.
 Cause . . . . . :     The run-unit was stopped because of reason 1 in the
   following list: (1) No active ERROR on-unit was found.   (2) An ON ERROR was
   specified for the ERROR condition.   (3) An ON ERROR SYSTEM was specified for
   the ERROR condition.   (4) A normal return was tried from an ERROR on-unit.
   (5) A STOP statement or a call to PLIDUMP with the stop (S) option was run.
 Recovery  . . . :     Create a new ERROR on-unit (reason 1) or change the
   existing ERROR on-unit (reasons 2, 3, or 4) so that it has a GOTO statement
   specifying the statement where your program is to continue running. Create
   your program again.  For reason 5, omit the STOP statement or S option and
   create your program again.
                                                                        Bottom
 Press Enter to continue.

 F3=Exit          F10=Display messages in job log          F12=Previous
```

Figure 19.22   Message help.

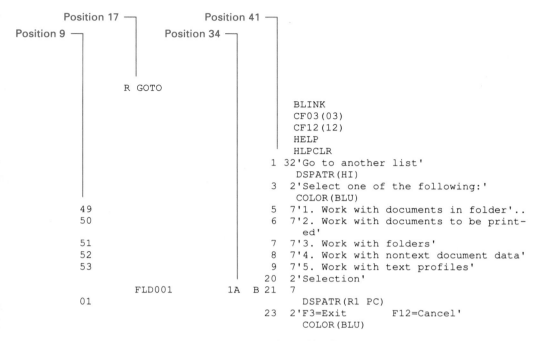

Figure 19.23 DDS specification.

specification is shown in Fig. 19.23. The location of each field within the panel is specified in terms of line number and position. Characteristics of the field such as cursor position and use of color or highlighting can be specified, as well as values displayed. Fields used as input or output variables are assigned names.

With DDS, there is little built-in support for standard panel elements or formatting guidelines that are part of CUA. For example, if a selection field is being defined, specific location and format information must be entered for the instructions, for each choice, and for the entry field. Similarly, for a function key area, the detailed contents of the area must be defined in DDS. A manual entitled *Defining AS/400 Compatible Displays Using Data Description Specifications Newsletter* is available that provides guidelines on defining displays that are consistent with the AS/400 system interface.

AS/400 COMPATIBLE DISPLAYS

Displays designed following the AS/400 compatible guidelines do not use action bars, pulldown menus, pop-up windows, or icons. Standard formatting elements that are described in the guidelines are the panel title, a function key area, a command line above the function key area, and a message line as the last line on the panel. Specific examples and guidelines are given for defining single-choice selection fields, entry fields, action lists, and general information displays.

DEFINING A MENU DISPLAY

The menu display example contains a single-choice selection field. Figure 19.24 shows the sample menu panel included in the AS/400 compatible guidelines. This is the panel that was defined by the DDS specification in Fig. 19.23. For the single-choice selection field, the choices are arranged vertically and are numbered. An entry field (FLD001) is defined for the user to enter the number of the selected choice. The value entered is passed to the application for processing. According to the AS/400 guidelines, the entry field is located just above the function key area.

Although not included in the example, there are also guidelines on how to format and define a command area in the panel. Multiple-choice fields are not specifically addressed in the guidelines.

DEFINING AN ENTRY DISPLAY

The entry display example demonstrates the use of entry fields. Figure 19.25 shows the entry panel example included in the AS/400 guidelines. The sug-

```
                          Go To Another List
Select one of the following:

        1. Work with documents in folder
        2. Work with documents to be printed
        3. Work with folders
        4. Work with nontext document data
        5. Work with text profiles




Selection
   __
F3=Exit    F12-Cancel
```

Figure 19.24   Sample menu panel.

```
                              Merge Options
Type choices, press Enter.

    Place on job queue  . . . . . .  _        Y=Yes, N=No
    Send completion message . . . .  _        Y=Yes, N=No
    Job Description . . . . . . . .  _____  Name, F4 for list
      Library . . . . . . . . . . .  _____  Name, *LIBL
    Adjust/Paginate option  . . . .  _        1=Do not adjust
                                              2=Line ending only
                                              3=Line and page ending

    Multiple line report  . . . . .  _        Y=Yes, N=No
    Collect footnotes
      in merged document  . . . . .  _        Y=Yes, N=No




F3=Exit    F4=Prompt    F12-Cancel
```

Figure 19.25   Entry panel example.

gested arrangement of instructions, field prompts, and possible values follows CUA formatting guidelines. Entry fields are defined with the underscore attribute. The guidelines also address how to define an entry field that uses multiple lines and how to format a multipart field, such as a date or social security number.

In addition to being responsible for panel formatting, the application must provide the appropriate processing to implement standard actions. The guidelines for entry panels address how to implement the Prompt action for an entry field. When F4 is pressed, an indicator is turned on and passed to the application. The application then displays a list panel that displays the possible values for the entry field. The user is able to select a value from the list. The application then places the selected value in the entry field in the entry panel and redisplays the entry panel.

DEFINING AN INFORMATION DISPLAY

Figure 19.26 shows the example used for an information display, which consists of two pages. As with dialog control actions, the application must control the switching from one page to the next. This is done based on the Enter action, rather than on system-controlled scrolling. The two

```
                              View Document Details                    Page 1 of 2
    Creation date  . . . . . :     00000000
    Document . . . . . . . . :     000000000000

    Document description . . :     00000000000000000000000000000000000000000000
    Subject  . . . . . . . . :     00000000000000000000000000000000000000000000000
00000000000
    Change formats/
      options  . . . . . . . :     0            Y=Yes, N=No
    Authors  . . . . . . . . :     0000000000000000000   0000000000000000000
    Keywords . . . . . . . . :     000000000000000000000000000000000000000000000000
000000000000000000000000000000000000000000000000000000000000000000000000000000
00000000000000000000000000000000000000000000000000000

    Document class . . . . . :     0000000000000000
    Print as labels  . . . . :     0            Y=Yes, N=No


    Press Enter to continue.

    F3=Exit    F12-Cancel
```

```
                              View Document Details                    Page 2 of 2
    Project  . . . . . . . . :     0000000000
    Reference  . . . . . . . :     0000000000000000000000000000000000000000000000000
000000000
    Status . . . . . . . . . :     00000000000000000000
    Document Date  . . . . . :     00000000
    Expiration Date  . . . . :     00000000
    Sent to  . . . . . . . . :     00000000000000000000000000000000000000000000000
000000000

    Date action due  . . . . :     00000000
    Date action
      completed  . . . . . . :     00000000
    Mark for
      offline storage  . . . :     0           1=Do not mark
                                               2=Mark and keep
                                               3=Mark and delete document content
                                               4=Mark and delete document
    Press Enter to continue.

    F3=Exit    F12-Cancel
```

Figure 19.26 Information display example.

pages are defined as separate panels, and the application controls the panel displayed in response to a navigation dialog control action (Enter, Exit, Cancel), as it does with any other type of panel.

DEFINING A LIST PANEL
The list panel example shows how to define an action list field. Figure 19.27 shows the example used for a list panel. The instructions define multiple action codes, which can be entered into the option fields in the list. The first entry in the list is one in which the user is allowed to enter data, defining a new entry in the list.

In this example, the panel body is scrollable, allowing for more list entries than will fit on the screen at one time. Again, it is the application's responsibility to implement the scrolling. When the user presses a scrolling key, an indicator is passed to the application. The application must then pass the appropriate data to the panel using variables and redisplay the panel, showing a different set of entries. The application must also define and control the displaying of the appropriate scrolling indicator (More . . . or Bottom).

There is a facility, involving the use of subfiles, that would allow the system to control scrolling directly through the different entries in a list. A subfile consists of a set of records. The system displays as many records as will fit on

```
                    Work with Documents in Folders
Folder  . . .       _____
Position to . . . . . .     _____     Starting character(s)    _____

Type options (and Document), press the Enter key.
   1=Create        2=Revise        3=Copy        4=Delete        5=View
   6=Print         7=Rename        8=Details     9=Print opts    10=Send
   11=Spell        12=File remote  13=Paginate   14=Authority

Opt  Document       Document Description                    Revised    Type
 ___  00000000000   000000000000000000000000000000000000   00000000   0000000000
 ___  00000000000   000000000000000000000000000000000000   00000000   0000000000
 ___  00000000000   000000000000000000000000000000000000   00000000   0000000000
 ___  00000000000   000000000000000000000000000000000000   00000000   0000000000
 ___  00000000000   000000000000000000000000000000000000   00000000   0000000000
 ___  00000000000   000000000000000000000000000000000000   00000000   0000000000
 ___  00000000000   000000000000000000000000000000000000   00000000   0000000000
 ___  00000000000   000000000000000000000000000000000000   00000000   0000000000
                                                                      00000000

F3=Exit       F4=Prompt                   F5=Refresh    F6=Print list
F9=Goto       F10=Search for document     F12-Cancel
```

Figure 19.27   List panel example.

the panel and then changes which records are displayed in response to the PGDN and PGUP keys. However, with system-controlled scrolling, the scrolling indicators consist of either a plus sign (+) or a blank. To use the recommended scrolling indicators, the application must control scrolling.

COLOR AND EMPHASIS

The guidelines include suggestions for color and emphasis. For example, the panel title should be high intensity, and instructions and the function key area should be blue. However, the suggestions do not address all the CUA guidelines.

STANDARD ACTIONS

The application is basically responsible for implementing standard actions. Indicators are used to notify the application when different keys are pressed. For dialog navigation actions, including Enter, Exit, and Cancel, the application must determine the next panel to display, if any processing should take place, or if the user should be given an option to save data. With the Refresh action, the application must determine the appropriate entry field values to use and then pass them to the display in variables. For the Prompt action, the application must provide an appropriate panel listing the choices with a selection capability and then must pass the selected value back to the original entry panel.

HELP FACILITIES

As part of a panel definition in DDS, it is possible to define a particular area within the panel and then associate a help panel with that area. Using this facility, an application can define help panels for individual selection field choices and entry fields. A help panel can also be defined and used when help is requested with the cursor outside any of the defined areas. This help panel should define the panel in general.

The general help panel performs the function of extended help. However, it is not reachable from a help panel associated with a defined area. A form of keys help can be provided by defining the function key area as a panel area and then associating a help panel with that area. If help is requested with the cursor in the function key area, this help panel is displayed. Again, this is not available from another help panel. The help index facility is not available to an application.

The AS/400 guidelines provide specific suggestions on the types of information to include in help panels for different areas, such as selection choices, entry fields, specific columns in a list panel, the function key area, the panel in general, and so on.

MESSAGES

The guidelines recommend displaying messages in the standard AS/400 area, which is the last line in the display. There are various system facilities that can be used for messages, where the display and removal of the message are controlled automatically. The guidelines recommend using a subfile for messages. This allows a series of messages to be displayed if multiple error conditions occur. The system scrolling facilities can then be used to move back and forth within the series of messages. A help panel can be defined and associated with each message. If help is requested when the cursor is on the message, this help panel is displayed.

INDEX

The Conceptual Prism of
Information Systems:

THE JAMES MARTIN BOOKS

Information Systems Management and Strategy	Methodologies for Building Systems	Analysis and Design	CASE
AN INFORMATION SYSTEMS MANIFESTO	STRATEGIC INFORMATION PLANNING METHODOLOGIES (second edition)	STRUCTURED TECHNIQUES: THE BASIS FOR CASE (revised edition)	STRUCTURED TECHNIQUES: THE BASIS FOR CASE (revised edition)
INFORMATION ENGINEERING (Book I: Introduction)	INFORMATION ENGINEERING (Book I: Introduction)	DATABASE ANALYSIS AND DESIGN	INFORMATION ENGINEERING (Book I: Introduction)
INFORMATION ENGINEERING (Book II: Planning and Analysis)	INFORMATION ENGINEERING (Book II: Planning and Analysis)	DESIGN OF MAN-COMPUTER DIALOGUES	**Languages and Programming**
STRATEGIC INFORMATION PLANNING METHODOLOGIES (second edition)	INFORMATION ENGINEERING (Book III: Design and Construction)	DESIGN OF REAL-TIME COMPUTER SYSTEMS	APPLICATION DEVELOPMENT WITHOUT PROGRAMMERS
SOFTWARE MAINTENANCE: THE PROBLEM AND ITS SOLUTIONS	STRUCTURED TECHNIQUES: THE BASIS FOR CASE (revised edition)	DATA COMMUNICATIONS DESIGN TECHNIQUES	FOURTH-GENERATION LANGUAGES (Volume I: Principles)
DESIGN AND STRATEGY FOR DISTRIBUTED DATA PROCESSING	**Diagramming Techniques**	DESIGN AND STRATEGY FOR DISTRIBUTED DATA PROCESSING	FOURTH-GENERATION LANGUAGES (Volume II: Representative 4GLs)
CORPORATE COMMUNICATIONS STRATEGY	DIAGRAMMING TECHNIQUES FOR ANALYSTS AND PROGRAMMERS	SOFTWARE MAINTENANCE: THE PROBLEM AND ITS SOLUTIONS	FOURTH-GENERATION LANGUAGES (Volume III: 4GLs from IBM)
Expert Systems	RECOMMENDED DIAGRAMMING STANDARDS FOR ANALYSTS AND PROGRAMMERS	SYSTEM DESIGN FROM PROVABLY CORRECT CONSTRUCTS	ACTION DIAGRAMS: CLEARLY STRUCTURED SPECIFICATIONS, PROGRAMS, AND PROCEDURES (second edition)
BUILDING EXPERT SYSTEMS: A TUTORIAL	ACTION DIAGRAMS: CLEARLY STRUCTURED SPECIFICATIONS, PROGRAMS, AND PROCEDURES (second edition)	INFORMATION ENGINEERING (Book II: Planning and Analysis)	
KNOWLEDGE ACQUISITION FOR EXPERT SYSTEMS		INFORMATION ENGINEERING (Book III: Design and Construction)	